Tim Kashani
Ola Ekdahl
Kevin Beto
Rachel Vigier

Microsoft® SharePoint 2010 PerformancePoint® Services

UNLEASHED

SAMS | 800 East 96th Street, Indianapolis, Indiana 46240 USA

Microsoft® SharePoint 2010 PerformancePoint® Services Unleashed

ISBN-13: 978-0672-33094-0
ISBN-10: 0-672-33094-6

Library of Congress Cataloging-in-Publication Data is on file

Printed in the United States of America

First Printing August 2010

Trademarks

All terms mentioned in this book that are known to be trademarks or service marks have been appropriately capitalized. Sams Publishing cannot attest to the accuracy of this information. Use of a term in this book should not be regarded as affecting the validity of any trademark or service mark.

Microsoft is a registered trademark of Microsoft Corporation.

Warning and Disclaimer

Every effort has been made to make this book as complete and as accurate as possible, but no warranty or fitness is implied. The information provided is on an "as is" basis. The authors and the publisher shall have neither liability nor responsibility to any person or entity with respect to any loss or damages arising from the information contained in this book.

Bulk Sales

Sams Publishing offers excellent discounts on this book when ordered in quantity for bulk purchases or special sales. For more information, please contact

U.S. Corporate and Government Sales
1-800-382-3419
corpsales@pearsontechgroup.com

For sales outside the United States, please contact

International Sales
international@pearsoned.com

Associate Publisher
Greg Wiegand

Senior Acquisitions Editor
Loretta Yates

Development Editor
Sondra Scott

Managing Editor
Kristy Hart

Project Editor
Andrew Beaster

Copy Editor
Keith Cline

Technical Reviewer
Alexis Jarr

Indexer
Brad Herriman

Proofreader
Apostrophe Editing Services

Publishing Coordinator
Cindy Teeters

Interior Designer
Gary Adair

Cover Designer
Gary Adair

Page Layout
Gloria Schurick

Contents at a Glance

	Introduction	1
1	Integrated Performance	5
2	PerformancePoint Services 2010	13
3	Case Study: Managing What You Measure	19
4	Installing Microsoft SharePoint Server 2010 and Configuring PerformancePoint Services	39
5	Introducing PerformancePoint Dashboard Designer	71
6	Data Sources	89
7	Using Indicators, KPIs, and Scorecards	121
8	Reports	165
9	Page Filters, Dashboards, and SharePoint Integration	199
10	Securing a PerformancePoint Installation	235
11	Working with the Monitoring API	261
12	Maintaining a PPS Deployment	285

Table of Contents

Introduction   **1**

Who Should Buy This Book 2
How This Book Is Organized 2
Conventions Used in This Book 4
     Text Conventions 4
     Special Elements 4

1   Integrated Performance   **5**

Business Intelligence as a Discipline 5
Performance Management Methodologies 9
Business Intelligence as an Enabler 9
Integrated Business Planning 10
Summary 12

2   PerformancePoint Services 2010   **13**

PerformancePoint Services 2010 Architecture 13
What's New? 15
What's the Same? 16
What's Gone? 17
Summary 17

3   Case Study: Managing What You Measure   **19**

Overview and Business Background 20
Business Situation and Requirements 21
     Market Expansion 22
     Increase Popularity 24
Where to Start 24
Proposed Solution Architecture Roadmap 25
Basic Project Plan 26
     Gather Data 26
     Analyze Data and Identify Measures 29
     Design KPIs and Scorecards 30
     Design Reports 32
     Design the Dashboard 34
Summary 38
Best Practices 38

4   Installing Microsoft SharePoint Server 2010 and Configuring
    PerformancePoint Services   39

    Examining PPS Installation Prerequisites 39
        Examining Server Hardware Prerequisites for PPS 40
        Examining Server Software Prerequisites for PPS 40
        Running the Preparation Tool 42
    Installing SharePoint 44
        Examining the Standalone Installation for SharePoint 44
        Running the Standalone Installation for SharePoint 45
        Examining the Server Farm Installation for SharePoint 47
        Running the Server Farm Installation for SharePoint 48
    Configuring PPS 53
        Configuring the Secure Store Service 53
        Creating the Service Application 56
        Starting the PerformancePoint Service 57
        Creating the PerformancePoint Service Application 58
        Set the Unattended Service Account 61
        Associating the Service Application Proxy with a Proxy Group ... 63
        Activating the Feature in the Web Application 64
    Validating the PPS Installation 67
    Summary 68
    Best Practices 68

5   Introducing PerformancePoint Dashboard Designer   71

    Understanding PerformancePoint Dashboard
        Designer Prerequisites 72
    Installing Dashboard Designer 73
    Uninstalling Dashboard Designer 75
    Examining Dashboard Designer 76
        Examining First Class Objects 78
        Examining the Home Tab 79
        Examining the Edit Tab 81
        Examining the Create Tab 82
        Examining Dashboard Designer Item Properties 83
    Content Migration with Dashboard Designer 84
        Importing Content with Dashboard Designer 84
    Summary 86
    Best Practices 87

6   Data Sources   89

    Overview of Data Sources 90
        Multidimensional Data Sources 90

Tabular Data Sources 91
Data Source Security and Trusted Locations 92
Analysis Services Data Source 92
Create a New Analysis Services Data Source 92
Authentication 93
Formatting Dimension and Cache Interval 95
PowerPivot Data Sources 95
Server Requirements 95
Creating a New PowerPivot Data Source 96
Manipulating PowerPivot Data 96
Excel Services Data Source 97
Create a New Excel Services Data Source 97
Import from Excel Workbook 102
Import Data from an Existing Workbook 102
SharePoint List Data Source 105
SQL Server Table Data Source 107
Time Intelligence 108
Configuring Time Intelligence for an Analysis
Services Data Source 109
Configuring a Tabular Data Source 110
STPS Syntax 111
STPS Example 115
Summary 118
Best Practices 119

7   Using Indicators, KPIs, and Scorecards   121
Understanding and Working with Indicators 122
Examining Indicator Styles 122
Examining Indicator Sources 122
Creating Custom Indicators 123
Editing a Custom Indicator 126
Understanding and Working with KPIs 128
Creating an Analysis Services KPI 128
Understanding Multiple Targets and Actuals 133
Examining Data Mapping 135
Understanding and Working with Scoring 142
Changing a Scoring Pattern 143
Editing Thresholds 146
Examining How a Score Is Calculated 147
Examining a Scoring Walkthrough 150
Examining Rollup Scoring 153

Understanding and Working with Scorecards 154
    Creating KPIs with the Scorecard Wizard 154
    Adding a Dimension to a Scorecard 158
    Examining the Scorecard Editor 160
    Designing Scorecards 161
Summary 163
Best Practices 163

8 Reports   165

Overview of Reports 165
Examining Analytic Chart Reports 167
    Adding Data Elements 169
    Adding Additional Measures and Dimensions 170
    Using Measures and Dimensions as Filters 172
    Using Interactivity Features and Context Menus 173
Examining Analytic Grid Reports 175
    Using Interactivity Features and Context Menus 176
Examining Excel Services Reports 176
Examining KPI Details Reports 180
Examining ProClarity Analytics Server Page Reports 183
Examining Reporting Services Reports 185
Strategy Map 188
Examining Web Page Reports 192
Examining Decomposition Tree Reports 193
Examining Show Details Reports 194
Summary 196
Best Practices 197

9 Page Filters, Dashboards, and SharePoint Integration   199

Overview 199
Creating Filters 200
PPS Filters 200
    Creating a PPS Filter in Dashboard Designer 201
SharePoint 2010 Filters 204
    Creating a SharePoint Filter from SharePoint Designer 205
Creating Dashboards 207
Web Part Connections 208
    Source Values 209
    Connect To Values 209
Dashboards in Dashboard Designer 210
    Creating and Deploying a Dashboard 210
    Dashboard Zones 216

Dashboard Pages 218
Working with Filters on Dashboards 220
Using the TheGreenOrange Data Source Option 224
Creating Dashboards in the Browser 227
Create a Dashboard Using PPS Objects 228
Summary 232
Best Practices 233

10   Securing a PerformancePoint Installation   235

Security Overview 235
Applying Security to PPS Elements 236
Defining Permissions Specific to an Element 239
Applying Security to Data Connections 242
Unattended Service Account 244
Unattended Service Account with the Username
    Added to the Connection String 244
Per-User Identity 245
Authentication Troubleshooting 251
Securing a Deployment with TLS 252
Configuring TLS on Web Applications 253
Configuring TLS on PPS Web Services 254
Secure Connections to Data Sources 255
Configuring Per-User Authentication with Kerberos 255
Create SPNs for the Farm and Data Sources 256
Enable Constrained Delegation for Computers
    and Service Accounts 258
Configure and Start the Claims to Windows Token Service 259
Summary 259
Best Practices 260

11   Working with the Monitoring API   261

Introduction: Extending PPS Functionality 261
Installing SharePoint on a Client Operating System 262
Installing Prerequisites 263
Setting Up Your Development Environment 265
Copying PPS DLLs from the GAC 265
Working with PPS Objects 267
Creating Indicator Example 267
Updating Custom Properties on KPIs 268
Custom Objects and Editors 269
Creating a Custom Tabular Data Source 269

Creating a Class Library for the Custom Tabular
Data Source Provider 270
Signing the Assembly 274
Custom Object Editors 274
Creating a Custom Editor for the File System Data Source 275
Deploying the Data Source and Editor 279
Using the Custom Object 282
Summary 284
Best Practices 284

12   Maintaining a PPS Deployment   285

Planning for High Availability 285
Examining the Management Pack 286
Examining Network Load Balancing 286
Configuring Multiple Application Servers 287
Managing PPS 288
PerformancePoint Service Settings 288
Trusted Data Source and Content Locations 296
Migrating from PPS 2007 299
Step-by-Step Migration from PPS 2007 300
Using Windows PowerShell and Cmdlets 302
Launching PowerShell 302
Cmdlet Reference 302
Cmdlets Available Out of the Box 303
Cmdlet Samples 310
Troubleshooting 312
Event Viewer 312
Trace Log Files 313
Summary 313
Best Practices 313

Index   315

About the Authors

Tim Kashani, founder and CEO of IT Mentors and author, has trained more than 100,000 students worldwide. He builds scorecards to track how many vegetables his son consumes daily. Tim thinks increasing is better. His son wants more information before making a strategic decision on the issue.

Ola Ekdahl has worked with PerformancePoint since its early alpha stages, as a trainer, content creator, and author, and has extensive experience developing business intelligence solutions. He is currently developing a KPI measuring how much catnip his cats can consume. The cats think they should use increasing is better but Ola disagrees.

Kevin Beto, a 10-year Microsoft veteran, is currently a test lead on the Microsoft SharePoint BI team. He builds scorecards to track his performance in arm wrestling and twister contests. The calculations and thresholds for these scorecards test the outer limits of performance monitoring and business intelligence.

Rachel Vigier is a writer. She has authored two volumes of poetry, a book about dance, and many technical and business works. She uses scorecards to track how many books her family reads. Increasing is definitely better and so far everybody consistently exceeds targets.

Dedication

To my loving wife, Pamela, and laughing son, Timothy, who remind me daily that some things go way beyond anything we can plan, monitor, and analyze.

Tim Kashani

To my mom, dad, and brothers for always supporting my crazy ideas 100 percent. I love you all.

To my newly compiled nephew Sixten. I hope you'll live well and prosper on planet earth.

Ola Ekdahl

This book is dedicated to my talented wife, Rachel, who has self-lessly put her own writing career on hold to raise some fine children. And don't worry, he'll learn to write his name eventually.

Kevin Beto

To my family and to the creative members of the technology community worldwide who help make our work fun and full of hope.

Rachel Vigier

Acknowledgments

The authors want to thank the Sams Publishing editorial and production team, particularly Loretta Yates, Andrew Beaster, and Alexis Jarr, for their diligent and thoughtful work during the process of writing and producing this book.

Thank you to our colleagues at IT Mentors, particularly Joshua Eklund for his work on the case study, and to the Microsoft PerformancePoint team for their work on the product itself.

And finally, we want to thank each other for our technical expertise and excellent humor during the writing of this book!

We Want to Hear from You!

As the reader of this book, *you* are our most important critic and commentator. We value your opinion and want to know what we're doing right, what we could do better, what areas you'd like to see us publish in, and any other words of wisdom you're willing to pass our way.

As an associate publisher for Sams, I welcome your comments. You can e-mail or write me directly to let me know what you did or didn't like about this book—as well as what we can do to make our books better.

Please note that I cannot help you with technical problems related to the topic of this book. We do have a User Services group, however, where I will forward specific technical questions related to the book.

When you write, please be sure to include this book's title and author as well as your name, e-mail address, and phone number. I will carefully review your comments and share them with the author and editors who worked on the book.

Email: feedback@samspublishing.com

Mail: Greg Wiegand
              Associate Publisher
              Sams Publishing
              800 East 96th Street
              Indianapolis, IN 46240 USA

Visit our website and register this book at informit.com/register for convenient access to any updates, downloads, or errata that might be available for this book.

Foreword

Nobody chooses to work in the absence of good, supporting information. Given the choice, and to improve the decisions they make every day, most business users want relevant information about their business to be easily available. Business intelligence (BI), business information, and the tools that deliver it can provide that information, but most business users do not have BI available to them, or if they do, they don't use it.

Today, roughly 20% of information workers utilize BI. This represents only about 8% of all business users. It seems clear that having the appropriate data to support decisions could lead to superior outcomes for nearly all information workers. However, for this to happen, that data needs to be provided in an intuitive, familiar, and context-sensitive way. And it needs to be provided where the user already works, not in some hidden location.

Given this, why are more people not using BI today? Business users don't currently use BI because most BI solutions are still provided by unfamiliar, specialized software that is separate from the software with which those business users normally do their work. Typically, the BI solutions provide information related to a business process that most users infrequently perform, such as budgeting, resource planning, or product planning. You have a situation where business users must use an unfamiliar product, for an unfamiliar activity performed so infrequently that they can't remember what they learned in the previous experience. It is no wonder that only the most advanced and data-savvy users take advantage of BI.

It is for this reason that we, Microsoft, believe that broadly applicable capabilities such as dashboarding and scorecarding should appear in a familiar and commonly used product. SharePoint 2010 is that product. It makes sense to see the metrics that define your team's success right alongside the rest of your documents and other information in your team portal.

SharePoint 2010 is the culmination of several evolutionary product steps for Microsoft. Each of these intermediate products had elements of broadly applicable features, but they solved only part of the problem, and they, too, were released as software that was separate from the familiar Office and SharePoint environments. Report Builder, Business Scorecard Manager, ProClarity, Data Analyzer, and even PerformancePoint Server 2007 are all examples. But now with the 2010 release of Office and SharePoint, PowerPivot is integrated into Excel, and PerformancePoint Services is integrated into SharePoint. From this point forward, BI will be a mainstream capability available to nearly all the users of Office and SharePoint.

The authors of *Microsoft SharePoint 2010 PerformancePoint Services Unleashed* have done an amazing job walking the reader through the capabilities of PerformancePoint Services and touching on important learning scenarios along the way. Their approach is pragmatic and straightforward, but not superficial. By the time you complete this book, you should be well prepared to embark on your own solutions.

Have fun reading the book, learn a lot, and be sure to make many great dashboards available to people who have never used them before! Together we will fix this oxymoron called *business intelligence*!

—Russ Whitney

Russ Whitney is a group program manager in the Microsoft Office organization. He and his team are responsible for BI capabilities in SharePoint and Office. He has worked as a development manager and a general manager in the four years he has been with Microsoft. Previously, Russ was the SVP of Research and Development of ProClarity Corporation. Since 1997, he has pursued the goal of bringing fact-based decision making to more people in more organizations than ever before. When not at work, you can find Russ hiking, fly-fishing, and taking pictures in the mountains of Idaho.

Introduction

IN THIS INTRODUCTION

▶ Who Should Buy This Book   2

▶ How This Book Is Organized   2

▶ Conventions Used in This Book   4

How is a dashboard like a poem? In the immortal words of the poet Elizabeth Barrett Browning "let me count the ways." Like a good poem, a good dashboard is elegant, brief, and to the point. In a good dashboard, every object (word) counts, and in a good dashboard you get a lot of meaningful information compressed into a small space.

How does this relate to PerformancePoint Services 2010, and why should you care? If you are reading this book, you might not care about poems, but you certainly care about business intelligence. Dashboards are at the heart of business intelligence solutions, and business intelligence solutions are at the heart of business performance.

To thrive, all organizations need to understand how they are performing. This is important in all organizational areas, including financials, sales, employees, and operations. With PerformancePoint Services, you can create web-based dashboards that enable you to define key metrics such as sales, revenue, and employee head count to measure performance in these and other key area. With key metrics in place, you can monitor and analyze your organization's performance. You can see how your business is doing, understand why it's performing the way it is, and set real goals based on real data.

Our intention with this book is to help you imagine what is possible for you and your organization in terms of business intelligence solutions. We also give you the technical know-how you need to begin implementing a business intelligence solution with PerformancePoint Services 2010. In these chapters, we try to help you understand the different aspects of business intelligence solutions, balancing an under-the-hood look at PerformancePoint Services features with sections that will have you rolling up your sleeves to do actual work. We say here that this is the kind of introduction you get when you put the four of us together. Between the four of us, we have years of experience in technology, business intelligence solutions and products, entertainment, and (you guessed it) poetry. We bring it all to bear in this book.

Emily Dickinson said that a good poem should take off the top of your head. A good dashboard may not take off the top of your head or the collective head of your business users, but it should provide you and your business users with plenty of "aha" moments.

Enjoy the book and use it well. Let us know what you think and what it has enabled you to do. Write to us at PPSUnleashed@itmentors.com with your thoughts, comments, sample dashboards, tips, and tricks. The occasional poem is welcome, too!

Who Should Buy This Book

Microsoft SharePoint 2010 PerformancePoint Services Unleashed focuses on what architects, implementers, and developers need to know to successfully deploy a business intelligence solution with PerformancePoint Services. If your organization has a SharePoint license or is considering a SharePoint license, you need to read this book. If you already have a PerformancePoint 2007 installation or other business intelligence solution, you need to read this book. If your business users ask for information and reports to help predict and analyze business performance, you need to read this book.

We assume that you have basic Windows Server and SharePoint skills. We also assume you are comfortable experimenting with various features and options in a new product, that you have a safe computing environment to experiment in, and that you are curious about what PerformancePoint Services can do for you and your organization.

How This Book Is Organized

Microsoft SharePoint 2010 PerformancePoint Services Unleashed is organized into 12 chapters. In this even dozen, you can go from understanding the business reasons for implementing PerformancePoint Services to getting the technical information you need to start. Read the book cover to cover to step through the entire process from planning a PerformancePoint Services deployment to implementing and maintaining your first installation. Or if you are a more experienced user, just dip into the chapters that interest you the most or that can help you fill in the gaps of your own knowledge.

Chapter 1, "Integrated Performance Management," introduces business principles of performance management and discusses the value and process of planning for a business intelligence solution in your organization.

Chapter 2, "PerformancePoint Services 2010," gives you an overview of PerformancePoint Services 2010, including a summary of what's new and different.

Chapter 3, "Case Study: Managing What You Measure," provides a case study that enables you to follow Apples and Oranges Productions, a fictitious production company, as they work through the process of implementing a business intelligence solution with PerformancePoint Services.

Chapter 4, "Installing Microsoft SharePoint Server 2010 and Configuring PerformancePoint Services," takes you through the first step toward implementing a business intelligence solution by installing Microsoft SharePoint Server and configuring PerformancePoint Services.

Chapter 5, "Introducing PerformancePoint Dashboard Designer," covers the specifics of the Dashboard Designer, which is the design tool you use to create and deploy dashboards on SharePoint.

Chapter 6, "Data Sources," provides information on data sources, which are the foundation of any business intelligence solution. In Chapter 6, you learn about two types of data sources, multidimensional and tabular, that you can use in PerformancePoint Services. This chapter also steps through several examples that illustrate how you can apply these data sources appropriately in various scenarios.

Chapter 7, "Using Indicators, KPIs, and Scorecards," provides an overview of how to work with indicators and KPIs and how to integrate these objects into a scorecard view. This chapter is rich in examples that explain the main features of indicators, KPIs, and scorecards. It also provides in-depth information on scoring patterns, thresholds, and methods. (If you're not sure what a scoring pattern is or a threshold, you definitely need to read this chapter.)

Chapter 8, "Reports," illustrates how you can work with the 10 different types of PerformancePoint Services reports to visualize data. The chapter explains the main features for each report type and provides examples of appropriate implementation and usage that help you translate data into information for your business users.

Chapter 9, "Page Filters, Dashboards, and SharePoint Integration," shows you different ways to create dashboards and connect filters using Dashboard Designer, SharePoint Designer, or the browser on the SharePoint page. This chapter covers each way to create dashboards and how to connect filters to dashboards, including Time Intelligence and other typical filters.

Chapter 10, "Securing a PerformancePoint Installation," focuses on security that an organization can implement to protect information stored in a PerformancePoint Services solution. This includes PerformancePoint Services element security (that is, how to configure user access to scorecards, KPIs), data sources, and other objects; and PerformancePoint Services data security (that is, how to secure data that appears on the dashboard).

Chapter 11, "Working with the Monitoring API," illustrates how to extend native PerformancePoint Services capabilities and functionality by using the Monitoring API. The focus here is on creating custom objects and creating editors or custom ASPX pages hosted inside of SharePoint.

Chapter 12, "Maintaining a PPS Deployment," covers the tools SharePoint provides for monitoring and maintaining a PerformancePoint Services deployment. This coverage includes the PerformancePoint Service settings you can apply from the Manage PerformancePoint Services page in SharePoint.

Conventions Used in This Book

The following section explains the special conventions used to help you get the most from this book and from PerformancePoint Services 2010.

Text Conventions

Various typefaces in this book identify terms and other special objects. These special type-faces are as follows:

▶ *Italic*: New terms or phrases when initially defined

▶ Monospace: Examples of code that you can use

Special Elements

Throughout this book, you find Tips, Notes, Cautions, and Cross References. These elements provide a variety of content, ranging from information you should not miss to information that can help you set up your own PerformancePoint Services solutions.

TIPS

Tips point out features and tricks of the trade that you might otherwise miss. This is not run-of-the-mill information that you learn out-of-the-box and don't need us to tell you about.

NOTES

Notes point out items that you should be aware of. Generally, we have added notes as a way to give you some extra information on a topic without weighing you down.

CAUTIONS

Pay attention to Cautions! These could save you precious hours. Don't say we didn't warn you.

CHAPTER 1

Integrated Performance

IN THIS CHAPTER

▶ Business Intelligence as a Discipline   5

▶ Performance Management Methodologies   9

▶ Business Intelligence as an Enabler   9

▶ Integrated Business Planning   10

This chapter introduces business intelligence (BI) as a discipline and discusses how business management and performance management strategies work hand in hand in BI solutions. You learn about the different decision types that occur across all levels of an organization and how BI products have evolved to their present capacity in which they can enable business decisions across all levels of an organization.

Business Intelligence as a Discipline

In any organization, decisions happen daily at every level, from the person working at the front desk to the most senior executive in the corner office. And for every person in an organization, making sound and timely decisions depends on access to good and reliable information. At its best, BI exists where decisions and information converge (see Figure 1.1).

The type of information needed for a decision varies depending on the decision required. The decisions themselves vary depending on who is making the decision, how much time there is to make the decision, and how much of an impact the decision may have on the organization as a whole. There are three different decision types referred to in the BI world:

▶ Strategic

▶ Tactical

▶ Operational

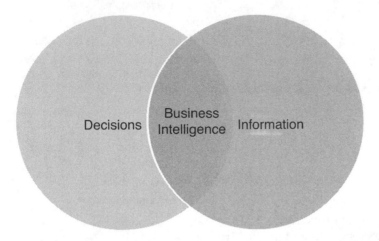

FIGURE 1.1   Fundamentally, business intelligence is about decisions and information.

Strategic decisions are typically made by senior management and generally impact the company as a whole. Only a few of these decisions are made during the year, and they often involve long-range planning from 1 to 3 years at the executive level. Strategic decisions might be centered on questions such as the following:

- Should we start a new product line?

- Should we open regional offices in Europe or the Middle East?

- Should we close our plants in the Midwest?

Tactical decisions are usually made more often than strategic decisions and have less of an impact on the company as a whole. They involve planning on a quarterly or semi-annual basis and might be centered on questions such as the following:

- How can we adjust the budget for the Chicago office to meet projections this quarter?

- Do we need to increase our sales staff for the upcoming holiday season this year?

- How can we increase production in the overseas plant to meet demand next quarter?

Operational decisions are made most often, and on a daily basis, by all types of employees, at all the various levels in the organization. These are like the decisions that keep the assembly plant running every shift and might be centered on questions such as the following:

- Do we need to add a team to the night shift to pack the orders that need to go out tomorrow morning?

- Who is available to replace Jane on her shift tonight?

- Do we need to change the supplier for our store?

Consider an example based on the case study of an organization called Apples and Oranges Productions detailed in Chapter 3, "Case Study: Managing What You Measure." The executive team of Apples and Oranges Productions, a fictitious production company with TV and film divisions, decides to grow the organization. Strategic questions might be centered on the following:

- How can we grow our organization?
- Which division is best positioned for growth?

The executive team decides to grow the organization by expanding into new markets and that compared to the Film division, the TV division is best positioned right now for this expansion. The decision to expand the TV division into new markets is an example of a decision taken at the highest level of the organization that will impact the company as a whole and will be evaluated and implemented over the long term. The executive team arrived at this decision by looking at industry performance, overall company revenue, and overall strengths and weaknesses. The decision defines a direction for Apples and Oranges for the next 2 years and will have an impact on the company as a whole as resources, financial and human, are turned toward realizing the goal of expanding the TV division into new markets.

Following up on this strategic direction, the management team of the TV division looks at what they need to do to realize this strategic goal. At this level, the TV division makes tactical decisions centered on these types of questions:

- Which of our shows is best positioned for expansion into new markets?
- How can we increase viewership for our best shows?

Looking at current viewership and advertising revenue, they decide that a show called *The Green Orange* that is currently in the top 10 television markets is best positioned for expansion. This is an example of a tactical decision. It is a decision taken at a lower level in the organization with the objective of enabling the strategic decisions communicated to the company. Other examples of tactical decisions at this level would be the decision to increase guest appearances on the show or to increase the presence of a particularly popular character based on viewership data.

Operational decisions for *The Green Orange* occur on the set and are centered on these types of questions:

- How do we increase viewership for *The Green Orange*?
- What can we do to make the show as appealing as possible to our viewership?
- What can we do to make the characters as appealing as possible to our viewership?

The set designer makes decisions about the appropriate architecture and furnishings for the show. The costume designer makes decisions about how to dress the characters. The writers make decisions about story lines and scripts. The actors decide how to interpret their lines. These are operational decisions made by a wide variety of Apples and Oranges employees, and all are geared toward producing the best possible episodes to realize operational, tactical, and strategic goals.

Information is required for each of these types of decisions. With BI, an organization can provide a continuous flow of information to business decision makers at all levels of the organization to answer questions such as the following:

▶ What has happened?

▶ What is happening?

▶ Why?

▶ What will happen?

▶ What do we want to have happen?

(From http://technet.microsoft.com/en-us/library/cc811595(office.12).aspx)

BI is where information and decisions converge to provide answers to these questions.

Organizations have been making business decisions from data ever since the first computer was introduced into the workplace, and in the past five years, BI products and understanding has evolved exponentially. In particular, the capacity to transform data into information has evolved. It is important to note that data and information differ in the following way:

▶ Data equals raw numbers.

▶ Information is repurposed data presented in a format that helps human beings make better decisions.

Various products have facilitated the evolution of data into information. Let's consider Microsoft products specifically: People have been making decisions from data since Excel was introduced to the desktop. Microsoft has offered an OLAP solution since SQL Server 7.0 and OLAP Services, which later evolved into Analysis Services with the release of SQL Server 2000. This was further enhanced by a line of BI-specific products. Again at Microsoft in particular, the Business Scorecard Manager, one of the first products in the BI line, embraced the idea of key performance indicators (KPIs) and scorecards as measures of business performance to enable better decisions. The next iteration of the product, PerformancePoint Server, extended the use of dashboards as visual decision-making support systems, and further expanded the analytic capabilities of the BI tools through the integration of ProClarity. With the most recent integration of PerformancePoint Services into SharePoint 2010, the next step in the evolution makes reliable information accessible throughout the organization in a secure, flexible, and readily available format integrated into daily activities and tools.

With this more unified and familiar structure, people in organizations have the support they need to make decisions and track the impact of their decisions quickly and with ease. This does not mean that people will always make predictable decisions dictated by data. It is important to remember that people make business decisions and that this can involve impulsive and intuitive behaviors. Think of how often on a personal level you might have gone against the facts at hand. For example, every month, Sam allocates money from his paycheck to pay the bills. This month he sees that he has additional money in hand. Following the strategic plan he laid out with his accountant, he knows he should invest this money in his retirement account. Instead Sam decides on impulse to buy tickets for a Broadway show and enjoy a night on the town with friends. This is the human factor. As long as BI involves *people* making decisions, the human factor will remain as an unpredictable (and sometimes surprising and profitable) aspect of the BI discipline.

Performance Management Methodologies

The BI products have matured along with the understanding by businesses of how they need a deep understanding of internal business drivers and processes. Although the products now provide a way to support the decision-making process at all levels, businesses have matured in their understanding of how business management and performance management methodologies work together to create frameworks for analyzing and understanding business performance and drivers.

Starting from business management strategies such as Balanced Scorecard, Six Sigma, CMMI (Capability Maturity Model Integration), Agile Management, and CRM (Customer Relationship Management), organizations can build performance management frameworks for monitoring and analysis. As long as your organization has the supporting metrics, you can use almost any form of organizational principle and measure, including, for example, employee satisfaction, future sales, and customer satisfaction.

The methodology you choose to support can provide a framework for thinking about and understanding your business and can help you maintain focus on displaying and communicating the current state of your business and its desired future state. A BI tool such as PerformancePoint Services is flexible enough to take whatever plan or methodology you choose is most appropriate and turn the analysis into tangible information that employees at all levels can use for informed decisions and actions.

Business Intelligence as an Enabler

By providing information across the organization, BI enables better decisions that support organizational objectives. It also can facilitate communication that in turn can enable buy-in of organizational directives.

Even though business intelligence enables better decisions, it is important to remember that BI is not a silver bullet, nor is it an exact science. Decisions are made by people, who have an amazing capacity to consume and process all kinds of data and information. A BI solution provides one part of what goes into making a decision. For example, a CFO checks her financial dashboard and sees that her company has experienced a drop of 4% in sales for this quarter. This does not necessarily mean that the best decision is to cut 4% of the staff for the coming year. Looking at her other performance measures, she sees that customer satisfaction has shot through the roof, and looking further into the overall performance of her industry, she sees that the industry as a whole lost 20% in sales. Processing all these points of information, her 4% drop in sales begins to look quite different, and she concludes that it is best to actually increase staff because she expects that sales next year will skyrocket.

BI also enables better communication across an organization. In another company, the CFO looks at KPIs and scorecards to measure employee productivity against revenue versus nonrevenue projects. In consultation with the Human Resources group, the company uses the scorecards to communicate to employees the necessity of moving the organization toward a more efficient operational model. Employees have access to the scorecards that track hours spent in revenue versus nonrevenue projects, and they can see the imbalance in how time is spent and the need for more effective models of work.

Integrated Business Planning

With the maturity of the products that makes up a BI solution, organizations can create and maintain a technically integrated BI solution. With SQL Server, an organization can create a central repository for data and repurpose the data for use in PerformancePoint Services to communicate valuable business information.

On the back end, SQL source systems collect and store data in normalized forms through transactional systems that provide the capacity to insert, update, and delete data. The SQL solution enables these transactional systems, and with extract and load processes provides the potential to extend the business value and potential of this data. Using extract and load processes, an organization can then transform and optimize data into cubes and prepare it for use in scorecards and dashboards.

To better understand this, consider a transactional sales system that tracks and stores sales quantities and orders as they are entered (see Figure 1.2). The data elements are stored in a relational database, and the underlying architecture of the system might look something like the structure shown here.

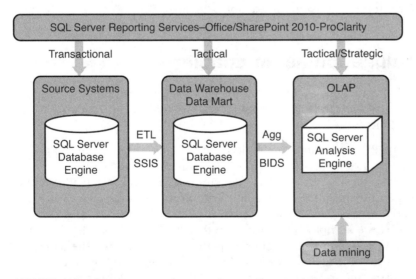

FIGURE 1.2   SQL Server systems collect and store data that can be transformed into valuable business information.

This system captures and stores valuable information that a manager may want to use when making daily or long-term decisions. The challenge is to extract the most valuable data and to transform it into a usable form for performance management—in other words, to transform the data into information.

To optimize data for reporting and analysis, data elements are typically structured into measures and dimensions. Measures identify data that you want to analyze, such as sales, head count, defective products, and profit margin. Dimensions enable you to add context to one or more measures. For example, if we have a measure called Sales, and its value is $1,000, what does that mean? Is it total sales for a year, quarter, or month? Is it for all products or a specific product category? A number by itself does not mean much to most users. By adding one or more dimensions that contain information about time, products, and regions, for example, you can start to add context to the number $1,000. You can now analyze sales based on time, products, and region. A dimension can also include hierarchies that provide navigational paths. It can make it easier for the user to browse data by looking at sales for all years and then navigate to a specific year, quarter, or month.

To use the data for analyses, the data elements must be converted into measures (see Figure 1.3). This is done by associating data elements with a dimension. Raw data elements are considered facts, whereas dimensions group these facts by time or geography, for example. Associating a fact with a dimension enhances its informational value. In this case, it is a fact that the sales organization sold 10,000 shoes. It is important to know that 5,000 of these shoes were sold in Quarter 4. It is also important to know that of these 5,000 shoes, 3,000 were sold in Europe. The measure that surrounds the fact communicates a dimension. In this case, Quarter is an example of the Time dimension, and Europe is an example of the Geography dimension.

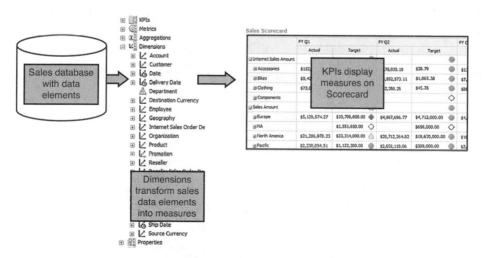

FIGURE 1.3   In this scenario, sales data is transformed into sales information displayed as KPIs on a Sales scorecard.

Dimensions allow you to measure facts in different ways to create and communicate valuable business information. You can then use these measures in the final step in this process, which occurs in PerformancePoint Services (which is where KPIs are built on available measures and presented in scorecards and dashboards). In this example, KPIs might display sales by quarter and by region. This information is populated dynamically from the underlying transactional database reflecting at all times a current view of the organization's sales performance.

Summary

This chapter provided you with an overview of BI as a discipline, including discussion of the types of decisions and information that are part of making an organization function and thrive. You learned how BI products have matured and how businesses have also matured in their understanding of how business management and performance management methodologies can work together in a technically integrated BI solution. With this theoretical overview of BI, you should be ready to roll up your sleeves and start exploring how PPS can help you build a BI solution.

CHAPTER 2

PerformancePoint Services 2010

IN THIS CHAPTER

▶ PerformancePoint Services 2010 Architecture   13

▶ What's New?   15

▶ What's the Same?   16

▶ What's Gone?   17

This chapter summarizes how PerformancePoint Services 2010 (PPS) integrates with SharePoint Server 2010 (SPS). The chapter identifies the new features shipped with PPS, discusses what's the same in PPS 2010, and identifies what has been removed from PPS 2010.

The goal is not to explore every detail of the PPS architecture or every new feature. Instead, this chapter provides just an overview, and directs you elsewhere in this book for more information about specific topics.

PerformancePoint Services 2010 Architecture

When PerformancePoint Server 2007 was released, it was deployed as a product that integrated with Microsoft Office SharePoint Server 2007 (MOSS). PerformancePoint Server 2007 enabled you to publish dashboards to SharePoint sites, but it was not fully integrated. For example, you managed users and permissions to dashboard elements outside of SharePoint, and all definitions of key performance indicators (KPIs), reports, and scorecards were stored in a proprietary database, not in a SharePoint content database.

With the release of SPS, PPS is now fully integrated into SPS as a service application (SA). SAs replace the shared service provider (SSP) architecture introduced with MOSS. The purpose of SAs is to enable for ease of deployment, management, and scalability of services deployed to application servers within a SPS farm. Figure 2.1 shows an example of SA deployment and its relationship to Web Front End (WFE) and database servers.

Typical SPS SAs include Excel Services, Business Connectivity Services, Search, and Visio Services (to name a few). You can also create your own custom SAs.

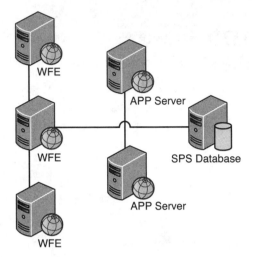

FIGURE 2.1   An SPS deployment using three WFEs, two application servers, and one database server for content and configuration databases.

In terms of manageability, PPS is managed using the SA page available in Central Administration (see Figure 2.2).

FIGURE 2.2   List of deployed SAs. The name of the PPS SA is PerformancePoint Service Application.

The SA architecture makes scalability easy. You can add additional application servers into your SPS environment and deploy PPS to those servers to accommodate more users. You might want to do this to handle heavy workloads. For example, if the user response time is unacceptably high during peak load times during the workday, you can deploy another application server to handle the increased workload. You might also want to do this to provide uninterrupted service (for example, when you take an application server offline to upgrade the machine's memory and then bring it back online without any interruption to service).

For more information about these topics, see Chapter 4, "Installing Microsoft SharePoint Server 2010 and Configuring PerformancePoint Services," and Chapter 12, "Maintaining a PPS Deployment."

What's New?

Besides the new SA architecture described earlier in this chapter, PPS now has several new features and components. Improvements have been made to the scorecard, KPI, and report feature sets, including the following:

- ▶ PPS object storage in SharePoint lists and libraries
- ▶ Filters as objects that can be shared across dashboards
- ▶ Calculated KPIs, which enable you to perform calculations from several different data sources
- ▶ Dynamic hierarchy support, which updates a hierarchy when the data source is updated
- ▶ Multiple KPI actuals
- ▶ Hierarchies as connection points in the filter framework
- ▶ Variance between actual and target values displayed on a scorecard
- ▶ Empty-row filtering
- ▶ KPIs natively on columns
- ▶ Scorecard drill-down
- ▶ Toolbar sorting and filtering redesign
- ▶ KPI details report
- ▶ Native support for the decomposition tree
- ▶ Pie charts
- ▶ SQL Server Analysis Services Conditional Formatting in Analytic Reports

In PPS 2010, browser support has been enhanced. Here is a list of supported browsers for dashboard viewing:

▶ Internet Explorer 7 and 8

▶ Firefox 3.5

▶ Safari

To learn how to use these new features, see the following chapters:

▶ Chapter 7, "Using Indicators, KPIs, and Scorecards," covers how to work with indicators and KPIs and how to integrate these objects into a scorecard view.

▶ Chapter 8, "Reports," covers how to work with the different types of PerformancePoint Services reports, including the new reports.

▶ Chapter 9, "Page Filters, Dashboards, and SharePoint Integration," examines the different ways to create dashboards and connect filters.

What's the Same?

Although the architecture of PPS is now based on SharePoint, the look and feel of PPS 2010 is not much different from the experience offered in PPS 2007. The Dashboard Designer makes an encore appearance as the primary vehicle to create and edit objects in PPS (see Figure 2.3). You can import almost all the content from PPS 2007 into PPS 2010 without loss of functionality.

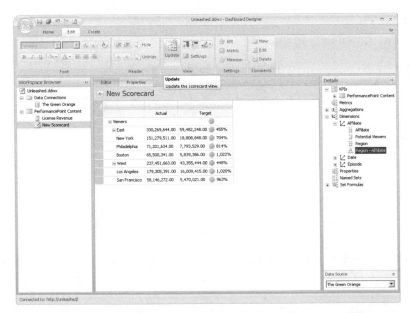

FIGURE 2.3   In PPS 2010, you still use Dashboard Designer to create and edit objects.

The following objects exist in both PPS 2007 and PPS 2010:

▶ Scorecards, KPIs, and indicators

▶ Analytic reports

▶ SQL Server Reporting Services, ProClarity Analytic Server (PAS), and Excel Services reports

▶ Strategy Maps

▶ Dashboards and filters

Chapter 5, "Introducing PerformancePoint Dashboard Designer," covers the Dashboard Designer in detail.

What's Gone?

Some features available in PPS 2007 are no longer available in PPS 2010, including the following:

▶ Dashboard previews

▶ OWC (Office Web Components), which include Pivot Tables and Pivot Charts

▶ ODBC (Open Database Connectivity) data source connection

▶ Trend analysis report

Summary

This chapter is just a starting point. It briefly covered the PPS 2010 architecture and examines what's new, what's the same, and what's been removed (since PPS 2007). You are encouraged to check out the various other chapters referenced herein for more information about how to make PPS 2010 work for you.

CHAPTER 3

Case Study: Managing What You Measure

IN THIS CHAPTER

▶ Overview and Business Background 20

▶ Business Situation and Requirements 21

▶ Where to Start 24

▶ Proposed Solution Architecture Roadmap 25

▶ Basic Project Plan 26

This chapter provides a case study that enables you to follow Apples and Oranges Productions, a fictitious production company, as it begins to implement a business intelligence (BI) solution with PPS. The popular saying "You can't manage what you can't measure" says it all. Sometimes attributed to Peter Drucker, this saying drives home the point that appropriate metrics are at the core of BI and performance management solutions. This saying is also central to the ideas of Drs. Robert S. Kaplan and David P. Norton, the architects of the Balanced Scorecard methodology, a management system based on performance measurement that we discuss in relation to Apples and Oranges.

You can follow Apples and Oranges as it first examines its goals in a key area of its organization, and then plans what it needs to measure to manage effectively and reach these stated goals. You can follow its process as it moves from the work of identifying business goals and requirements to gathering and analyzing data, identifying measures, designing key performance indicators (KPIs) and scorecards, and designing reports and final dashboards using PPS.

To borrow from another saying, "Rome was not built in a day." A performance management system also cannot be built in a day or even a year. Building a performance management system is an iterative process that continues as long as your organization changes and grows. You should expect that this process will be punctuated by moments in which you need to pause to consider what you do not know but need to know to make good decisions. Further, it will be punctuated by points in which you need to make plans to collect data you need but do not yet have in place.

In this chapter you find the story of what can happen when one company starts to implement a real-world BI solution along with a blueprint of a basic project plan that you can use as a jumping-off point for your own implementation with PPS.

Overview and Business Background

Apples and Oranges, a film and television production company located in Los Angeles, has been in existence for 5 years and currently employs 250 employees. Figure 3.1 is a high-level organizational chart of Apples and Oranges.

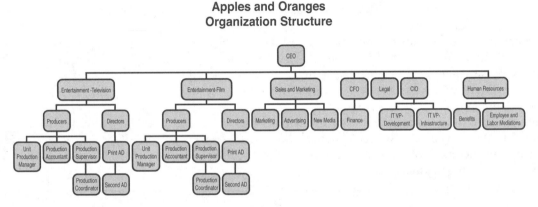

FIGURE 3.1   The organizational chart for Apples and Oranges.

Since its inception, the Entertainment–Television group has created several local television shows and formed distribution and syndication relationships for these shows. Two years ago, Apples and Oranges expanded into nationwide syndication with a new show called *The Green Orange* (see Figure 3.2). The show was created to give people quick environmental tips in a humorous way and has just completed its second season. *The Green Orange* is broadcast in 10 markets across the country: New York, Los Angeles, Chicago, Philadelphia, Boston, San Francisco, Dallas, Washington DC, Atlanta, and Houston.

NOTE

We have a confession to make. Apples and Oranges and *The Green Orange* are not entirely fictitious. For a few laughs and for tips and tricks on living green visit *The Green Orange* at http://www.thegreenorange.com.

As part of an overall company initiative to grow Apples and Oranges, the CEO asked the producers of *The Green Orange* to outline several short-term and long-term goals they would like to achieve with the show. The producers would like to start laying the foundation for these changes now, during the hiatus between the recently completed season two

FIGURE 3.2   *The Green Orange* from Apples and Oranges.

and the upcoming season three. They know that these goals relate to market expansion and increasing popularity.

A BI consultant has been brought on board as an associate producer to help the producers of *The Green Orange*. Currently, the consultant knows that performance management is new to Apples and Oranges and that all the data captured for the show exists in numerous Excel spreadsheets. In addition to unifying the data into a central location and analyzing the show data, the consultant can help the producers of *The Green Orange* identify new goals for growth and understand how they can use performance management to meet these goals.

Business Situation and Requirements

The BI consultant knows that if Apples and Oranges understands its goals and what it wants to measure, then most of the work has been done toward implementing a business intelligence solution that can guide the organization in making targeted, informed, and timely decisions. In his experience of working with organizations, the primary challenge is to agree on a methodology, that is to agree on what counts in an organization and how best to count it. PerformancePoint Services simplifies the creation and centralization of what counts in organizations. The difficult questions have to do with setting business goals and objectives. Having the data sources to support what an organization has decided counts is another issue that can present significant challenges.

Organizations can create scorecards and dashboards from any business management and performance management methodology. Starting from business management strategies such as Balanced Scorecard, Six Sigma, CMMI (Capability Maturity Model Integration), Agile Management, and CRM (Customer Relationship Management), organizations can build performance management frameworks for monitoring and analysis. PPS is flexible enough to capture the characteristics of each of these methodologies and the objectives and measures specific to any organization.

At Apples and Oranges, the BI consultant reviews the Balanced Scorecard methodology with the CEO and her executive management team before working directly with *The Green Orange* producers. The Balanced Scorecard is a scorecard based on the performance management methodology developed by Drs. Robert S. Kaplan and David P. Norton. Kaplan and Norton's comprehensive approach analyzes an organization's performance in four areas:

- ▶ **Finance:** Financial performance
- ▶ **Operations:** Operational excellence
- ▶ **Sales:** Customer satisfaction
- ▶ **Human Resources:** People commitment

Collectively, these areas are called the FOSH (Finance, Operations, Sales, and Human Resources) metrics.

For now, the CEO and her management team agree to focus on the financial performance of Apples and Oranges, and specifically to focus on increasing the financial potential of *The Green Orange*. The CEO and her team understand that a full business intelligence system is a long-term process and that this journey of a thousand miles begins with a single step. The BI consultant is experienced in this process and knows that it is best to get the client started on the road to business intelligence as soon as possible with the data and questions it has available. He begins by interviewing the management and production teams, and a summary of the interviews can be found in the "Market Expansion" and "Increase Popularity" sections.

Market Expansion

As part of their overall strategy, Apples and Oranges is planning to expand into new markets on several fronts. The production company has negotiated a license fee with 10 affiliate stations in different markets across the country. The fee is broken down into categories for the three types of broadcasts, as follows:

- ▶ **First Run:** First run describes an episode that is shown for the first time in a specific market. First run shows can run at any time during the week, but each episode plays in all 10 markets within the same week, regardless of which day.
- ▶ **Ancillary:** Ancillary describes an episode that already had its first run and is rebroadcast within 7 days of its first run broadcast. Often referred to as "an encore presentation" by the local affiliates, it does not necessarily air in the same week as a first run broadcast, but always airs before the next first run broadcast. For example, if

a week is considered to run from Monday to Sunday, an affiliate may broadcast a first run episode on Saturday night. The ancillary broadcast may not be until the following Wednesday. It is not uncommon for ancillary broadcast to run the hour before a new first-run episode airs.

▶ **Rerun:** Rerun describes an episode that has already had a first-run and ancillary broadcast. From that point on, all broadcasts of that episode are referred to as reruns.

Currently in the top 10 television markets, producers of *The Green Orange* want to expand to the top 30 for next season. To do so, they must negotiate license fees in the 20 new markets. These should be based on the number of viewers in the market and comparable to the existing 10 markets.

CEO: "We should be able to quickly glance and see a list of the top 30 markets in order of viewers."

Affiliates make a profit by selling advertising time during the broadcast, usually to local companies. Apples and Oranges would like to land a national advertising partner. Placing a national ad into the broadcast would mean less advertising time available for the local affiliates, so the license fee needs to be renegotiated in existing markets. To understand these negotiations better, the CFO needs to have answers to the following types of questions:

▶ How much do we need to drop the license fee to compensate for the loss of 1 minute of local advertising time?

▶ What is the minimum we must charge for a national commercial to offset the potential drop in revenue if we discount the license fee?

CFO: "It would be great to see some kind of sliding/adjustable scale so that you can fiddle with the numbers. You could adjust how much you charge for a national spot and how much you charge the affiliates to hit the perfect sweet spot."

To get the maximum amount from a national advertiser, the show needs to have the best ratings possible. As the show is on at different times on different nights in the various markets, Apples and Oranges would like to analyze ratings data and try to figure out the best nights and spots in each market. It plans to offer a license discount if affiliates are willing to move the show to the more popular slots. Again, to understand their negotiation position better, Apples and Oranges needs to have answers to these questions:

▶ How much can we offer while still increasing revenue?

▶ How can the ratings from multiple markets be aggregated into an average for a national sponsor to use as a gauge?

Marketing: "This key performance indicator would track ratings for the upcoming third season and compare it to the previous two seasons with the goal of increasing ratings by 10% over the previous two seasons (average)."

Looking further into the future, Apples and Oranges will be expanding its show offerings. First, it will be creating a spin-off from *The Green Orange*. It needs to decide what night and spots the new show should take.

> Marketing: "By analyzing our ratings from the previous two seasons, we should be able to determine what the first and second best slots are for the show. We could then decide to move the current show with its loyal fans to the second best slot and put the new spin-off into the best possible slot to attract as many viewers as possible."

Increase Popularity

In addition to increasing ratings by improving the timeslots in various markets, the executives and producers also want to target the show to fit the audience's tastes. This means analyzing the episodes with the highest ratings to try to spot trends in style, cast, and guest stars so that the most popular elements can be worked into more episodes.

> CFO: "This is an extension of the lower-costs initiative. By analyzing the show types and ratings, we should be able to strike a balance of lowering costs while satisfying fans.
>
> We want to analyze show demographics to determine whether certain elements increase viewership in our lower demographic categories.
>
> We need to break our ratings down into demographics to see if any show elements are more or less appealing to others than our core group of fans."

Where to Start

To better define and plan for its expansion strategies, Apples and Oranges needs to understand current performance of *The Green Orange* and overall market performance. Producers and executives need to answer the following questions quickly:

- ▶ How is the show performing now?
- ▶ How is the show performing relative to market indicators?
- ▶ How is the market performing?
- ▶ How can we better understand the market to position the show in the best way possible?
- ▶ Which type of broadcast brings in the most viewers for *The Green Orange*?
- ▶ What are the top markets in terms of viewers?
- ▶ Based on the analysis, what targets do we want to set for the show?
- ▶ Based on the analysis, what factors can help Apples and Oranges meet advertising and rating targets for the show?

Asking questions such as these is a good starting point for Apples and Oranges and for the producers of *The Green Orange*. From these questions, executives and producers can derive straightforward metrics to build on. For example, by measuring the number of viewers per episode, producers can answer the first question in this list, "How is the show performing now?" If *The Green Orange* is performing well, producers can start planning for market expansion and increasing advertising revenue. If the show is not performing well, the course of action needs to start with a plan to increase the show's ratings.

> **TIP**
>
> To start implementing a business monitoring solution:
>
> First, analyze your organization and ask what business problems you need to solve.
>
> Second, ask how your organization can quantify or measure these problems.
>
> Third, go to your Information Technology group and ask how technology can support the metrics you have defined.

Proposed Solution Architecture Roadmap

After consulting with senior management and key stakeholders, the IT group agrees that the best strategy is to start with a small implementation of PerformancePoint Services (PPS). Business monitoring is new to Apples and Oranges, so one of the goals of this strategy is to provide the company with a manageable start that it can build on. Its plan is to start with two servers, as shown in Figure 3.3, and create a deployment that can scale for rapid growth. At this stage, PPS and Excel Services are the only services that will be enabled on the SharePoint server.

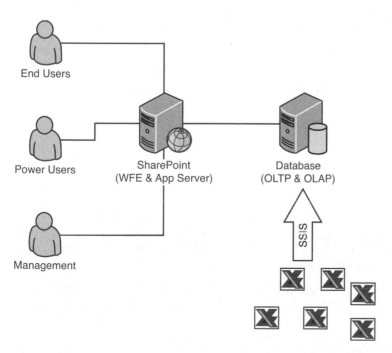

FIGURE 3.3   IT proposes a two-server deployment of PPS that can scale easily for growth.

All the data that will be used is stored currently in individual spreadsheets. The plan is to load the data using SQL Server Integration Services (SSIS) and then continue to update it directly in the online transaction processing (OLTP) database. To make the data as accessible and flexible as possible, the IT group has also decided to build a dimensional data warehouse and an online analytical processing (OLAP) cube. Structuring the data in this way can make it easier to build analytics dashboards. It can also provide the producers with the business information they need to make timely, well-informed decisions.

> **NOTE**
>
> SSIS is a tool that can manage a data Extract, Transform, and Load (ETL) process. It ships as part of the SQL Server platform.

Basic Project Plan

To build monitoring solutions, organizations can begin with an examination of data or by examining existing business issues and decisions. Beginning at either end of the spectrum is appropriate and provides great flexibility. However, it is important to keep in mind that the data and business decisions must converge eventually.

Regardless of the approach, appropriate metrics are at the core of BI and performance-management solutions. You always need to examine what you want to measure and how you plan to measure it. You always need to understand what data you currently have available to build your metrics.

A basic project plan for building a BI solution needs to include the following high-level tasks:

- Gather data
- Analyze data and identify measures
- Design KPIs and scorecards
- Design reports
- Design the final dashboard

Gather Data

Data must be set up so that it can be used as a measure of performance. This is true regardless of the data source or storage solution. PPS can work with different types of data sources, regardless of whether your organization stores data in Analysis Services cubes or in Excel spreadsheets as Apples and Oranges does (see Figure 3.4).

At Apples and Oranges, the spreadsheets contain data about actors, affiliates, regions, broadcast, characters, episode, license fees, and slots. This information is gathered from various data sources such as Nielsen ratings. The information is then consolidated manually into the spreadsheet. After the data warehouse, cube, and dashboards are built, the plan is to automate the data gathering process, too.

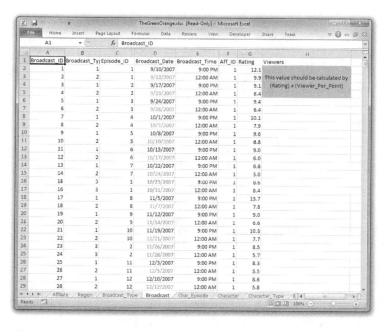

FIGURE 3.4   Currently the data exists in a series of spreadsheets collected by the production team.

Because the data in the spreadsheet is already fairly denormalized, the process of structuring it into a dataset that can be useful for an Analysis Services cube should be a straightforward process.

> **NOTE**
>
> Keep in mind that when you import data from Excel, you often have to pay attention to data types. Frequently, data that you want to treat as Ints is interpreted by SSIS as Double or String. For this reason, make sure you do the proper data type conversions in SSIS.

Build Dimensional Data Warehouse

The first step is to load the Excel spreadsheet data into SQL Server. This needs to be done so that Apples and Oranges can build a multidimensional data warehouse better suited to use with Analysis Services than Excel.

The most straightforward way to load data from Excel into SQL Server is to use SSIS. The IT group has decided to load all the spreadsheet data, as is, into the staging area. This means it will not be doing any transformations or data conversions. The dimensional transformation will take place from the staging area. Figure 3.5 depicts the final dimensional schema.

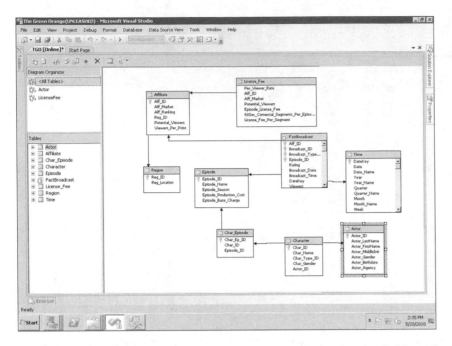

FIGURE 3.5   The final dimensional schema built from the data loaded from the Excel spreadsheets.

Based on the data warehouse, the IT group will build a cube that will be used to build KPIs, scorecards, reports, and dashboards. The initial structure of the cube is depicted in Figure 3.6. This cube will enable Apples and Oranges to analyze episode and viewer data.

At first it might look as if the schemas in Figures 3.5 and 3.6 look almost identical. The difference is that Figure 3.5 shows the data warehouse schema and Figure 3.6 shows the schema used by SSAS.

TIP

This is the initial structure of the cube that will be used to analyze episode and viewer data.

Here are some points to keep in mind when building a cube:

▶ It is easier to focus on a few measures and dimensions and make sure these are done right. Then you can add other measures and dimensions later.

▶ It usually pays to start small. Do not try to implement all measures and dimensions at once.

▶ After you have a solid foundation, adding more measures and dimensions is a straightforward process.

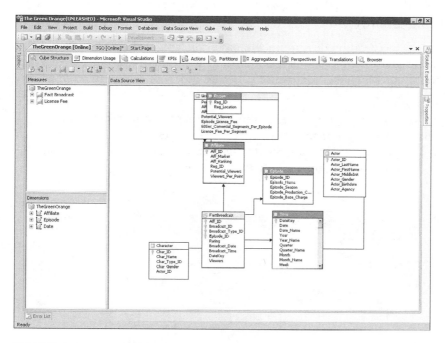

FIGURE 3.6   The initial structure of the cube.

Analyze Data and Identify Measures

When the IT team has gathered the data, it is ready to analyze it and identify from it the measures needed to answer the strategic business questions raised by the executives and producers. Fundamentally, these measures are the Key Performance Indicators (KPIs) that will be used to build scorecards and dashboards for the producers of *The Green Orange*.

Listed here are KPIs that might assist in answering key questions:

- ▶ KPI—Number of viewers for different types of broadcasts.

- ▶ KPI—Advertising time for different types of markets and broadcasts. KPI displays market by advertising time.

- ▶ KPI—Ratings by night and spot in each market. KPI displays market by ratings.

- ▶ KPI—Most popular night. KPI displays audience numbers by day of the week.

- ▶ KPI—Most popular spot. KPI displays audience numbers by spot and day of the week.

- ▶ KPI—Most popular episode. KPI displays audience numbers by episode.

- ▶ KPI—Most popular character in the show. KPI displays audience numbers by character appearance.

- ▶ KPI—Most popular guest star. KPI displays audience numbers by guest star appearance.

Design KPIs and Scorecards

During the functional specification design process, basic concepts such as what should appear on a scorecard and which KPIs to use can be modeled using tools such as Excel or Visio. The next four figures include examples of scorecard mockups that were created using Excel.

This first example, as shown in Figure 3.7, is a ratings scorecard that measures the numbers of viewers by each location and for each broadcast types. The final scorecard includes actual and target values. This can help the producers analyze and understand how *The Green Orange* is performing now in different locations.

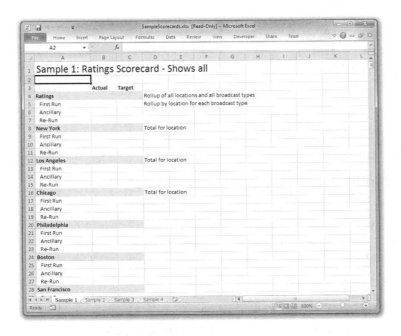

FIGURE 3.7   The ratings scorecard measures numbers of viewers by each location and for each broadcast types.

In the second example, as shown in Figure 3.8, the data for each location and broadcast type in the sample ratings scorecard has been rolled up to display objectives only.

In the third example, as shown in Figure 3.9, a character scorecard measures the number of viewers by each episode. The final scorecard includes actual and target values. This can help the producers of *The Green Orange* to determine which characters are the most popular.

In the fourth example, as shown in Figure 3.10, the data for each character in the sample character scorecard has been rolled up to display objectives only.

FIGURE 3.8   Roll up the data to the objective level to view overall values for each location.

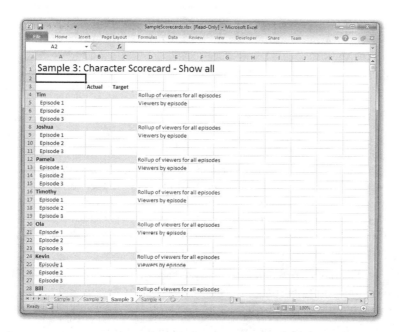

FIGURE 3.9   The character scorecard measures the number of viewers by each character and for each episode.

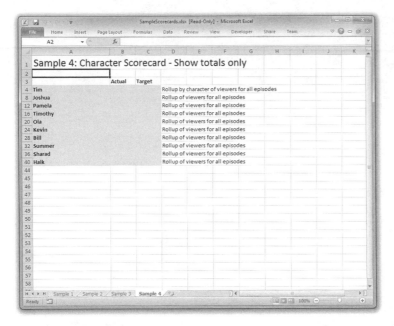

FIGURE 3.10   Roll up the data to the objective level to view overall values for each character.

The first and most important KPI that the producers of *The Green Orange* want to analyze is viewers. As with the cube, the IT group has decided to begin with a small and simply designed scorecard that enables the producers to measure viewership against a target (see Figure 3.11). It also shows a KPI detail report on the right side of the scorecard. The KPI details report shows information such as metric, measure, and row and column path about a specific metric.

Design Reports

Presenting properly designed reports is a critical aspect of a successful dashboard. Reports enable users to further investigate data and to apply visualizations that "makes sense" to them. Each person in an organization interprets and consumes information differently, and PPS makes is easy to change visualizations on-the-fly. The five figures included in this section are examples of how you can create a variety of different reports for Apples and Oranges while still using just the viewer KPI.

The report shown in Figure 3.12 enables producers to analyze viewers by episode and region. It enables them to understand how the viewership trends over a season and provides answers to questions such as the following:

▶ Does the viewership decline or increase during the course of a season?

▶ Can a pattern be identified during the course of a season?

▶ If so, what factors might influence a decline or an increase?

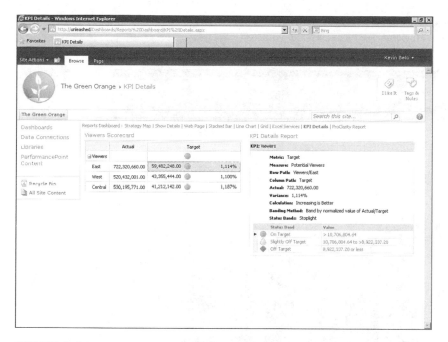

FIGURE 3.11   This scorecard is simple but allows the producers of *The Green Orange* to measure a critical metric—the number of viewers.

FIGURE 3.12   Use this report to analyze viewership by episode and region.

The stacked bar chart enables producers to analyze how the different regions proportionally compare to each other (see Figure 3.13).

FIGURE 3.13   The stacked bar chart presents a different view on the same data showing how different regions compare to each other.

This second line chart, as shown in Figure 3.14, enables producers to drill into a specific region and look at viewership trends based on time and individual affiliates.

The ability to analyze data in a grid format is useful when you want to drill down into data. The grid format used in Figure 3.15 enables producers to analyze data based on date and episodes. They can quickly understand how different seasons or episodes within a season compare to each other.

Visio strategy maps enable producers to visualize data in many interesting ways. The strategy map shown in Figure 3.16 uses a map to inform the producers how the West, Central, and East regions compare to each other.

Design the Dashboard

Fundamentally, the goal of a dashboard is to display valuable business information in the best possible way to foster and strengthen the decision-making process of an organization. The look and feel of the dashboard is critical to the success of a BI solution. PPS is a visual decision-making tool. The display of the data is just as important as how the data is stored and organized.

FIGURE 3.14   This line chart displays viewership trends based on time and individual affiliates.

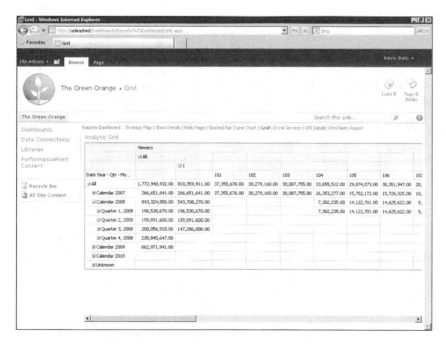

FIGURE 3.15   With the grid format, you can quickly drill down into data.

FIGURE 3.16   Visio strategy maps enable you to present data in highly visual and accessible ways.

When designing a dashboard, it is important not to add too much information on one page. Users should analyze what is on a dashboard and figure out how the information pertains to them without spending unnecessary time scrolling up and down or trying to understand the meaning of a particular scorecard or report (see Figure 3.17).

In the dashboard shown in Figure 3.17, several pages have been added, including Strategy Map, Show Details, Web Page, and Stacked Bar. This selection enables users to choose the scorecard or type of report they want to look at and makes it easy for users to navigate the data.

Another good tool to use is filters, which enable the user to look at high-level information or select values that are more specific (see Figure 3.18).

On the strategy map example, IT added a filter that enables the producers to analyze viewership based on all seasons, individual seasons, or individual episodes. Figure 3.18 uses the episode filter to show information for a single episode.

FIGURE 3.17   In this example, the dashboard offers the user a selection of pages, making it easy for them to navigate the data.

FIGURE 3.18   Filters enable users to specify the information they want to see.

Summary

This chapter introduced Apples and Oranges Productions and provided an overview of how the company initiated the process of implementing a BI solution with PPS.

Apples and Oranges started by focusing its BI implementation in the financial area for one of its productions, *The Green Orange*. It already had some of the data necessary for analysis in Excel spreadsheets. The chapter covered the process of moving this data into SQL Server and transforming it into multidimensional data using SSIS. When the IT team built the data warehouse, they were building a cube that could be used to create KPIs, scorecards, reports, and dashboards.

Later chapters in this book provide additional information and instructions on each of the topics introduced in this case study.

Best Practices

▶ First, analyze your organization and ask what business problems you need to solve.

▶ Second, ask how your organization can quantify or measure its business problems.

▶ Third, go to your IT group and ask how technology can support the metrics defined by the business analysis.

▶ If your company is new to BI, begin with a manageable implementation that you can then build on.

▶ A basic project plan for building a BI solution includes the following tasks: gather data, analyze data and identify measures, design KPIs and scorecards, and design reports and final dashboards.

▶ During the functional specification design process, use modeling tools such as Excel and Visio to diagram the basic concept for your scorecards and KPIs.

▶ When you design a dashboard, it is important not to add too much information on one page.

CHAPTER 4

Installing Microsoft SharePoint Server 2010 and Configuring PerformancePoint Services

IN THIS CHAPTER

▶ Examining PPS Installation Prerequisites   39

▶ Installing SharePoint   44

▶ Configuring PPS   53

▶ Validating the PPS Installation   67

In this chapter, you take the first step toward implementing a business intelligence (BI) solution by installing Microsoft SharePoint Server (SharePoint) and configuring PerformancePoint Services (PPS). Because PPS is integrated into SharePoint, you must first install SharePoint and then configure the PPS service application. For the most part, the installation and configuration process is straightforward via various built-in tools and utilities.

This chapter covers PPS installation prerequisites, how to use the Preparation tool to install SharePoint first, followed by how to configure PPS. This chapter also includes step-by-step instructions on how best to configure PPS and discusses various issues and points to consider when working through your installation and configuration.

By the end of this chapter, you will have a fully functional SharePoint deployment with a properly configured PPS service application. You will be ready to start creating objects with PPS.

Examining PPS Installation Prerequisites

Specific PPS server hardware and server software prerequisites must be satisfied before installation, configuration, and use can begin. These prerequisites are a subset of the prerequisites SharePoint requires.

Examining Server Hardware Prerequisites for PPS

Component	Recommended Minimum
Processor	64 bit, dual processors at 3GHz
RAM	8GB
Hard disk	80GB

Examining Server Software Prerequisites for PPS

Because PPS is integrated into SharePoint, you must begin by installing SharePoint. SharePoint is a sophisticated business server product. This chapter covers only a fraction of the supported deployment types for SharePoint, specifically the parts of SharePoint that interact with PPS. For more information about deploying SharePoint, we recommend the following book: *Microsoft SharePoint 2010 Unleashed* (0672333252).

Examining SharePoint Operating System Prerequisites

> **CAUTION**
>
> SharePoint 2010 dropped support for Windows Server x86 platforms. All installations need to be on x64 platforms. This is due to the enhanced scalability, reliability, and security advantages that x64 processors have over their x86 ancestors. Probably the most significant reason for dropping support for x86 platforms is the 4GB per process RAM limit inherent in the x86 platform architecture. After all, 4GB of RAM is not enough to provide reasonable performance in many SharePoint production scenarios.

To install successfully, SharePoint requires one of the following operating systems:

- ▶ Windows Server 2008 x64, Standard
- ▶ Windows Server 2008 x64, Datacenter
- ▶ Windows Server 2008 x64, Enterprise
- ▶ Windows Server 2008 x64, Web Server

> **NOTE**
>
> Virtualization, primarily through Hyper-V, is a fully supported platform for running the operating system.

Examining SharePoint Prerequisites

SharePoint requires the installation of several software components. The SharePoint installation media includes a handy SharePoint Products and Technologies 2010 Preparation tool that will install most of these components for you. There are two categories of prerequisites for SharePoint: ones that are installed for you automatically and ones you are expected to install on your own.

The following table describes the required software components for SharePoint that are not installed automatically by the Preparation tool.

Name	How Used
Windows 2008 SP2	Contains some compatibility updates.
AMO 2008	Allows for advanced communication between SharePoint and SQL Analysis Services. Although not an enforced prerequisite, this is necessary for importing key performance indicators (KPIs) from SQL Analysis Services cubes.

The following table describes the required software components that are installed for you through the Prerequisite Installer tool.

Name	How Used
Web Server Role	Internet Information Services (IIS) components to host web applications.
Application Server Role	.NET Framework support and Windows process activation service support, which facilitates communication between servers within the farm.
SQL 2008 Native Client	Connectivity with SQL.
.NET Framework 3.5 SP1	.NET Framework compatibility fixes for SharePoint.
Windows PowerShell 2.0	Server administration via cmdlets support.
Geneva Framework Runtime	Support for Windows claims authentication. This is used for back-end communication between servers in the farm.
Sync Framework Runtime v1.0	Used for Groove library synchronization.
Chart Controls for .NET 3.5	Rendering of analytic charts and grids.
Microsoft Filter Pack 2.0	Used for search functionality within SharePoint.
ADOMD.NET 2008	Connectivity with Analysis Services data sources.

4

Running the Preparation Tool

All the prerequisites are installed through a standalone tool included with SharePoint. The tool installs all the prerequisites listed earlier and adds any Windows Server roles and features necessary for SharePoint to function properly. The Preparation tool requires connectivity to the Internet to install most of the components.

> **NOTE**
>
> For SharePoint 2007, some prerequisites were installed as part of the Setup.exe process, whereas others had to be installed before launching Setup.exe. SharePoint 2010 improves this process. The PrerequisiteInstaller.exe utility installs everything necessary and configures the operating system automatically.

To run the SharePoint Products and Technologies 2010 Preparation tool, follow these steps:

1. Launch PrerequisiteInstaller.exe from the root of the installation CD. The first screen of the utility lists all components that will be installed or configured as a part of this utility (see Figure 4.1).

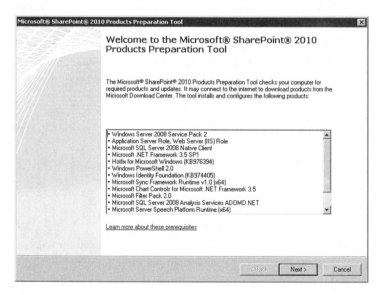

FIGURE 4.1   The Preparation tool checks for required products and updates.

2. Click Next to proceed to the Microsoft software license terms. The license terms here are the combined terms for all the products that will be installed.
3. Read the license terms. If you accept the terms, click I Accept the Terms of the License Agreement(s), and then click Next. The tool now checks for products and installs any required updates. Depending on your computer hardware and network connection, the installation may take several minutes to complete.

TIP

Downloading.NET Framework 3.5 SP1 from the Microsoft Download Center is the most time-consuming aspect of this part of the installation process. If the .NET Framework is installed from a local source before you run the Preparation tool, the tool will skip this step, greatly reducing the overall installation time.

4. When the tool has completed running, you see a status check (see Figure 4.2). Read the items to see whether any errors occurred or if a reboot is required before proceeding to install SharePoint. If there are no errors and you do not need to reboot, click Finish.

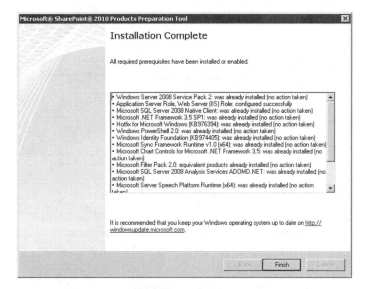

FIGURE 4.2   Review the status check carefully.

CAUTION

Sometimes the Preparation tool fails or requires a reboot without clearly notifying you. Make sure you read the completion screen carefully before continuing. If you miss any error messages at this stage, you might have problems installing SharePoint.

The installation of all required software prerequisites is now complete, and you are now ready to install SharePoint.

Installing SharePoint

SharePoint is a flexible product that you can install in a number of different ways. The methods range from a standalone installation that results in a functional deployment completed with a minimal number of clicks, to a more advanced server farm installation. The server farm installation is more complex and takes longer to complete, but it does allow for future expansion. In this section, you learn about both the standalone installation and the server farm installation. The following table outlines some of the common scenarios for each installation type.

Installation Type	Scenario
Standalone	Quick setup for evaluation purposes
	Simplified Kerberos deployment
	Small datasets
Single-machine farm	Reduced hardware needs
	Simplified administration
	Simplified migration to a multimachine farm
Multimachine farm	Maximum performance scaling
	High security deployments
	High availability deployments
	Extranet deployments

Examining the Standalone Installation for SharePoint

The standalone installation for SharePoint is intended to provide a quick evaluation of the SharePoint software and may be useful during a proof-of-concept phase. The standalone installation automatically configures many settings and makes the installation process simple and quick. This convenience does incur some risk.

When doing a standalone installation, here are some issues to consider:

▶ The standalone installation installs and uses SQL 2008 Express Edition. This edition has the following limitations: 1 CPU, 1GB of RAM, and a maximum database size of 4GB.

CAUTION

If you use the standalone installation type for a production scenario or for long-term use, you will likely run into the 4GB database size limit. All content uploaded slowly eats into this limit.

▶ When doing a repair on a standalone install, you risk overwriting previously created content. The repair process prompts the user to overwrite the default site that was created. This is the default option, which overwrites any previously created content.

▶ The standalone installation instantiates and starts every service application. There are many of these service applications. If the server is not a high-capacity computer, this may overtax the computer's resources and prevent the installation from completing successfully.

▶ The standalone installation allows only a single-server configuration. This means that no expansion is possible. If you expect the single server to grow into a mission-critical application server, we recommend you go through the server farm installation.

Running the Standalone Installation for SharePoint

To run the standalone installation for SharePoint, follow these steps:

1. Launch Setup.exe from the SharePoint installation location.
2. Read the Microsoft software license terms. If you accept the terms, click I Accept the Terms of This Agreement, and then click Continue.
3. Enter the license key for this installation.

> **CAUTION**
>
> Make sure the key is for an Enterprise deployment of SharePoint. The Standard SKU for SharePoint does not include PPS. If a Standard SKU key is entered here, and you want to upgrade to the Enterprise SKU later, you need to perform an SKU-to-SKU upgrade with a new license key. Consult the SharePoint documentation for more information on how to accomplish this.

4. Select Standalone as the installation you want (see Figure 4.3). The installation begins.
5. When the installation is complete, select the Run the SharePoint Products and Technologies Configuration Wizard Now check box, and then click Close (see Figure 4.4).
6. The SharePoint Configuration Wizard launches automatically. Click Next to proceed.
7. The wizard provides a warning about starting or resetting services during configuration. Review the warning carefully (see Figure 4.5). If it is acceptable to start or reset the services listed, click Yes.

> **CAUTION**
>
> The SharePoint Configuration Wizard restarts IIS. If you run the installation on a mission-critical server, try scheduling this step during off hours or during scheduled downtime to avoid disruption of critical Internet services.

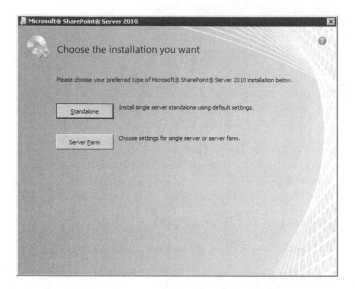

FIGURE 4.3   Select Standalone to install a single server standalone.

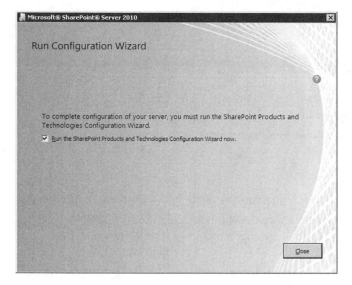

FIGURE 4.4   You are now ready to complete the configuration of your server.

The wizard proceeds with configuring SharePoint. This step may take some time because it includes installing SQL Server 2008 Express and configuring SharePoint.

When the wizard has completed the configuration, you see a message confirming a successful configuration. At this point, the SharePoint installation is almost functional.

FIGURE 4.5   Review the list of services to be started or reset.

CAUTION

PPS is not yet fully operational. Therefore, at this point you can create web applications and site collections. However, before a default connection to a data source can work, it is important to configure the Secure Store Service. To complete the PPS installation, see the "Configuring the Secure Store Service," later in this chapter.

Examining the Server Farm Installation for SharePoint

The server farm installation for SharePoint is intended for people who have a deeper understanding of SharePoint and how it works. The term *SharePoint server farm* refers to a more advanced installation. This installation has multiple machines working together from the same SharePoint configuration database. There are two main flavors of farms, both of which have the same installation steps. The differentiation comes in configuration after the installation completes.

▶ **Single-machine farm:** All SharePoint components run on a single server that may or may not contain the SQL databases.

▶ **Multi-machine farm:** Multiple machines with potentially varying SharePoint configurations work together from a single SharePoint configuration database. Machines within the farm can be hosting different SharePoint service applications.

The server farm installation starts with a minimal configuration. You must then perform a series of steps to bring the environment to a functional state.

When doing a server farm installation, consider the following issues:

▶ The server farm install requires a SQL Server 2008 or higher database. You can download the free Express Edition from Microsoft.com, or you can use an edition of SQL Server that has more appropriate database size limitations for your needs.

▶ When setup completes, a wizard guides you through the initial configuration steps for the server farm. Depending on what you select as part of your installation, PPS may or may not be partially configured for you.

TIP

For more information about how to install SQL Server for a server farm installation, we recommend the following book, *Microsoft SQL Server R2 2008 Unleashed* (0672330563).

Running the Server Farm Installation for SharePoint

To run the server farm installation for SharePoint, follow these steps:

1. Launch Setup.exe from the SharePoint installation location.
2. Read the Microsoft software license terms. If you accept the terms, click I Accept the Terms of This Agreement, and then click Continue.
3. Select Server Farm as the installation type you want.
4. From the Server Type tab, select Complete, and then click Install Now. The installation begins (see Figure 4.6). The installation takes a few minutes to complete.

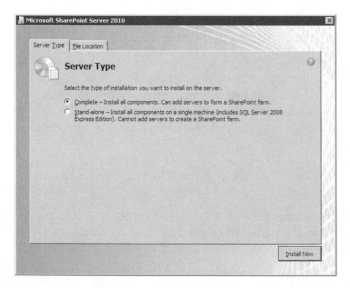

FIGURE 4.6 The installation now begins.

CAUTION

At this point, you are again given the option between doing a farm install or a stand-alone install. Even though you selected a server farm install on the previous screen, the default is to do a standalone install on this screen, which negates the choice you made in the previous step and does a standalone install. Before proceeding, be sure to change the radio button selection to select Complete install.

5. When the installation is complete, select the Run the SharePoint Products and Technologies Configuration Wizard Now check box, and then click Close.

6. The wizard provides a warning about starting or resetting services during configuration. Review the warning carefully. If it is acceptable to start or reset the services listed, click Yes.

CAUTION

The SharePoint Configuration Wizard restarts IIS. If you run the installation on a mission-critical server, try scheduling this step during off hours or during a scheduled downtime to avoid disruption of critical Internet services.

7. Select Create a New Server Farm, and then click Next.

8. In the Specify Configuration Database Settings dialog box, enter the name of the database server and the name of the database you want to use. In addition, specify the database access account in this dialog box (see Figure 4.7). This is the account that will be granted access to the database, and it will be the SharePoint server farm account. Click Next to continue.

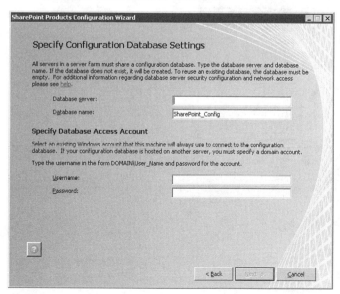

FIGURE 4.7   Specify the SQL instance and database access account in this dialog box.

TIP

The user running setup needs system administrator level access on the database specified here. Setup uses the user's credentials to grant minimal required permissions to the database access account.

---

9. The Configuration Wizard requests a passphrase that is asked for when other servers attempt to join the farm. Make sure you enter a strong passphrase, and then click Next to continue.

10. In this step, you configure the SharePoint Central Administration Web Application. The Administration Web Application is the site you use to perform all farm-level configurations. Enter a port number you can remember easily or accept the default random port. It is also possible to configure the authentication method for accessing Central Administration, with the default being NTLM. It is recommended that you use the default. Otherwise, Kerberos requires additional manual steps that need to be performed by a domain administrator to make Central Administration work after the Configuration Wizard closes. Make your choice, and then click Next.

11. Review the configuration settings that will be applied. When you are satisfied with the settings, click Next to start the installation. The installation takes several minutes to complete.

12. When the wizard has completed the configuration, you see a message confirming a successful configuration (see Figure 4.8). If configuration was successful, click Finish.

13. SharePoint Central Administration launches automatically. At this point, you can choose to participate in the Customer Experience Improvement Program. After you make your selection, click OK to continue.

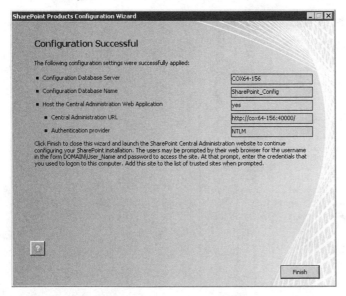

FIGURE 4.8   This configuration completed successfully.

NOTE

Microsoft uses the data collected through the Customer Experience Improvement Program to determine which bugs should get fixed in service packs and to shape testing efforts for future releases. This effort focuses on the most frequently used features. None of the data is personally identifiable information (PII). Make sure to enable this option if you want to cast a vote on which features should be tested.

14. Accept the default option, Walk Me Through the Settings Using This Wizard, and then click Next.

TIP

If you want to configure everything yourself, see the sections later in this chapter that explain how to configure the service application manually.

15. In the Service Account section, enter the credentials of a new account to use as an application pool for the service applications or use the SharePoint server farm account. In the Services section, select the services you want to run in the farm. Make sure to select PerformancePoint Service (see Figure 4.9).

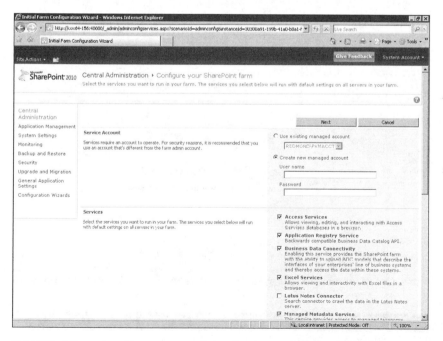

FIGURE 4.9   In the Services section, make sure to select PerformancePoint Service.

TIP

Regarding security, a best practice is to enter a new managed account in the Service Account section instead of using the existing server farm managed account.

CAUTION

Depending on the computer hardware, this step may time out if all services are selected. This may happen especially if you select the Search service. If the process does time out, you can restart the wizard. At this point, only unconfigured services are available for configuration.

16. Enter a title for the site in the Title and Description section. In the Template Selection section, select a template for the root site of the site collection, and then click OK (see Figure 4.10).

FIGURE 4.10   In this screen, enter a title for your site, and select a template for the root site.

TIP

From the Enterprise tab, select the Business Intelligence Center template for the site collection to have select features activated automatically. This can save a few configuration steps later.

When the Wizard has completed the configuration, you see a message confirming a successful configuration.

CAUTION

Before you can begin working with PPS, you must configure the Secure Store Service and set the unattended service account properly. The following section provides information and step-by-step instructions about how to do so.

Configuring PPS

After SharePoint has been installed, the next step is to configure the PPS service application. You must complete this step regardless of the installation type you selected.

In this example, you select to do a server farm installation in preparation for future expansion. The SharePoint farm starts as a single application server deployment. However, additional web and application servers can be added later to scale for future growth and expanding data requirements.

In this type of installation, the administrator needs to complete the following tasks in the order shown here:

1. Configure the Secure Store Service.
2. Create the service application.
3. Start the PerformancePoint Service.
4. Configure all other service applications that will be useful in the deployment, such as Excel Services or SQL Server Reporting Services Integration.

Configuring the Secure Store Service

The Secure Store Service is a service that encrypts selected data stored within it. A user-generated encryption key is required to ensure that the data is secure. This is a new addition to the SharePoint feature set in SharePoint 2010.

NOTE

For security reasons, PPS requires the Secure Store Service to be manually configured before it can be used. This ensures that passwords are not stored as plain text in the database.

The data that is encrypted is

▶ Unattended Service Account credentials. This is a domain account used by default to access data sources.

To configure the Secure Store Service, follow these steps:

1. Launch SharePoint Central Administration from the Start menu. Select Start, All Programs, Microsoft SharePoint 2010 Products, SharePoint 2010 Central Administration.

2. From Application Management, select Manage Service Applications.

3. Scroll to find and select Secure Store Service, and then click Manage on the ribbon (see Figure 4.11).

FIGURE 4.11   Select the Secure Store Service link from this screen.

TIP

Two different types of Secure Store Service objects are created for you: the Secure Store service application and the Secure Store proxy. Both of these objects have links that should lead to the same page, which means that you may select either link.

4. From the Secure Store Service configuration page, select Generate New Key (see Figure 4.12).

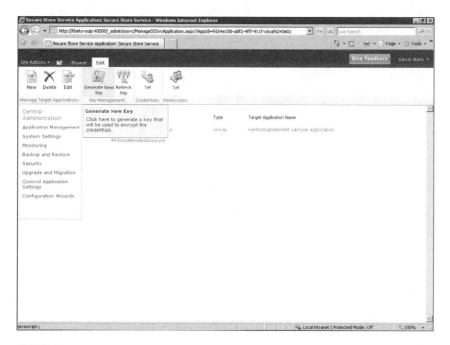

FIGURE 4.12   Select Generate New Key from this screen.

5. Enter a secure passphrase in the dialog box (see Figure 4.13). Because it is protecting potentially sensitive data, make sure this is a strong password. Accept the check to Re-encrypt the Database Using the New Key, and then click OK. The database will be encrypted.

NOTE

Wikipedia suggests the following guidelines for creating strong passwords:

▶ Include numbers, symbols, and upper- and lowercase letters in passwords.

▶ Password length should be between 12 and 14 characters.

▶ Avoid any password based on repetition, dictionary words, letter or number sequences, usernames, relative or pet names, or biographical information.

("Password Strength" from Wikipedia, the free encyclopedia, http://en.wikipedia.org/wiki/Strong_password#Examples_that_follow_guidelines)

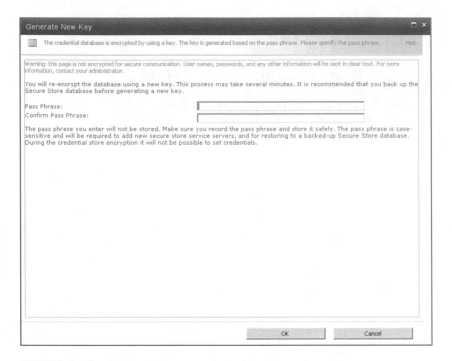

FIGURE 4.13   Make sure you create a strong passphrase.

CAUTION

To increase security, you should first configure the Central Administration pages to use Secure Sockets Layer (SSL). Alternatively, you need to ensure that the browser is running directly on the server so that Internet traffic is not going through a proxy server. If you do not do this, the passphrase you enter here can be viewed by a *packet analyzer*. A packet analyzer is a hardware or software utility that intercepts network traffic and allows an unauthorized user to see the password you are setting. The password appears in plain text on the HTTP packet. The packet analyzer can pick up the password you are sending to the server to configure the Unattended Service Account.

6. When the Secure Store Service key is generated successfully and the database is encrypted, click Home to return to the Service Application Management.

Creating the Service Application

You are now ready to complete the final steps for your PerformancePoint installation. You must complete four tasks:

▶ Start the PerformancePoint Service.

▶ Create the PerformancePoint service application.

▶ Set the Unattended Service Account.

▶ Associate the service application proxy with a proxy group.

These tasks may be performed in any order. Depending on your installation type, some of these tasks may not be required. If you selected to perform a server farm installation and bypassed the Configuration Wizard or cleared the PerformancePoint Service check box in the Configuration Wizard, you need to create the PerformancePoint Monitoring service application manually.

Best practice is to verify these tasks regardless of the type of installation you performed. This can help to give you both peace of mind and ensure smooth functioning of the PerformancePoint Monitoring service application.

After you perform or verify these tasks, you are ready to launch the Dashboard Designer and create your first dashboard.

Starting the PerformancePoint Service

The PerformancePoint Service is the web service that all requests go through. This service needs to be started on at least one application server in the farm. Any server that has this service started will be servicing requests and conceptually "running" PPS.

The PPS Service needs to run on at least a single application server in the server farm. Although you may choose to run it on multiple application servers in the farm, this is not necessary. Requests are load balanced equally by a round-robin distribution between all instances of the service that are running. This is a good way to help control the load and avoid performance issues.

NOTE

You must start the PPS Service on every computer that shares the workload for PPS processes across the farm.

To start the PerformancePoint Service, follow these steps:

1. Browse to the SharePoint Central Administration site, and then click the System Settings tab in the navigation pane on the left.

2. From this page, click the Manage Servers in This Farm link available below the Servers option.

3. From the list of servers in the farm, click the name of the server where you want to start the service application.

4. Scroll and find PerformancePoint Service in the list of available services, and then click Start from the Action column. The status changes from Stopped to Started (see Figure 4.14).

FIGURE 4.14   The status changes from Stopped to Started.

CAUTION

Although not an option available through the setup UI, it is possible to configure SharePoint to have web front-end (WFE) servers through command-line setup.

It is possible to start the PerformancePoint Service on a WFE box that is not capable of successfully running the PerformancePoint Service. If this happens, the user periodically sees errors when using PerformancePoint whenever a web service request goes to the WFE box that has this service incorrectly running on it. Before proceeding, make sure that this is running only on the appropriate application servers.

This completes the first of the four tasks you must perform.

Creating the PerformancePoint Service Application

Conceptually, the PerformancePoint service application is a collection of settings that will be used when a request is issued to PPS. For example, you might configure the following:

▶ Unattended Service Account used to connect to data sources

▶ Secure Store settings

▶ Various application and timeout limits

The PerformancePoint service application differs from the PerformancePoint Service in one significant way. There can be multiple PerformancePoint service applications in the farm but only one PerformancePoint Service.

> **NOTE**
>
> Creating a service application automatically creates a proxy associated with that service application.

To create the PerformancePoint service application, follow these steps:

1. Browse to the SharePoint Central Administration site, and then click Application Management in the left navigation pane.

2. Under Service Applications, click Manage Service Applications.

3. From the ribbon, click New. Click PerformancePoint Service Application to launch the PPS Service Application creation dialog box (see Figure 4.15).

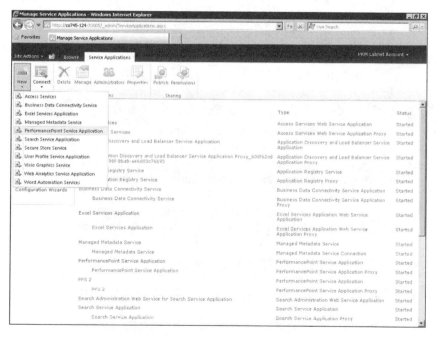

FIGURE 4.15   This option launches the PPS Service creation dialog box.

4. Enter a name for the service application. If this is going to be the default service application, select Add This Service Application's Proxy to the Farm's Default Proxy List (see Figure 4.16).

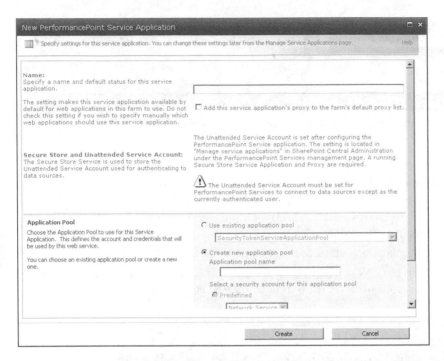

FIGURE 4.16   Specify settings for the new PerformancePoint service application in this screen.

TIP

If you select the Add This Service Application's Proxy to the Farm's Default Proxy List check box, the service application will be associated automatically with any web application that is created. There can be only one active service application per web application. These are managed by proxy groups, as discussed later in this chapter.

---

5. In the Application Pool section of this screen, you can select to either Use Existing Application Pool or Create New Application Pool. If you select Create New Application Pool, enter the application pool name. After you have made your selection, click Create to create the service application. This may take a few minutes. When the process has completed, you see a message confirming a successful creation.

> **NOTE**
>
> If you use a new security account for the application pool that was not created by the SharePoint wizard, it is necessary to grant permission for that account to access the content database for each web application it will be associated with. This can be done by executing the following two PowerShell commands in a SharePoint 2010 Management Shell instance:
>
> ```
> $w = Get-SPWebApplication -Identity http://webapplicationurl
> $w.GrantAccessToProcessIdentity("domain\serviceaccount")
> ```

This completes the second of the four tasks you must perform.

Set the Unattended Service Account

To set the Unattended Service Account, follow these steps:

1. From the Service Application Management screen, select Application Management, Manage Service Applications.

2. Scroll to find and select PerformancePoint Service Application from the list, and then select Manage from the ribbon.

3. From the PerformancePoint Service Application Management page, select PerformancePoint Services Settings (see Figure 4.17).

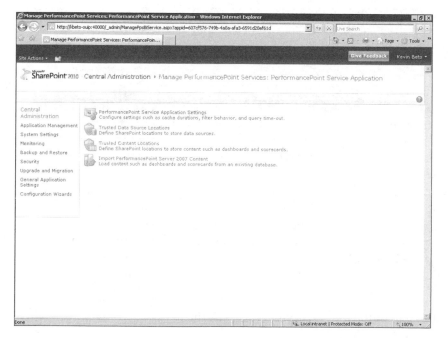

FIGURE 4.17   Select the PerformancePoint Services Settings link from this screen.

4. Secure Store Service is selected as the default in this screen. If you plan to use the Unattended Service Account to access data sources, enter credentials in this screen, and then click OK (see Figure 4.18).

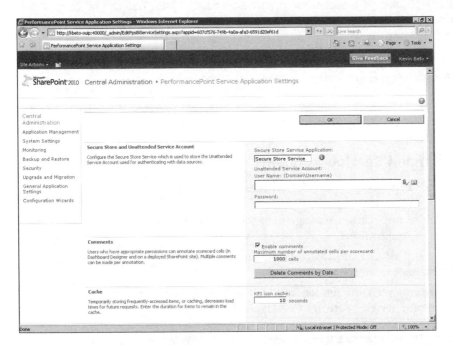

FIGURE 4.18   Select the default Secure Store Service or enter new credentials for the Unattended Service Account.

TIP

If you do not enter credentials in this screen, the Network Service Account on any computer running PerformancePoint Service is used to connect to data sources. If you choose this method of access, ensure that the Network Service Accounts on all your application servers can access the appropriate data sources.

If you are not planning to use the Unattended Service Account and do not want to use the Network Service Account method to access data sources, you likely need to configure per-user authentication via Kerberos. This complex process usually requires domain administrator level permissions to complete. See Chapter 10, "Securing a PerformancePoint Installation," for information about how to configure per-user authentication.

This completes the third of the four tasks you must perform.

Associating the Service Application Proxy with a Proxy Group

NOTE

Only perform the task discussed in this section if you did not select the Add This Service Application's Proxy to the Farm's Default Proxy List check box when you created the service application. Leaving this check box clear means that the service application will not be used by any web applications by default. This step is necessary to identify which web applications use the service application.

Because there can be many service applications in the farm and a web application can only have one PerformancePoint service application associated with it, it is important to associate the correct service application with the correct web application. There are several ways to do this, but the easiest way is to configure the service connections while managing web applications. You can do this through the SharePoint Central Administration site.

CAUTION

The following instructions assume that you have already created a web application. The Configuration Wizard also makes this assumption.

To associate the PerformancePoint service application with a proxy group, follow these steps:

1. Browse to the SharePoint Central Administration site, and then click Application Management in the left navigation pane.
2. Under Service Applications, click Configure Service Application Associations.
3. Select the name of the application proxy group next to the web application you need to edit.
4. Select the name of the service application to be associated with the web application check box, and then scroll to the end of the dialog box and click OK (see Figure 4.19).

CAUTION

It is possible to put many service applications in a single proxy group. Unfortunately, it is not possible to make them all work at the same time. Therefore, be careful about where each service application is used. Only the default service application is used, which can be changed in an application proxy group.

This completes the fourth and final task that you must perform.

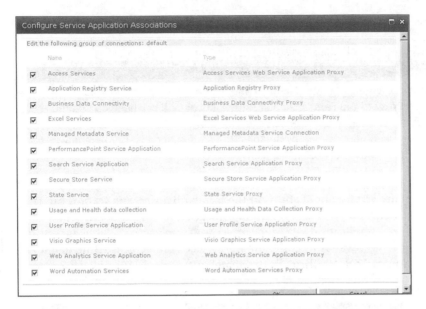

FIGURE 4.19   Configure service application associations in this screen.

Activating the Feature in the Web Application

The last step to getting PPS up and running is to activate the PerformancePoint Services Site Collection and Site features in the sites or site collections that use them. A *feature* is a package of SharePoint settings that represent a unit of functionality. When activated, a feature adds additional functionality to a SharePoint web application, site collection, or site. PPS has features available only at the site collection or site levels.

Activating the feature creates the content types, Web Parts, and site definitions necessary to launch Dashboard Designer (and to render dashboards). Feature activation must be performed inside the site collection that hosts PPS dashboards (see Figure 4.20). In addition, the activation must be performed by a site collection administrator.

> **CAUTION**
>
> If there are many site collections in a web application, the site collection administrator must activate the feature in each site collection that will be running PPS. There is no way to do this in bulk, although it is possible to script the activation through PowerShell. See Chapter 12, "Maintaining a PPS Deployment," for more information.

> **NOTE**
>
> If you use the Business Intelligence Center site template as the initial template for the site collection for your web application, this step is done automatically.

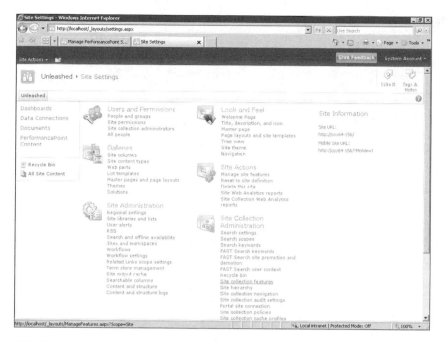

FIGURE 4.20   Select to activate the site collection features in this screen.

Activating the Feature at a Site Collection Level

To activate the feature in the site collection, follow these steps:

1. Browse to the root of the site collection. Remember you must be the site collection administrator.
2. Click Site Actions, and then click Site Settings.
3. Under Site Collection Administration, click the Manage Site Collection Features link.

NOTE

If you are not at the site settings for the root site of the site collection, this link will not be available.

4. Scroll to find PerformancePoint Services Site Collection Features. If the feature is not already activated, click the Activate button (see Figure 4.21).

NOTE

The action activates the SharePoint Server Publishing Infrastructure feature automatically because this feature is a prerequisite feature for the PerformancePoint Services site collection features.

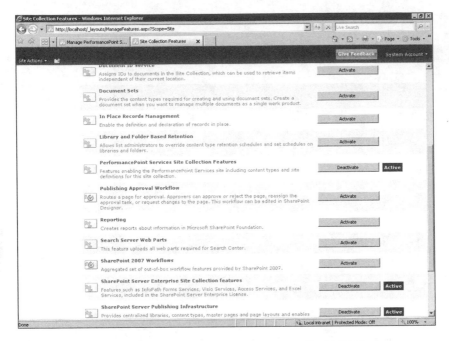

FIGURE 4.21   You see an Active banner after you activate the feature.

5. When activation completes, browse to each site that needs to host PerformancePoint content. For each site, go to the Site Actions menu and select the Site Settings menu item.

TIP

Past this point, being a site collection administrator is no longer required. Site administrator access is required only on sites that host PerformancePoint content.

You also need to perform the steps included in the next section for any site that you want to use to host PerformancePoint content.

Activating the Feature at a Site Level

To activate the feature in the site, follow these steps:

1. Browse to the site at which the PPS feature is to be used. Remember that you must be the site administrator.

2. Under Site Actions, click the Manage Site Features link.

3. Scroll to find PerformancePoint Services Site Collection Features. If the feature is not already activated, click the Activate button (see Figure 4.22).

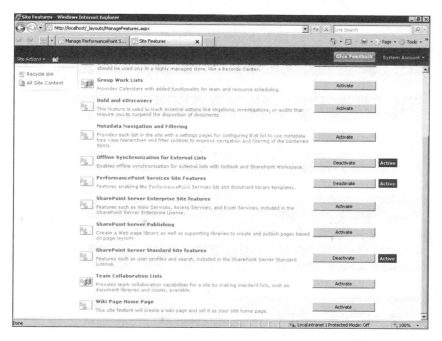

FIGURE 4.22   You see the Active banner after you activate the feature.

4. When activation completes, browse to each site that needs to host PerformancePoint content. For each site, go to the Site Actions menu, and then select the Site Settings menu item.

Validating the PPS Installation

With a multistep installation, a best practice is to verify that all components are configured and working properly before moving the application into full production for use by business users. You can validate the PPS installation by launching and using PerformancePoint Dashboard Designer to create a data source, scorecard, and dashboard. Dashboard Designer is the design tool you use to build these PPS objects. If you can successfully create a data source, scorecard, and dashboard, you can rest assured that you have configured PPS correctly.

To prepare for validating the PPS installation, read Chapter 5, "Introducing PerformancePoint Dashboard Designer," which serves as an introduction to Dashboard Designer. Then read Chapter 6, "Data Sources," Chapter 7, "Using Indicators, KPIs, and Scorecards," and Chapter 9, "Page Filters, Dashboards, and SharePoint Integration," where you can find instructions on creating a data source, scorecard, and dashboard.

Summary

PPS is integrated into SharePoint, so first you must install SharePoint and then configure the PPS service application. It is important to note that the installation of SharePoint 2010 is similar to the installation of SharePoint 2007, but the configuration of the PPS service application is different. The service application concept has been changed significantly in the PPS 2010 release, and these changes impact the configuration process.

For the most part, the installation process is straightforward, and the Preparation tool guides you through the installation of SharePoint, including the identification and installation of software prerequisites. SharePoint can be installed as a standalone installation or a server farm installation. The server farm installation is more complex and takes longer to complete, but it allows for future expansion.

Regardless of the type of installation you select, you must complete four tasks to complete the PerformancePoint installation:

▶ Start the PerformancePoint Service.

▶ Create the PerformancePoint service application.

▶ Associate the service application proxy with a proxy group.

▶ Activate the feature in the web application.

Upon completion of these tasks, you will have a fully functional SharePoint deployment with a properly configured PPS service application, which means you are ready to start creating objects with PPS.

Best Practices

▶ For more information about SharePoint and deploying SharePoint, we recommend the following book, *Microsoft SharePoint 2010 Unleashed* (0672333252).

▶ Remember to use an x64 operating system; x32 is no longer supported.

▶ Downloading .NET Framework 3.5 SP1 from the Microsoft Download Center is the most time-consuming aspect of this part of the installation process. If necessary, install the .NET Framework from a local source before running the Preparation tool (to reduce overall installation time).

▶ Use the standalone installation for SharePoint to provide a quick evaluation of the SharePoint software during a proof-of-concept phase.

▶ If you run the installation on a mission-critical server, run the SharePoint Configuration Wizard during off hours or during scheduled downtime to avoid disruption of critical Internet services.

▶ Join the Customer Experience Improvement Program to participate in helping to shape feature and testing efforts for future releases.

▶ A best practice regarding security is to enter a new managed account in the Service Account section instead of using the existing server farm managed account.

▶ Verify the four tasks for creating the service application regardless of the type of installation you performed.

▶ Validate the PPS installation by launching and using PerformancePoint Dashboard Designer to create a data source, scorecard, and dashboard.

4

Introducing PerformancePoint Dashboard Designer

IN THIS CHAPTER

▶ Understanding PerformancePoint Dashboard Designer Prerequisites 72

▶ Installing Dashboard Designer 73

▶ Uninstalling Dashboard Designer 75

▶ Examining Dashboard Designer 76

▶ Content Migration with Dashboard Designer 84

After you have deployed a fully functional Microsoft SharePoint Server 2010 installation with a proper configuration of PerformancePoint Services (PPS), you are ready to launch PerformancePoint Dashboard Designer. Dashboard Designer is the design tool you use to create and deploy dashboards on SharePoint. Dashboard Designer is a ClickOnce application, making installation a straightforward process. Dashboard Designer is a visual and intuitive design tool that also makes the creation of scorecards and dashboards for monitoring performance a straightforward process.

This chapter covers the specifics of launching Dashboard Designer, including understanding how to install and uninstall a ClickOnce application. It also provides an overview of the Dashboard Designer main screen and most important options and a section on migrating content with Dashboard Designer.

It is recommended to review the installation chapter (Chapter 4, "Installing Microsoft SharePoint Server 2010 and Configuring PerformancePoint Services") before launching Dashboard Designer. This chapter serves as an introduction to Dashboard Designer. For additional information and instructions on using some of the most important and most frequently used Dashboard Designer features, see

▶ Chapter 6, "Data Sources"

▶ Chapter 7, "Using Indicators, KPIs, and Scorecards"

▶ Chapter 8, "Reports"

▶ Chapter 9, "Page Filters, Dashboards, and SharePoint Integration"

Understanding PerformancePoint Dashboard Designer Prerequisites

PerformancePoint Dashboard Designer is the design tool you use to build key performance indicators (KPIs), indicators, scorecards, reports, filters, data sources, and dashboards. It also enables you to deploy your finished dashboards to SharePoint.

Dashboard Designer is a .NET Framework ClickOnce application that requires the .NET Framework 3.5 SP1. It also has a few other optional components that enable additional functionality that users can install on their own, including the following:

▶ Visio 2007 or 2010 Professional for creating or editing strategy map reports

▶ Report Viewer 2008 for creating or editing SQL Server Reporting Services reports

---

NOTE

If you deploy Dashboard Designer in a highly secure environment, it is important to ensure that the proper prerequisites are installed. If the .NET Framework 3.5 SP1 (Service Pack 1) is not installed, you see an error indicating that the System.Data.Entity assembly does not exist on the client machine (see Figure 5.1). To resolve this, ensure that the .NET Framework 3.5 is installed and has been upgraded at least to SP 1. Figure 5.1 shows the error message you see if the appropriate .NET Framework version is not installed.

FIGURE 5.1   This error appears if the .NET Framework 3.5 SP1 is not installed.

You can determine which service pack of the .NET Framework is installed on a client machine by querying the HKEY_LOCAL_MACHINE\SOFTWARE\Microsoft\NET Framework Setup\NDP\v3.5 Registry entry for the service pack value. The service pack value should be 1 or greater than 1.

Visio 2007 or 2010 Professional is required on the client machine for creating or editing strategy maps. Strategy maps are reports that enable you to connect KPI data to Visio shapes to visualize data. Due to interoperability requirements from the .NET Framework, it is important that the processor architecture for the operating system match the processor architecture for the version of Visio that is installed. If the processor architecture does not match, it will not be possible to edit strategy maps with that particular client machine. It is possible to work with strategy maps by adding them to dashboards and creating links between the strategy map and other PPS objects on the dashboard editor, but you cannot create new ones. The following table summarizes the client processor architecture compatibility for Visio and Windows (what combinations work on the client machine).

	Windows x86	Windows x64
Visio 2007 (x86 only)	Works	Does not work
Visio 2010 x86	Works	Does not work
Visio 2010 x64	N/A	Works

Installing Dashboard Designer

Dashboard Designer is a ClickOnce-deployed application. One advantage to ClickOnce technology is that the application is hosted and client deployment is lightweight. Therefore, you do not have to install the application from any type of installation media or files, and there is not an EXE file. Instead, you launch the Dashboard Designer installation by clicking a hyperlink located on the home page on a site created using the Business Intelligence template.

In addition, patches are applied automatically. If the SharePoint server has a patch or service pack applied, the next time a user launches Dashboard Designer, the ClickOnce framework checks the version number on the server and downloads an updated version before launching.

CAUTION

Patching, which refers to deploying a new version of Dashboard Designer on the server, works fine as long as the build version is moving forward. If the new build number is lower than the last run version on the client machine, the application will not be updated automatically. Patching breaks down in cases where the patch applied to the server has been rolled back or in a multiple server scenario where there are two environments at different patch levels. If this happens and strange behavior occurs, follow the steps for uninstalling Dashboard Designer described later in this chapter.

All first class objects created by Dashboard Designer are stored in one or more SharePoint document libraries and lists. A *first class object* is an item that you can manage in Dashboard Designer and reuse in different dashboards. Examples of an item include a KPI, an indicator, a scorecard, reports, filters, data sources, and dashboards. You learn more about first class objects in the "Examining First Class Objects" section later in this chapter.

To initiate the Dashboard Designer download and installation process, follow these steps:

1. Browse to a Business Intelligence Center site, such as http://localhost/BICenter (see Figure 5.2).

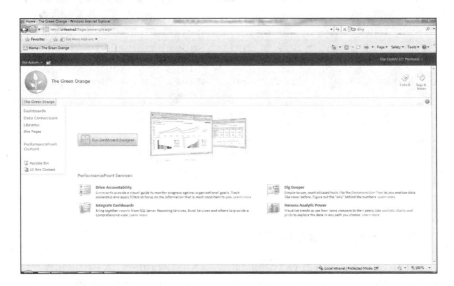

FIGURE 5.2   Click Run Dashboard Designer from this screen.

2. Under the Create Scorecards with PerformancePoint Services section, click the Start Using PerformancePoint Services link.

3. Click the Run Dashboard Designer button.

Dashboard Designer downloads and starts. When this process is complete, you see the main screen of the Dashboard Designer application, as shown later in Figure 5.4.

After you download and start Dashboard Designer the first time from the website, you can start it from your computer's Start and Programs menu. Dashboard Designer does not operate in offline mode. This means you must be connected to a SharePoint instance running PPS to run Dashboard Designer.

It is also possible to start Dashboard Designer when viewing a SharePoint list that supports PPS content types. You can create a new item by clicking the Add New Item button at the bottom of the web page, or you can use the New Item button on the Item tab located in the page ribbon.

You can edit an existing item by accessing the item's drop-down and selecting the Edit in Dashboard Designer option. In both cases, when Dashboard Designer launches, add the current list to the workspace, and any dependent items, and then open the item for editing in Dashboard Designer.

TIP

It is possible to launch Dashboard Designer from Firefox. To do this, you must have the Microsoft .NET Framework Assistant 1.1 add-on for Firefox installed. This add-on ships with Windows Vista and Windows 7. You can find the add-on for Firefox by searching for add-ons on the client computer.

If the add-on is not installed on your computer, you can download it from https://addons.mozilla.org/en-US/firefox/addon/9449?collection_uuid= 55afefb5-620d-ae0c-d5d1-b602b44e6428.

Although Safari is supported for viewing dashboards and PPS Web Parts, it is not possible to install a ClickOnce application using Safari.

Uninstalling Dashboard Designer

It is not possible to remove ClickOnce applications from the Windows Control Panel using the Add/Remove Programs option. However, because the files and settings created by Dashboard Designer are well contained, it is possible to remove Dashboard Designer from a client machine. To do this, perform the two steps listed here for each user who has used Dashboard Designer:

1. Delete the shortcut created on the Start menu under the SharePoint menu item.
2. Delete all files underneath %userprofile%\local settings\apps\2.0.

CAUTION

Keep in mind that the second step mentioned here also removes other ClickOnce applications that have been installed. However, these ClickOnce applications should download again automatically the next time they are launched by the user.

The first step removes the shortcut to Dashboard Designer. By removing access, it appears to the end user that Dashboard Designer has been removed from the computer. Although Dashboard Designer will not be readily accessible, the Dashboard Designer files and settings will remain on the computer. These files and settings do not take up much space on the hard drive, so this step is probably sufficient for the average end user. The second step removes the Dashboard Designer binaries from the computer (see Figure 5.3 for a list of folders to delete). This should be mostly transparent to the end user.

FIGURE 5.3   This is a sample list of folders to delete to remove Dashboard Designer from a client machine. Do not delete the manifest directory.

Examining Dashboard Designer

When you launch Dashboard Designer, the main Dashboard Designer screen consists of the following elements:

▶ A ribbon with three tabs: Home, Edit, and Create (see Figure 5.4)

▶ Workspace Browser pane on the left

▶ SharePoint tab that displays a view of the items that have been deployed to SharePoint

▶ Workspace tab that displays a view of the items that exist in the local workspace

When you select an item from the Workspace Browser on the left, the screen changes to include a view of the item in the workspace and a Details pane on the right, as shown in Figure 5.5.

The Details pane appears when you select a workspace item such as a KPI, scorecard, or data source. In the example shown in Figure 5.5, you see the settings for The Green Orange Data Connection in the center of the screen. On the right, the Details pane provides information on The Green Orange item.

FIGURE 5.4   This is a view of the main Dashboard Designer screen with items deployed to SharePoint.

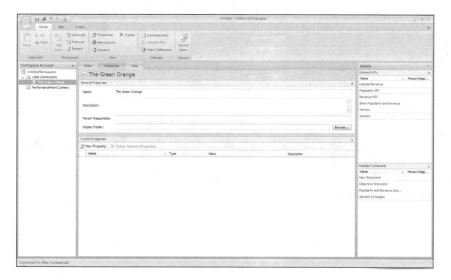

FIGURE 5.5   The Details pane changes depending on the item you select from the Workspace Browser.

Examining First Class Objects

Dashboard Designer allows you to work with first class objects. *First class objects* are items that you can manage in Dashboard Designer and reuse in different dashboards. The following items are considered first class objects:

▶ **Dashboards:** A compilation of KPIs, scorecards, reports, and filters. A dashboard is deployed to SharePoint.

▶ **Scorecards:** A compilation of KPIs.

▶ **KPIs:** KPIs enable you to measure the success of your organization, project, employees, and products. This is done by defining a goal or target value that is compared to an actual value.

▶ **Filters:** Filters enable you to filter dashboard items so that you can view only select items. The filter values can be almost anything. For example, you can filter by time, region, employee, or product.

▶ **Indicators:** Visual element associated with your KPIs that enables you to determine the status of a KPI. A classic example of an indicator is the red, yellow, and green traffic light indicator.

▶ **Data Sources:** PPS enables you to connect to the following data sources: Analysis Services, Excel Services, Excel Workbook, SharePoint List, and SQL Server Table/View.

▶ **Reports:** Reports enable you to visualize data using charts such as bar and line charts. Types of reports include analytic grid, analytic chart, strategy map, KPI details, and Reporting Services. Other reports include Excel Services, ProClarity Analytics server page, and web page.

> **NOTE**
>
> All objects that you create are stored in a database. Objects cannot be deployed until they have been saved to the database. You can also save a workspace locally as a Dashboard Designer Workspace (DDWX) file.

You learn more about the first class objects listed here, including how to use them, in the following chapters:

▶ Chapter 6, "Data Sources"

▶ Chapter 7, "Using Indicators, KPIS, and Scorecards"

▶ Chapter 8, "Reports"

▶ Chapter 9, "Page Filters, Dashboards, and SharePoint Integration"

Examining the Home Tab

The Home tab is made up of the following sections:

- ▶ Clipboard
- ▶ Workspace
- ▶ Item
- ▶ Changes
- ▶ Import

The Home tab is context sensitive, which means the options available will vary depending on the item you select. This section covers only the most important options in the Home tab.

Workspace Section

The Workspace section of the Home tab offers the following options, among others (see Figure 5.6):

- ▶ **Add Items:** Enables you to add an item and its related items to the local workspace. If you add a scorecard, the KPIs, data sources, and indicators that the scorecard uses will also be added. This option, which is context sensitive, will activate when you have objects highlighted in the SharePoint tab.

- ▶ **Add Lists:** Enables you to add a SharePoint list to the workspace. You cannot create a new list. Instead, the list has to exist in SharePoint.

- ▶ **Refresh:** Enables you to refresh the contents of a list. Use this option to update the contents of your local workspace to include items that have been added to a SharePoint list.

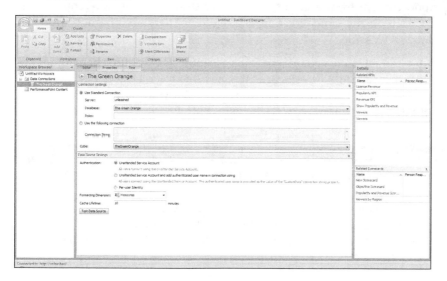

FIGURE 5.6   The Home tab contains the Workspace section.

Item Section

The Item section of the Home tab offers the following options among others:

▶ **Properties:** This option enables you to open the item's properties page in SharePoint. See Chapter 10, "Securing a PerformancePoint Installation," for more details.

▶ **Permissions:** Opens the item's permissions page in SharePoint. Because all Dashboard Designer items are SharePoint list items, the permissions from its parent, which is a site in this case, will apply. If necessary, you can break the inheritance.

▶ **Delete:** Enables you to delete an item from either the local or SharePoint workspace.

Changes Section

The Changes section of the Home tab offers the following options:

▶ **Compare Item:** Compare an item in the workspace with the latest saved version in SharePoint. This will produce a detailed report of property value differences between the workspace item and the SharePoint item.

▶ **Validate Item:** Checks that all data sources are valid and available for the item you select. For example, you can use this option to verify that data is available for all the KPIs on a scorecard.

▶ **Mark Differences:** Enables you to mark items in the local workspace that have a different property value compared to the SharePoint item.

Import Section

The Import section of the Home tab offers the following option:

▶ You can import content from different SharePoint lists on the same site, from different site collections on the same server, from a different SharePoint farm, or from a custom created DDWX file.

▶ The DDWX file format is created by serializing PPS objects from the SharePoint content database into a simple XML structure. It is possible to do custom editing of DDWX files before importing them. This proves useful if you want to do bulk editing of content and are comfortable working with XML.

CAUTION

The import feature in PPS 2010 works differently than the import feature in PPS 2007. In PPS 2007, you simply connected to a new server and republished the objects to import. In PPS 2010, the database and content are hosted natively in SharePoint. To import content, you must use the import user interface in Dashboard Designer. The "Content Migration with Dashboard Designer" section, later in this chapter, describes this process in more detail.

Examining the Edit Tab

The Edit tab is context sensitive, which means the options available will vary depending on the item that you select. For example, the options available will differ if you select a KPI or if you select a scorecard. The options available when a scorecard is selected are shown in Figure 5.7. Object-specific functionality for the various objects in PPS is discussed in their respective chapters.

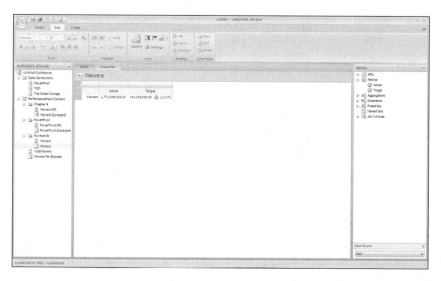

FIGURE 5.7   In this example, the Edit tab shows the options that are available when you select a scorecard.

Bulk Edit Section

When you select two or more items to edit, you will see the Bulk Edit section with the Bulk Edit option, as shown in Figure 5.8. The Bulk Edit option enables you to select and edit two or more items from a document library or workspace list. You can use this option to change the following properties: Description, Person Responsible, and Display Folder. This option appears when you select more than one item on the Workspace tab in Dashboard Designer.

This can prove useful when you need to change the same property on a number of objects (for example, changing the display folder for 15 KPIs simultaneously).

5

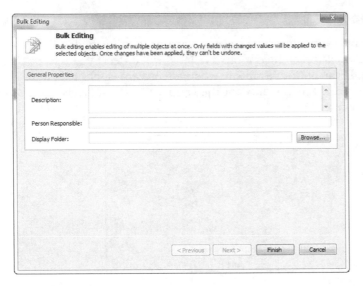

FIGURE 5.8   Use the Bulk Editing option to make changes to two or more items from a document library or workspace list.

Examining the Create Tab

The Create tab, shown in Figure 5.9, enables you to create any first class object. Examples of these first class objects include items such as dashboards, scorecards, KPIs, filters, indicators, and data sources. The Create tab also enables you to create different types of reports, including analytic charts, analytic grids, strategy maps, KPI details, Reporting Services, and other report types. The details for working with each of these dashboard items and reports are discussed in their respective chapters.

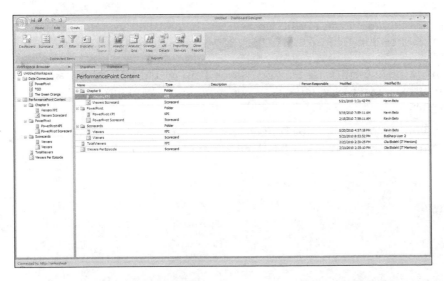

FIGURE 5.9   The Create tab enables you to create dashboard items and reports.

Examining Dashboard Designer Item Properties

Every first class item, except dashboards, has the same options available on the Properties page, as shown in Figure 5.10. A dashboard has an additional section called Deployment Properties. Remember that there are SharePoint properties available, as well as security.

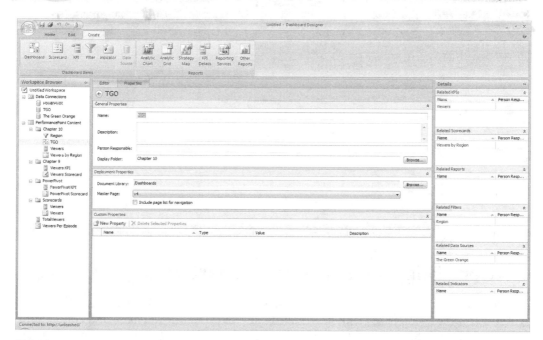

FIGURE 5.10   The Properties pane for most items consists of general properties and custom properties.

The Properties pane for all items, except dashboards, consists of two sections: General Properties and Custom Properties.

General Properties

In the General Properties section, you can specify the following properties:

▶ **Name:** The name of the item.

▶ **Description:** Item description.

▶ **Person Responsible:** The person who is responsible for an item. For example, you can list a person to contact if there are questions about a KPI.

▶ **Display Folder:** This setting enables you to organize items into folders. Remember that these are logical folders. Everything is stored in a database, so there is no actual file folder being created anywhere.

Custom Properties

In the Custom Properties section, you can select and add different property types, including text, decimal, date, or hyperlink. In the example shown in Figure 5.11, a custom property type called Expiration was added. Expiration is a date property type added to indicate how long a scorecard is valid. Another example is to add a property of type Hyperlink that shows a URL linking documentation that further explains the KPI. For example, this might include information on the data sources and calculations that are being used.

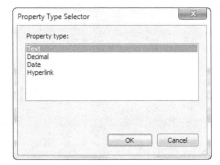

FIGURE 5.11   For custom properties, select the property type from the Property Type Selector.

Content Migration with Dashboard Designer

You can import content between farms, between site collections, or even within sites when you want to move content between lists. In PPS 2010, the database and content are hosted natively in SharePoint. To import content, you must use the import user interface in Dashboard Designer. First, in Dashboard Designer, you need to save the DDWX files on the source content server.

Importing Content with Dashboard Designer

To import content with Dashboard Designer, follow these steps (which assume that you have saved a DDWX file with the objects you want to import):

1. Open Dashboard Designer for the site to which you want to import. Ensure that the destination lists into which you are importing have been added to your current workspace. Click the Import Items button.

2. Select a local DDWX file you want to import and click OK in the file-selection dialog box.

3. In the Import Items to SharePoint dialog box shown in Figure 5.12, you see the Import From column. This column shows the document libraries and lists that exist in the workspace you selected in the previous step. The Copy To option enables you to browse for the document library or list to which you want to copy. Click the link to specify the document library or list on SharePoint where you want to copy the items.

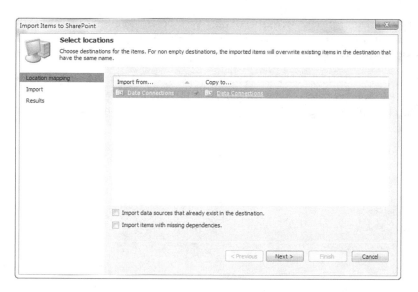

FIGURE 5.12   Click the link to specify the document library or list on SharePoint where you want to copy the items.

Location mapping will be done automatically if there are lists with the same names in your current workspace, as in the source location specified in the DDWX file to import. If not, select the lists into which you want to import.

In this example, the Data Connections option from the workspace was selected. The only valid destination on SharePoint is a document library also called Data Connections. This is the only valid destination because it is the only document library with an associated data connection document type. In addition, items from a document library cannot be imported into a list. Similarly, items from a list cannot be imported into a document library. This is because the different content types associated with the library and list are not compatible.

This dialog box provides the following available options:

▶ **Import Data Sources That Already Exist in the Destination:** When this item is selected, additional copies of data sources are created for any data source with the same name that already exists in the destination list. The data sources are using GUIDs as an identifier when they are being saved on the server and not the display name. That is how you can end up with two or more data sources using the same name. Do not select this option if you want to reuse existing and available data sources.

▶ **Import Items with Missing Dependencies:** This option enables you to import incomplete items. For example, you can import a KPI even if its data source is not present in the workspace. Select this option if you want to import an incomplete list of objects in a working state so that you can continue development in the destination location.

All document libraries and lists from the workspace must be mapped to a SharePoint destination before you can continue. When you have mapped all the items, click Next to import the items to SharePoint.

When the import process is complete, you see a screen detailing the results of the import (see Figure 5.13). If something did not happen as you expected, click the View the Log to See More Details link. This opens a log file in Notepad detailing exactly what happened to each object selected for import.

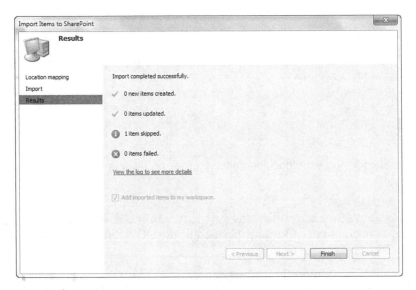

FIGURE 5.13   When the process is complete, you see the results.

Summary

Dashboard Designer is the design tool for building KPIs, indicators, scorecards, reports, filters, data source, and dashboards. It is also the tool used for importing content between farms, site collections, or even within sites.

As a ClickOnce application, installing Dashboard Designer and keeping it up-to-date is a straightforward process. The ClickOnce framework ensures that you are always working with the most recent version of the application.

There are a few prerequisites for installing Dashboard Designer, including the installation of .NET Framework 3.5 SP1 and the installation of Visio and Report Viewer for creating and editing specific report types. After you have fulfilled these prerequisites, you can take advantage of Dashboard Designer to start building a performance-monitoring system.

Best Practices

- ▶ Review Chapter 4 of this book before launching Dashboard Designer.

- ▶ Install .NET Framework 3.5 SP1 before launching Dashboard Designer.

- ▶ Install Visio 2007 or 2010 Professional to create or edit strategy map reports.

- ▶ Examine the processor architecture for the operating system to make sure it matches the processor architecture for the version of Visio that is installed.

- ▶ Install Report Viewer 2008 to create or edit SQL Server Reporting Services reports.

- ▶ To uninstall Dashboard Designer for the average user, just delete the shortcut.

- ▶ To uninstall Dashboard Designer and delete the Dashboard Designer binaries, remove all files under %userprofile%\local settings\apps\2.0. Do not remove the manifest directory.

5

CHAPTER 6

Data Sources

IN THIS CHAPTER

▶ Overview of Data Sources 90

▶ Analysis Services Data Sources 92

▶ PowerPivot Data Sources 95

▶ Excel Services Data Source 97

▶ Import from Excel Workbook 102

▶ SharePoint List Data Source 105

▶ SQL Server Table Data Source 107

▶ Time Intelligence 108

As the foundation for key performance indicators (KPIs), data sources are the most important part of business intelligence (BI) solutions. It is not an exaggeration to say that a BI solution is only as good as its underlying data. PPS supports two primary types of data sources: multidimensional and tabular.

In this chapter, you learn about the differences between these two types of data sources. You also learn how these data sources can be applied appropriately in various scenarios. Each section in this chapter includes information to explain the main features of the different data sources, and examples to illustrate implementation. The chapter includes in-depth information on the following data sources:

▶ Analysis Services

▶ Excel Services

▶ Excel workbooks

▶ SharePoint list data

▶ SQL Server tables and views

A final section shows how to apply time intelligence formulas to both multidimensional and tabular data sources to enable users to view data over time. Time intelligence formulas make use of the Simple Time Period Specification (STPS) syntax language. This chapter also provides examples of the most commonly used STPS expressions and operators.

Refer to the following chapters for information on other topics relevant to this chapter:

- ▶ Chapter 5, "Introducing PerformancePoint Dashboard Designer," provides information on using PerformancePoint Dashboard Designer to create data sources.

- ▶ Chapter 7, "Using Indicators, KPIs, and Scorecards," can help you understand how data sources interact with the key components of a monitoring system.

- ▶ Chapter 10, "Securing a PerformancePoint Installation," explains how to secure your data sources.

Overview of Data Sources

Data sources are an extremely important piece of any BI solution. A scorecard or dashboard can only be as good as the data it is presenting, so it is important to consider the quality, accessibility, and format of the data before embarking on a BI solution.

Data sources serve as the foundation for KPIs and analytic charts and grids. In addition, data sources can be used for dashboard filters. Specifically, tabular data sources can be used for the Custom Table filter, and the Analysis Services data source can be used for the Multidimensional Expressions (MDX) query, member selection, named set, time intelligence, and time intelligence connection formula filters.

> **NOTE**
>
> Filter configuration is discussed in more detail in Chapter 9, "Page Filters, Dashboards, and SharePoint Integration." Time intelligence configuration is discussed in more detail in the "Time Intelligence" section of this chapter.

The following two subsections discuss the two broad categories of data sources that PPS supports: multidimensional data sources and tabular data sources.

Multidimensional Data Sources

Multidimensional data sources are all variants of SQL Server Analysis Services. They feature dimensions, fact data, and support for the MDX language, as opposed to columns and values that are used in tabular data sources.

Multidimensional data sources are the primary use case for PPS, and many features such as analytic charts and grids and the decomposition tree in PPS require multidimensional data to operate. If you do not have any data in multidimensional format, consider porting some of your data to a multidimensional format to take full advantage of the features of PPS.

- ▶ Analysis Services (2005, 2008, and 2008 R2)

- ▶ SQL Server 2008 R2 PowerPivot

> **NOTE**
>
> Online analytical processing (OLAP) data sources, which were available in PPS 2007, have been removed from PPS 2010. This is largely due to functional gaps caused by variations in features and support for the MDX language between other OLAP-supporting data sources and true Analysis Services data sources. If you have a multidimensional data source in a format other than SQL Server Analysis Services, it will not be accessible directly by PPS 2010.

Tabular Data Sources

Tabular data sources come in a wide variety of formats. Tabular data sources all feature columns and values and conceptually are similar to a spreadsheet. It is also possible to create custom tabular data sources, as covered at length in Chapter 11, "Working with the Monitoring API."

Tabular data sources have limited functionality. You can represent them as KPIs on scorecards or have them appear as data values within filters to interact with various non-analytic report types. Generally, this is the extent of their functionality. Listed here are the tabular data sources supported by PPS:

- ▶ Excel Services (Excel Services 2007 or 2010)

- ▶ Import from Excel workbook (Excel 2007 or 2010)

- ▶ SharePoint list (SharePoint 2007 or 2010)

- ▶ SQL Server table (SQL Server 2005, 2008 or 2008 R2)

- ▶ Custom data source

Conceptually, tabular data is turned into *microcubes* within Dashboard Designer. Each tabular data source can define dimension and fact data types in the data source definition editor.

Dimension values are populated through members that are currently available in the data column. For instance, take the example of a dimension column that can contain Yes or No values. If the data only contains No values, it will not be possible to select a Yes value when adding a dimension filter to a KPI until the data contains at least one Yes value. In addition, dimensions created from tabular data are also always flat. Therefore, it is not possible to create a parent/child relationship and hierarchies between dimension values.

Fact data types are determined by the contents of the list. If all the data values are numbers, the data type is considered a number and can be aggregated as numbers. If just one value is text, the entire list will be considered as text fact data.

The Data Source template allows you to select the appropriate data source for your KPIs. For KPIs, you can use all types of PPS data sources. For analytic chart and grid reports, a multidimensional data source is required.

Data Source Security and Trusted Locations

All data connections must be stored in a trusted data connection library. This is true for all data connections that you want to reference from SharePoint. The reason for this is to ensure that all external data connections are approved before they can be used. In other words, a user cannot upload a data connection file to a random document library and use it in PPS; the user needs proper permissions to add the data connection file to the proper library.

By default, all data source locations are trusted and, if desired, need to be locked down by the farm administrator. This topic is discussed in more detail in Chapter 12, "Maintaining a PPS Deployment."

Analysis Services Data Source

To create a new Analysis Services data source, you need to have a deployed cube available. In addition, the unattended service account you use to connect should be configured to have at least read permissions. In this example, you connect to a cube named TheGreenOrange in a database named The Green Orange.

Create a New Analysis Services Data Source

The following steps describe how to create an Analysis Services data source:

1. There are two ways to create a new data source in Dashboard Designer. You can either select Data Source from the Create tab or right-click on a Data Connections library in the Workspace Browser and then select New Data Source.

2. Select the type of data source you want to create. In this example, select Analysis Services.

> **NOTE**
>
> After the data source has been created, you see three tabs called Editor, Properties, and Time, as shown in Figure 6.1. This example focuses on the Editor tab. The Properties tab was discussed in Chapter 5. In addition, the Time tab is discussed later in this chapter in the "Configuring Time Intelligence for an Analysis Services Data Source" section.

3. Specify the server and database connections by either specifying the name of the server and database or by providing a custom connection string. For this example, connect to localhost and a database named The Green Orange.

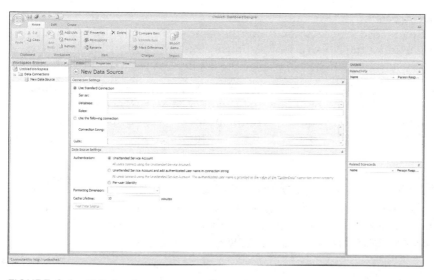

FIGURE 6.1   This is where you specify settings for the new data source.

NOTE

In step 3, if you use the connection string, you will have access to all connection string properties, such as packet size, timeout, and compression.

4. Select the cube by clicking the Cube drop-down, and then select the cube named TheGreenOrange from among the list of cubes available on the specific server.

You have now configured the connection settings for the data source. Authentication is discussed in the "Authentication" section.

NOTE

The Roles setting allows you to choose a specific Analysis Services database role that you want to use when you connect. The identity you are using to connect to the cube must be a member of the role you choose. This can be useful during development when you want to test different security settings.

Authentication

After you have successfully connected to a cube, the next step is to specify how you want to connect to the cube. You have the following options:

▶ Unattended Service Account

▶ Unattended Service Account and Add Authenticated User Name in Connecting String

▶ Per-User Identity

Unattended Service Account

In PPS 2007, the Unattended Service Account was the same as the application pool identity that was being used for the PPS web service, preview site, and SharePoint site. If you needed to change the identity, you had to change the application pool identity.

In PPS 2010, the Unattended Service Account is defined separately from the application pool identity. The farm administrator defines the Unattended Service Account in the Central Administration tool located on the PerformancePoint Service Application Settings page. See Chapter 10 and Chapter 12 for more information about how to configure this setting.

> **NOTE**
>
> A common issue that occurs when connecting to a newly deployed cube is that a role that was previously configured has been overwritten or deleted. Security settings may be set to prevent this issue. This is discussed in more detail in Chapter 10.

Using this configuration for authentication will scale better than the other two options because all users are connecting as the same user identity. Therefore, more caching can be done, which results in improved performance. On the other hand, this option does not allow you to filter data from the cube based on the user who is logged in. All users will have access to the same data.

Unattended Service Account and Add Authenticated User Name in Connecting String

The Unattended Service Account and Add Authenticated User Name in Connecting String setting is similar to the Unattended Service Account setting. The difference is that after you have connected to the cube, you can retrieve the name of the connected user using the CustomData() MDX function. This allows you to do a look up against a value in the cube and dynamically return a cell set. This is often called *dynamic OLAP security*, which can be useful if it is difficult to align security roles with Active Directory groups.

Following is a script that uses CustomData() to look up a user in the Employee dimension. If the user exists, Reseller Sales data for every country that has a match in the Geography dimension is returned:

```
Exists( [Geography].[Country].[Country].Members,
Filter(Employee.Employee.Employee.Members,
Employee.Employee.CurrentMember.Properties("Login ID") = CustomData()),
"Reseller Sales")
```

Because this setting depends on the CustomData() MDX function, it is available only when connecting to an Analysis Services cube.

Per-User Identity

The Per-User Identity setting allows you to connect to the cube using the identity of the logged-in user. You can also filter data in the cube based on its security settings. For example, you can restrict certain dimension members to show up in a filter. The potential downside to using this option is scalability. If you have a large number of users that interact heavily with a dashboard, little data can be cached.

CAUTION

There are two ways to utilize the Per-User Identity setting.

The easiest is to do a standalone installation of SharePoint, which automatically configures per-user security for any requests that do not leave the box. This is useful in demo scenarios where the cube is deployed locally on the SharePoint server. Because this requires a standalone configuration, there are some limitations to the amount of content. Keep in mind that this scenario does not work in a single-machine farm scenario.

The other way to accomplish this is to configure Kerberos authentication for the environment. This requires domain-level settings but enables this authentication mechanism for all farm scenarios. See the "Configuring Kerberos Security" section in Chapter 10 for more information.

Formatting Dimension and Cache Interval

The Formatting Dimension setting allows you to specify which of your cube dimensions has the data formatting information to use.

The Cache Interval setting allows you to specify the time interval before queries will be resent to the cube. If the cube data changes within the specified time interval, the change will not be reflected until the cache has expired. Setting this to zero has the effect of always returning real-time data but will cause increased load on both the data source and SharePoint server.

PowerPivot Data Sources

SQL Server 2008 R2 PowerPivot data sources are the only other type of multidimensional data source that can be accessed by PPS. The data is an Excel workbook saved on a SharePoint server with the PowerPivot components installed.

Server Requirements

There are some increased server prerequisite requirements to enable PowerPivot data sources. If you are using PPS on the same SharePoint farm that has the PowerPivot components installed, there should be no additional requirements or software.

If you are connecting to a different SharePoint farm, and the farm that PPS is running on does not have PowerPivot installed, the SQL native client on that server needs to be upgraded to SQL Server 2008 R2.

Creating a New PowerPivot Data Source

PowerPivot data sources are not natively supported by PPS. However, because they support most of the same interfaces and functionality as Analysis Services, it is possible to connect to a PowerPivot workbook hosted in Excel through a connection string as follows using an Analysis Services data source (see Figure 6.2):

```
provider=molap;datasource=http://<server>/<document library>/<Power PivotFile>.xlsx
```

Notice the name of the cube used in Figure 6.2. All cubes used with PowerPivot are called Sandbox, and that is the only cube you will see in the cube dropdown list.

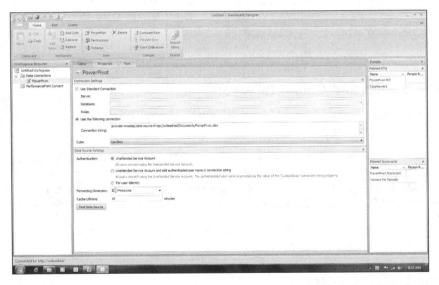

FIGURE 6.2   You can connect to a PowerPoint workbook hosted in Excel through a connection string.

Manipulating PowerPivot Data

You work with PowerPivot data the same way you work with native mode Analysis Services data. The major differences are that PowerPivot does not have support for parent-child hierarchies so all dimensions will be flat attribute hierarchies, and Time Intelligence functionality is disabled for PowerPivot data sources. This is due to limitations in the PowerPivot DAX language, and may work for future releases or Service Packs of PerformancePoint and PowerPivot.

Once you have connected to the PowerPivot data source, you can create any first class object based on that data source such as KPIs, scorecards, reports, filters.

Excel Services Data Source

Before you can successfully configure an Excel Services data source, you need to have an Excel workbook deployed to a SharePoint document library. Whether you are using an Unattended Service Account or Per-User Identity, you also need to ensure that the identity you are using to connect has the proper permissions to connect to the SharePoint document library housing the Excel Services data source.

> **NOTE**
>
> If you are using an external tabular or Analysis Services data source to populate the workbook, remember that the connecting user must also have the proper permissions to use the data source.

In this example, you are going to connect to a spreadsheet called TheGreenOrange.xlsx that is located in the Documents document library, as shown in Figure 6.3.

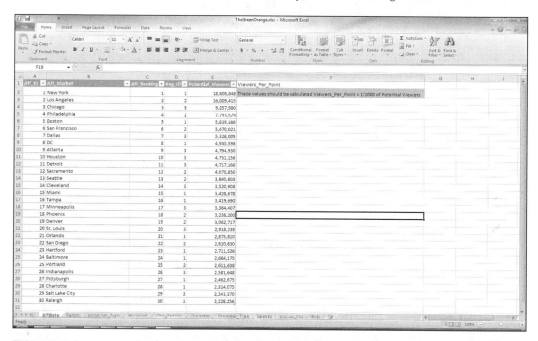

FIGURE 6.3   In this example, TheGreenOrange.xlsx is located in the Documents document library.

Create a New Excel Services Data Source

1. You create a new Excel Services the same way you created an Analysis Services data source. Either click Data Source on the Create tab or right-click Data Connections, and then select New Data Source.

2. Next, specify the SharePoint server and document library where the workbook is located. After you have successfully connected to the document library, you can enumerate all workbooks in that document library.

3. This step is important. You need to specify the name of a table or named range within the workbook that you want to use. For this example, use a table named Affiliate_Table. The complete settings look like those shown in Figure 6.4.

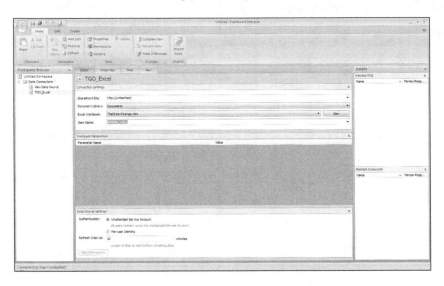

FIGURE 6.4   Your settings for this example should look like this.

4. You do this step with all tabular data source options, including Excel Services, Import from Excel Workbook, SharePoint List, and SQL Server Table. Because Dashboard Designer understands only dimensional data, configure how to interpret the tabular columns as dimensions and facts by clicking the View tab, as shown in Figure 6.5.

   As you can see in Figure 6.5, the five columns in the original workbook appear, and either a dimension or a fact suggestion is provided based on the data type for each column. Notice that all the cells say No data.

5. Click the Preview Data button to get a data sample based on the contents in the workbook. The first 25 rows of data in the table appear.

6. Dashboard Designer will suggest that all numerical columns are facts and that all text columns are dimensions. In this example you only want to use the Aff_Market as a dimension and Potential_Viewers as a measure. You also need to modify the column type and column headers to make them more descriptive and useful. You can do this by changing the column type and column headers in the Details Properties pane on the right side. Figure 6.6 shows what your data will look like after the column header names have been changed.

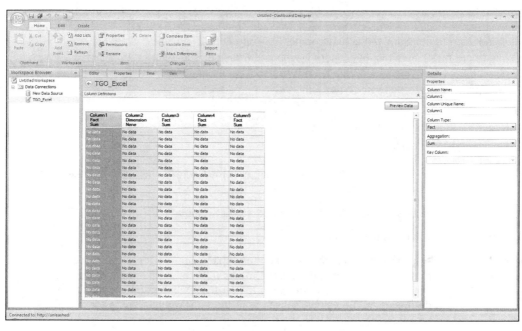

FIGURE 6.5 Either a dimension or a fact suggestion is provided based on the data type for each column.

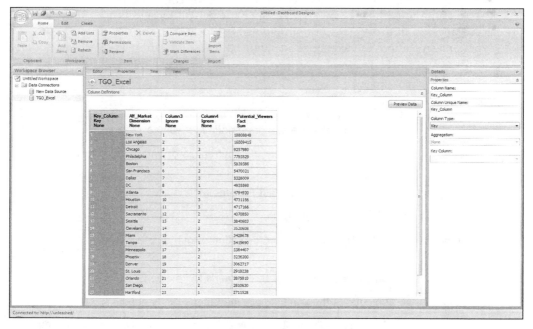

FIGURE 6.6 The column headers have been modified to be more descriptive and useful.

> **NOTE**
>
> In addition to changing the column names, you can change a column type. For example, there might be situations where Dashboard Designer suggests that a column should be a fact when you actually want to use it as a dimension. Table 6.1 lists the available column types you can specify.

TABLE 6.1   Tabular Data Source Column Types

Column Type	Function
Dimension	Values in this column are treated as if they were members of a dimension based on the column.
Fact	Values in this column are treated as fact values.
Ignore	Values in this column are ignored.
Key	Values in this column are treated as tuples. Data in the column has to be formatted as a tuple, [Product].[Category].[Bike]. An example of using this would be using filter values from a filter that is based on a multidimensional data source. The values passed from the filter would also be formatted as tuples.
TimeDimension	Values in this column are candidates for mapping to the master time dimension for time intelligence.

7. Configure the type of aggregation you want to use for your facts. The default is always going to be Sum, but you can change the default by selecting a different aggregation from the Aggregation drop-down list located in the details pane. The types of aggregations are explained in Table 6.2.

TABLE 6.2   Aggregation Types

Aggregation	Usage
Average	Calculates the average of numeric fact values
Count	Determines the number of occurrences of unique members in the column
Minimum	Determines the smallest numeric fact value
None	Performs no aggregation
Statistical Standard Deviation	Calculates the standard deviation of numeric fact values
Sum	Calculates the sum of the numeric fact values
Statistical variance	Calculates the variance of the numeric fact values
First occurrence	Determines the first fact value that occurs for each unique column member

TIP

None, Count, and First occurrences are the only aggregation types that can be used with textual data. Using any other aggregation types will result in errors when using the data source.

8. Configure the type of authentication model you want to use. The options are Unattended Services Account or Per-user Identity. The settings for these two options are the same as for the Analysis Services data source and are found on the Editor tab.

9. (Optional) The parameter configuration is optional because it applies only if the workbook has parameters defined (see Figure 6.7). When you deploy a workbook to SharePoint, you have the option to specify if you want to use a single-cell named range as a parameter. These parameters can then be referenced in the parameters settings. Figure 6.7 shows an example of a different workbook with parameters called param1 and param2.

TIP

Parameters can be used within an Excel workbook to pass some configuration data back to the workbook. In the data source scenario, they are primarily used to modify data when the parameters are used in formulas within the workbook. However, they first need to be configured in the workbook in the Excel Services Options dialog that is available when publishing the workbook to Excel Services.

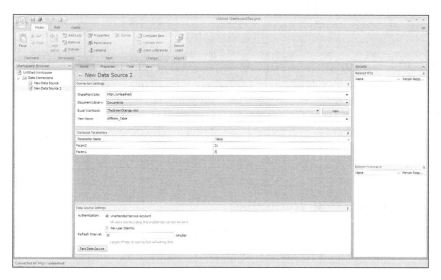

FIGURE 6.7   The parameter configuration applies only if the workbook has parameters defined.

Import from Excel Workbook

The Import from Excel Workbook data source option behaves differently from the other data source options because it does not maintain a live connection. In other words, if you import a workbook and values within that workbook change, the changes will not be reflected until you import that data again. The workbook will be serialized and stored inside of the PPS content repository. Use Excel Services if you need to maintain a live connection to an Excel data source. The primary case for using an Excel workbook as a data source is when using static data that is not likely to change over time. For example, you might use this option when creating a set of custom filter values that can be passed to various reports on the dashboard.

The Import from Excel Workbook option enables you to import data from an existing workbook or to create the workbook during the process of creating the data source. This option also requires Excel to be installed on the same computer as Dashboard Designer.

Due to interoperability requirements from the .NET Framework, it is important that the processor architecture for the operating system match the processor architecture for the version of Excel that is installed. Table 6.3 illustrates the combinations that work on the client machine.

TABLE 6.3   Possible Interoperability Requirements

	Windows x86	Windows x64
Excel 2007 (x86 only)	Works	Does not work
Excel 2010 x86	Works	Does not work
Excel 2010 x64	N/A	Works

CAUTION

Office introduced several new methods of running Office applications such as Excel in the 2010 release. Aside from the standard installation, you can use the Click2Run technology and run applications from Office Online. However, none of these work with PPS or Dashboard Designer. The only supported method for using Excel with PPS is the tried-and-true MSI-based installation.

Import Data from an Existing Workbook

This example leads you through the steps of importing data located in a workbook named Actors.xlsx, as shown in Figure 6.8.

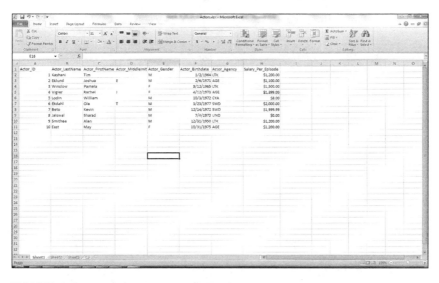

FIGURE 6.8   Data for the scorecard is stored in this Excel workbook called Actors.xlsx.

1. After creating a new data source based on the Import from Excel Workbook template, the Import screen appears.

2. You have the option to either Import or Edit data. For this example, import data from the Actors.xlsx workbook. To do this, click the Import button to browse for the workbook.

NOTE

It is also possible to start from a new Excel workbook by clicking the Edit button rather than the Import button. This launches a blank workbook where you can enter data.

3. If the first row contains header names, accept the default check, and then click Accept.

4. When the data is imported, preview the data to verify that the columns are tagged properly as either a dimension or a fact (see Figure 6.9).

   The data is imported successfully with the exception of the Actor_ID column, which was expected. This occurred because the data in this column is of type integer. Therefore, the import process assumes this column will be used as a fact, but you want to use it as a dimension.

5. To change the Actor_ID column type from a fact to a dimension, use the Column Type property in the Details Properties pane. Each column header indicates if it is of type Fact or Dimension.

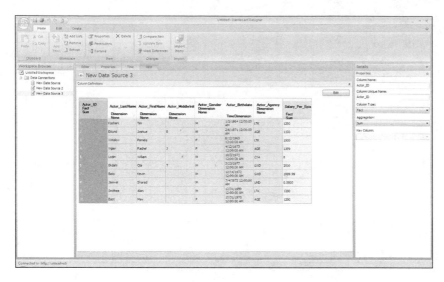

FIGURE 6.9   Verify that the columns are tagged properly as dimension or fact.

After you make this change, the data source is ready for use. Figure 6.10 shows the data used in a scorecard. Again, notice that you are now working with a dimensional and not tabular data structure.

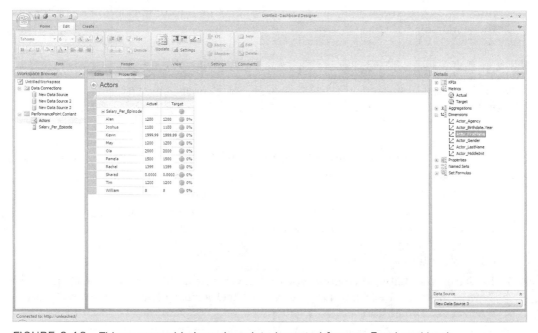

FIGURE 6.10   This scorecard is based on data imported from an Excel workbook.

SharePoint List Data Source

SharePoint lists are another form of tabular data that can be useful as a data source. SharePoint lists are quite easy to create and share with other business users. They also prove useful for gathering or sharing data in a persisted format.

CAUTION

SharePoint data sources always connect to the default list view and will take into account any filtering or column hiding done in this view. It is not possible to work around this limitation.

For example, if a column is hidden in the default view, it will not be shown in the list preview in Dashboard Designer, nor will it be available as a fact or dimension for a KPI or filter. In addition, if a filter is applied that obscures some rows in the list, that data will not be available in Dashboard Designer. This means that this data will be left out of aggregations.

To connect to a SharePoint list, you must have access to the list. In the following example, you connect to the SharePoint list, as shown in Figure 6.11.

FIGURE 6.11   This is an example of data stored in a SharePoint list.

1. After you create a new data source based on the SharePoint List data source template, a screen appears that allows the entry of connection information to the SharePoint list. On this screen, specify the SharePoint site that contains the list.

2. Select the list collection and list name from the drop-down menus.

3. Click Test Data Source to ensure that the connecting user has read permission to access the SharePoint list. See Figure 6.12 for an example of complete settings.

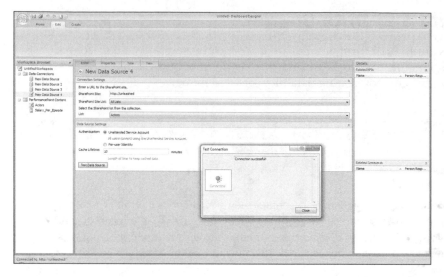

FIGURE 6.12   This is an example of complete settings for a SharePoint list data source.

4. Switch to the View tab to verify that all columns have been configured using the proper column type and that all facts use the correct aggregation function. This step applies to all tabular data sources.

TIP

A common problem when working with existing SharePoint lists is that they were not designed with BI in mind. When working with SharePoint lists that do not have true fact data, a useful trick is to create a Count aggregation on the Attachments column. This will have the effect of counting the number of rows that are in a given query.

5. Check to make sure that all the columns are configured properly. There is an additional SharePoint list metadata column, called Attachments, listed in the preview. Because you probably are not interested in using that column, verify that the Attachments column is set to Ignore.

NOTE

It is quite common for SharePoint lists to contain additional metadata columns that you can choose to ignore. These columns can either be ignored in SharePoint Designer or removed from the default view.

The Authentication options, Unattended Service Account, and Per-User Identity behave the same as all other tabular data sources.

SQL Server Table Data Source

The last type of data source examined in this chapter is the SQL Server table data source. As the name implies, this data source allows you to create a connection to SQL Server tables. You can also create a connection to SQL Server views. Like all other data sources discussed in this chapter, you need to have at least read access to the source before you can create a successful connection.

In this example, connect to the RequestUsage table located in the WSS_Logging database.

1. After you create a new data source based on the SQL Server table data template, the SQL Connection Settings screen appears.

2. Next, specify the server, database, and table or view name.

3. You can also choose to configure the connection string manually to get access to all connection string properties, as you did with Analysis Services. As with all other tabular data sources, the authentication options available are Unattended Service Account and Per-user Identity. Figure 6.13 shows how the settings should look after you specify all the properties.

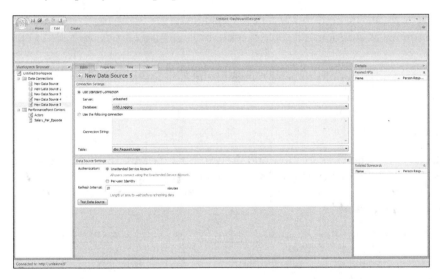

FIGURE 6.13   This is an example of complete settings for a SQL Server table data source.

4. As with all tabular data sources, verify that all columns have been properly configured as a dimension or fact. In addition, verify that all facts are using the proper aggregation column (see Figure 6.14).

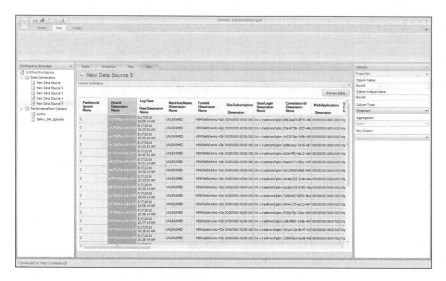

FIGURE 6.14   Verify that the columns are tagged properly as dimension or fact.

As shown in Figure 6.14, all the columns except for the RowID are configured correctly. The RowID is interpreted as a dimension since it contains GUID's, so it has been set to be a dimension.

After you change the RowID column to be of type Key, the data source is ready to be used in a scorecard.

Time Intelligence

A common requirement of clients is to allow end users to filter data from scorecards and reports on a dashboard based on a time intelligence formula. Time intelligence formulas allow users to view data over time, such as year over year (YOY), last period, rolling average, and year to date (YTD).

For example, to implement this capacity in an Analysis Services cube, the cube implementer needs to create that type of formula using a language native to Analysis Services. In Analysis Services, the language used is Multidimensional Expressions (MDX). To implement this capacity against a tabular data source, you need to implement it using a language native to the data source. For example, if your data source is a SQL database, you need to use T-SQL.

PPS provides its own expression language called Simple Time Period Specification (STPS). STPS enables you to create time intelligence formulas rapidly. For example, if you want to see aggregated data based on YTD, you can create a time intelligence filter and use the following formula:

```
Year.FirstMonth:Month
```

If you want to apply this data to 2009 sales numbers and the current month is July, this STPS expression aggregates all 2009 sales data from the first month of the current year to the current month. Under the covers, this expression is translated to the data source's native language. In this next section, you see this formula in action.

> **TIP**
>
> Time intelligence can be a confusing topic. To gain a better understanding of how it works, use the SQL Profiler to see how your STPS formulas are translated into MDX or T-SQL depending on which data source you are working against.

Configuring Time Intelligence for an Analysis Services Data Source

For STPS to work, you need to configure the data source so that your expressions properly match the time definition in the data source. Look at the previous code example:

```
Year.FirstMonth:Month
```

For this expression to work, you need to explain to STPS how year and month are defined in the data source. In other words, you need to map how time is defined in the data source to an internal, conformed master time dimension against which STPS works.

In this first example, you configure TheGreenOrange Analysis Services data connection that you created earlier.

The following steps describe how to configure the screen shown in Figure 6.15:

1. Notice that both the Analysis Services and tabular data sources have a Time tab. To successfully use time intelligence features, select a dimension named Date and a hierarchy named Year—Qtr—Month—Date to specify which dimension and hierarchy in the cube defines time.

2. Select a reference member and a hierarchy level because all Time Intelligence operations are calculated with these settings as a reference point. Any date within the cube should work fine because PPS can extrapolate other dates after one of them is selected.

> **CAUTION**
>
> A best practice is to ensure that the cube you are working with has its time dimension starting at the beginning of the calendar year. There were some issues in PPS 2007 where calendars starting at random intervals returned the wrong data.

3. Specify how the hierarchy levels in the data source's time dimension maps the internal, conformed master time dimension. The available hierarchy levels for the master time dimension are on the right side in the Time Member Associations area, as shown in Figure 6.15.

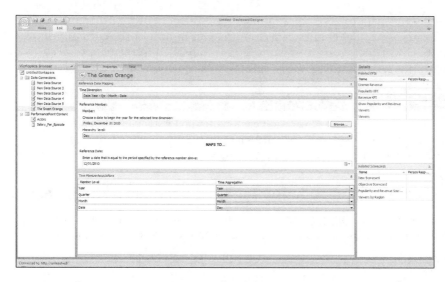

FIGURE 6.15   This is an example of complete settings for the Time Member example.

The Analysis Services data source is now configured to support STPS expression.

> **TIP**
>
> Suppose you have a data source that has multiple time dimensions and you want to use both time dimensions. The solution is to create a new data source for each time dimension you want to use in your PPS solution. For example, if the cube you are using has both calendar year and fiscal year dimensions, you can create two data sources using the same server and cube information with the only difference being the time dimension selected in the Time tab of each data source. When creating KPIs or filters, select the data source with the time dimension that makes sense for that object.

Configuring a Tabular Data Source

Configuring a time dimension for a tabular data source is slightly different from working with an Analysis Services data source. It is not necessary to select a reference member because PPS builds its own calendar and automatically maps it to the dimension. In this example, you configure a SQL Server table data source for which all tabular data is configured the same.

You have two columns that are treated as time dimensions in the data source: LogTime and RowCreatedTime. Select the LogTime column for this example. Figure 6.16 shows the completed settings.

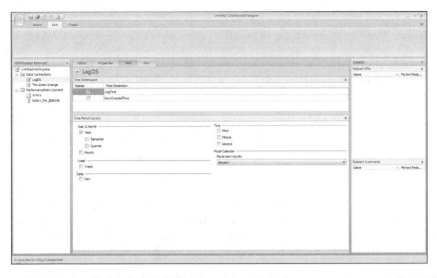

FIGURE 6.16   The tabular data source is now ready for time intelligence applications.

NOTE

Although it is possible to select multiple columns as time dimensions for tabular data sources, only the one with the check box selected is considered the "master" time dimension. If a time dimension is not the master time dimension, it is effectively just another dimension.

You now have the ability to use STPS expressions against the tabular data source.

STPS Syntax

The STPS syntax language is meant to be similar to the Excel Macro language. It enables you to select time members based on logical calendar patterns on business logic focused selection criteria such as last week or last quarter. In contrast, regular dimensions do not support the ability to select dimension members in this way.

Time members are always resolved to leaf members in the cube. For instance, if a month of time is selected and the cube has members stored in days, a collection of all days in that month will be returned. Likewise, if that cube stores data with hour granularity, all hours in that month will be returned instead.

NOTE

When dealing with non-English builds of PPS, it is important to note that the STPS language is not localized into different languages. For example, a Japanese installation of PPS still uses the English terms for members and functions.

Language Form

For those who are mathematically inclined, the formal declaration of the STPS syntax is as follows:

```
<TI_Expression> ::= <MemberExpression> , <TI_Expression> ¦ <MemberExpression> :
<MemberExpression>
```

For the rest of us, this means that a TI expression is a combination of time members. Time members, which are discussed later in this chapter, can consist of relative dates such as yesterday, relative date ranges such as last month, and functions such as quarter to date.

Time Members

Time members, which correspond to logical date units, are the core building blocks for the STPS syntax. Listed here are the levels of granularity available for users, which are referred to as *members* in the STPS syntax.

CAUTION

Members are available for use only if they have been configured in the data source. For example, if you configure an Analysis Services data source that only contains Year, Month, and Day levels, the Semester and Quarter members will result in errors if you attempt to use them.

▶ Year

▶ Semester

▶ Quarter

▶ Month

▶ Week

▶ Day

▶ Hour

▶ Minute

▶ Second

TIP

Although granularity down to the minute and second is included, it does not have many practical applications. Given the default caching times of 10 minutes, and overall performance of PPS, it is probably a good idea to stay with hour or greater granularity when using time intelligence.

Operators

The colon and comma are two operators used with time intelligence. These operators can be used to combine various members and functions of the STPS syntax. Table 6.4 summarizes the STPS operators you can use.

TABLE 6.4   STPS Operators

Operator	Usage
Colon (`:`)	The colon is used to indicate a range of dates. For example, the statement Day-1:Day-7 selects all the days between yesterday and a week ago inclusively.
Comma (`,`)	The comma is used to combine two members. For example, the statement Day-1,Day-7 selects today and a week ago today as distinct dates.

Functions

Several functions are available for traversing members. All parent and child references are relative to the configuration of the data source. For example, if a week level is configured directly above the day level, the Day.Parent function returns the current week. If there is no week configured and the next configured level up is a month, it returns the current month. The same applies to child references. Table 6.5 summarizes these functions.

CAUTION

Be careful of the FirstChild and LastChild functions. They work just fine until the data source definition changes to add in new levels. For a more robust implementation, stay with expressions that use members rather than the parent/child relationship where possible.

TABLE 6.5   STPS Functions

Function	Description	Example Expression	Example Result
Parent	The parent of the specified member.	Day.Parent	Week
FirstChild	The first child of the specified member.	Month.FirstChild	First day of month
LastChild	The last child of the specified member.	Month.LastChild	Last day of month
First<Member>	Returns the first child member of the parent time period. Any member must be below the referenced member; otherwise, the expression will not be valid. For example, Week.FirstYear will return an error.	(Year-1).FirstWeek	First week of the previous year
Last<Member>	Returns the last child member of the parent time period. Any member must be below the referenced member; otherwise, the expression will not be valid. For example, Week.FirstYear returns an error.	(Month-1).LastDay	The last day of last month
<Member>ToDate	Returns the range of dates between the beginning of the current period and now. Note that this function only supports members down to the Day level. This means that HourToDate, MinuteToDate, and SecondToDate are not valid expressions.	QuarterToDate	All days up until the current quarter

TABLE 6.5   Continued

Function	Description	Example Expression	Example Result
Full<Member>	Returns the last full period as specified by the member. Full is determined by calendar days, not by data in the data source. For example, FullMonth normally returns last month (month-1). However, in some cases it returns the previous parent periods last month. This function is primarily included to handle boundary cases around the beginning of periods when used in conjunction with the <Member>ToDate functions. For example, YearToDate.Month-1 is correct in all months except for January, in which case it returns an error because there are no months ahead of January in the current Year. YearToDate.FullMonth.	YearToDate.FullQuarter	The last full quarter for the current year

NOTE

The Full<Member> and <Member>ToDate functions are new with PPS 2010. All the other functions come from PPS 2007.

STPS Example

This section includes an example of how to create a time intelligence filter. More details about this topic are included in Chapter 9.

   1. To start, select the time intelligence filter template, and then select The Green Orange data source as seen in figure 6.17.

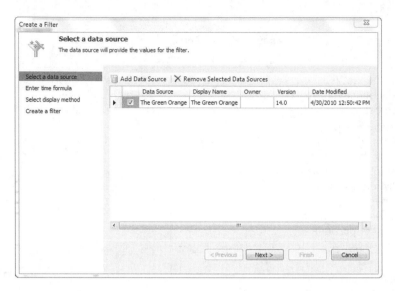

FIGURE 6.17   Start by selecting the Time Intelligence filter template and the data source.

2. Next, create the STPS expressions. For this example, the STPS expression is a year-to-date entry based on months, as shown in Figure 6.18.

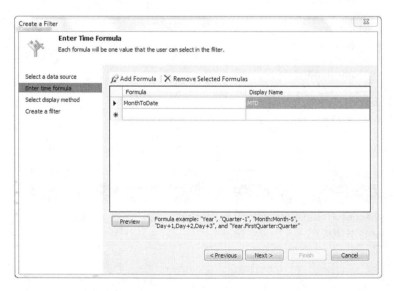

FIGURE 6.18   Enter the time formula.

3. Click the Preview button to see the dimension members that are returned, as shown in Figure 6.19.

FIGURE 6.19   Use the Preview feature to see the dimension members.

By using SQL Profiler, you can see how our STPS expression is translated to MDX (see Figure 6.20).

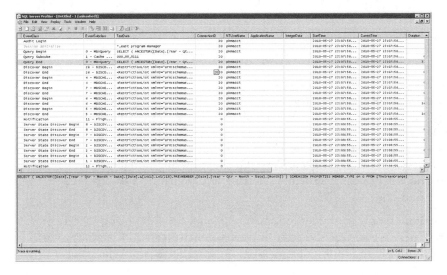

FIGURE 6.20   Use the SQL Server Profiler to see how the STPS expression translates to MDX.

After the filter has been added to a dashboard and it has been used with a scorecard, you can verify that it returns the correct data, as shown in Figure 6.21.

FIGURE 6.21   Verify the time intelligence filter and the formula on the dashboard.

Summary

This chapter provided an overview of working with the two primary types of data sources supported by PPS: multidimensional and tabular. After reading this chapter, you should have a good understanding of how to configure data sources to allow users to consume data from Analysis Services, Excel Services, Excel workbooks, SharePoint lists, and SQL Server tables and views. You should also understand the most appropriate scenarios for each data source and what to consider when selecting and preparing a data source for use in BI monitoring solutions.

With the information on how to configure time intelligence formulas using STPS expressions with Analysis Services and tabular data sources, you can create KPIs and scorecards that allow business users to monitor and view their organization's performance over time.

Best Practices

▶ Consider the quality, accessibility, and format of the data before embarking on a BI solution.

▶ If you do not have any data in multidimensional format, consider porting some of it to a multidimensional format to take full advantage of the features of PPS.

▶ Use Excel workbooks as data sources to hardwire in data that is not likely to change over time.

▶ Use SharePoint lists as a data source to share data in a persisted format.

▶ A best practice when using time intelligence formulas is to ensure that the cube you work with has its time dimension starting at the beginning of the calendar year.

▶ A best practice when using time intelligence formulas is to use hour granularity or greater.

CHAPTER 7

Using Indicators, KPIs, and Scorecards

IN THIS CHAPTER

▶ Understanding and Working
with Indicators   122

▶ Understanding and Working
with KPIs   128

▶ Understanding and Working
with Scoring   142

▶ Understanding and Working
with Scorecards   154

Scorecards, which are a key component of dashboards, are one of the most versatile objects in the PPS world. Scorecards display indicators and key performance indicators (KPIs), which are the metrics used for monitoring performance. Indicators are the images used to display the value of KPIs visually in a scorecard. Together these objects make up a monitoring system that can communicate critical business information quickly. This chapter provides an overview of how to work with indicators and KPIs and how to integrate these objects into a scorecard view. Examples are provided throughout the chapter.

Each section includes information to explain the main features of indicators, KPIs, and scorecards, and examples to illustrate implementation. The chapter includes in-depth information on scoring patterns, thresholds, and methods. This can help PPS users understand the calculations that occur behind the scenes and help users understand how to refine KPIs and scorecards to best meet their monitoring needs. The chapter also examines how to select the data you want to use for a metric in a KPI. This discussion includes adding dimensions and measures to create scorecards and using calculated metrics to provide refined and complex views into the business information of an organization.

Refer to the following chapters for information on other topics relevant to this chapter:

▶ Chapter 5, "Introducing PerformancePoint Dashboard Designer," provides additional information on using PerformancePoint Dashboard Designer to create indicators, KPIs, and scorecards.

▶ Chapter 6, "Data Sources," provides details about the different types of data sources you can use with KPIs.

▶ Chapter 9, "Page Filters, Dashboards, and SharePoint Integration" provides information on integrating scorecards into dashboards and different filter options available after a scorecard is rendered on a SharePoint site.

Understanding and Working with Indicators

Indicators are the images used to display the approximate value of a KPI visually in a scorecard. Typical indicators include the popular traffic light icons that display green (on target), amber (needs attention), and red (off target) to indicate status. Indicators prove useful when displaying a large amount of data on a scorecard. For example, a scorecard might contain hundreds of different KPI metrics. Visual indicators on a scorecard heavily populated with KPIs can communicate a high-level status and make performance understandable with a single glance.

Examining Indicator Styles

In PPS there are two types of indicators:

▶ Standard indicators

▶ Centered indicators

Standard indicators are indicators that have increasingly better statuses. For example, a metric with no upper limit to its goodness, such as profit, would be best represented by a standard indicator. Likewise, a metric such as spending that gets better as it decreases should also be represented by a standard indicator. The decision to choose which end is better can be made when creating the KPI to be associated with the indicator, not when you are creating the indicator.

Centered indicators are used for KPIs that aim for a specific target. For example, monitoring headcount in a department is the type of metric that could use a centered indicator. With headcount, a manager generally has a target number, which means it could be bad to go too far above or too far below the target number.

Examining Indicator Sources

Indicators are stored as objects within the SharePoint content database. In PPS, there are two indicator sources:

▶ Built-in indicators

▶ Custom indicators

PPS comes with a variety of free indicator images out of the box. All of these built-in indicators can be used royalty free.

> **NOTE**
>
> There is also a set of built-in indicators on trending. These trending indicators can be tricky to use. They also require a form of time intelligence to be applied to the scorecard. Trending indicators are discussed in the "Designing Scorecards" section of this chapter.

It is also possible to upload your own images and make custom indicators, either from scratch or by modifying an existing indicator. Custom indicators are useful for adding corporate branding or a personalized touch to scorecards.

Creating Custom Indicators

Custom indicators are best created through Dashboard Designer. Follow these steps to create a custom indicator:

1. Open Dashboard Designer, shown in Figure 7.1, and then open the PerformancePoint content list in which you want to create the custom indicator.

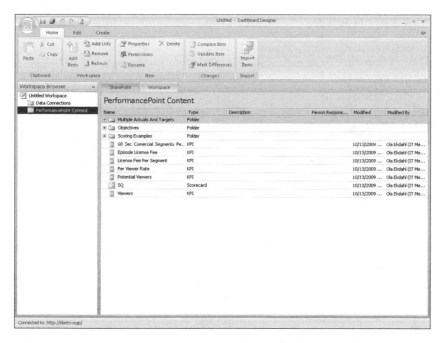

FIGURE 7.1   Use Dashboard Designer to create custom indicators.

2. Select the Create tab on the ribbon, shown in Figure 7.2, and then click the Indicator button to launch the Select an Indicator Template Wizard.

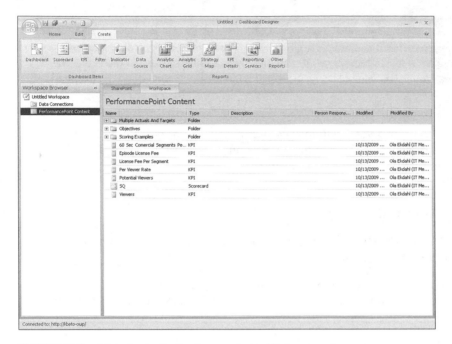

FIGURE 7.2   Click the Indicator button from the Create tab.

3. From the Select an Indicator Template Wizard, shown in Figure 7.3, select Blank Indicator, and then click OK.

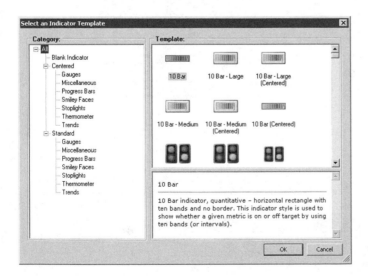

FIGURE 7.3   The Indicator Template Wizard helps you create custom indicators.

In this example, you use the Blank Indicator template, which allows the greatest amount of customization. However, if you just want to modify an existing indicator, choose a built-in indicator with which to start. For example, you can choose a built-in indicator to change the background highlight of the indicator's display cell.

After you have created an indicator, it is only possible to change images and colors. You cannot add or remove levels after an indicator has been created.

4. When the Create New Indicator dialog page appears, shown in Figure 7.4, you have the option to choose which style of indicator you want, such as standard or centered. You can also choose the number of levels in the indicator. Choose suitable values for this task, and then click Finish.

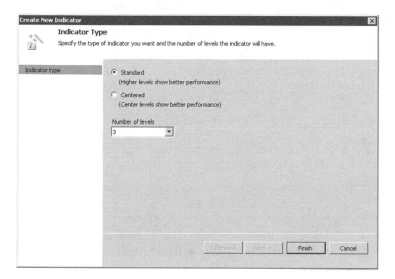

FIGURE 7.4   Select the suitable type and number of levels.

The number of levels for a centered indicator indicates the number of levels from the center. For example, if you create a centered indicator with three levels, you will have three levels above center and three levels below center. The "best" score for all centered indicators is made up of two halves, one on the top half and one on the bottom half of true center.

In addition, all indicators have a No Data level that is used when the indicators do not have associated data. This may occur in cases when the data source is not available or when there are no valid intersections between dimensions.

At this point, Dashboard Designer creates the indicator for you in the root of the PPS Content List currently selected, as shown in Figure 7.5. In addition, the Dashboard Designer displays the Indicator editing page.

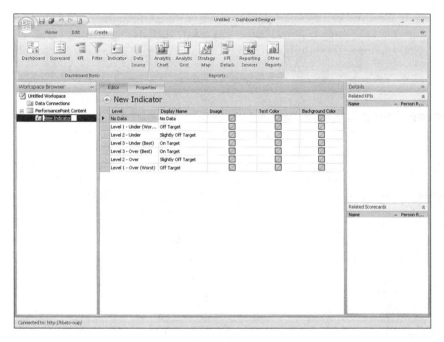

FIGURE 7.5   This is an example of the Indicator editing page in Dashboard Designer.

Editing a Custom Indicator

When your custom indicator has been created, Dashboard Designer has functionality that enables you to modify some of the custom indicator's properties. Much like other objects within the PPS world, changes you make are viewed and applied locally in Dashboard Designer. These changes become "live" for all users when they are saved to the server. You can make changes to the following values on the Editor tab when viewing an indicator:

▶ Display name

▶ Image

▶ Text color

▶ Background

Edit Display Name

The display name is an edit box field. Edit the field by selecting the cell and then changing or entering the new text to display in the field.

Edit Image

The image used for the indicator can be in JPG, BMP, GIF, or PNG format. Select the image by selecting the Image cell on the level where you want to edit the indicator. Next, you can either use the Edit—Picture from File option or double-click the cell. Select the picture file you want to use as an indicator.

Indicator images must be 255-by-255 pixels or smaller. When using larger images for indicators, consider how many of those types of indicators you want to have on a scorecard.

TIP

Keep in mind that a scorecard can become crowded and lose its effectiveness in communicating performance.

CAUTION

The Reset Indicator button that is available in the Edit tab clears the selection of the Image and Text Color fields. However, because there is not a good reason to do this, it is better to avoid using this button.

Edit Text Color

The Text Color field controls the color of the text displayed in a cell on a scorecard. When a KPI on a scorecard has a value corresponding to that level, the text color of the target cell for that value changes to the color selected.

Edit Background Color

The Background Color field is similar to the Text Color field. When a KPI on a scorecard has a value corresponding to that level, the background color of the target cell for that value changes to the color selected.

CAUTION

By default, target metrics are not configured to honor text and background color changes as defined by indicators. If you want these changes to take effect, right-click the target metric header on the scorecard where you want the text changes. When you want background color changes to be displayed, select the Metric Settings from the context menu, and then select the Indicator section of the dialog box. At this point, you can configure several options such as text and background color that control how this metric is displayed.

Understanding and Working with KPIs

As mentioned earlier, a KPI is a metric for monitoring performance. In other words, a KPI is a metric or set of metrics used to provide the status of how close the actual value of a metric is to its target value.

Financial metrics are typical applications of KPIs. For example, suppose that *The Green Orange* has a production budget for each show. The producer allocates a fixed budget for the show and the director must work within this budget to complete the show. If the financial metric indicates that the director is tracking toward spending less than the budgeted amount, he is considered to be on target with his spending. If the financial metric indicates that the director is tracking toward spending more than the budgeted amount, he is considered to be off target with his spending. In each case, the KPI enables the producer to monitor the budget for the show and take action if required.

KPIs can be complex, and they aggregate data from multiple sources such as other KPIs. On the other hand, they can be quite simple measures based on a single point of data. The complexity or simplicity of a KPI depends on business needs and requirements.

Creating an Analysis Services KPI

In this example, you create a KPI that tracks the number of viewers per episode and compares this number to a fixed target:

1. Launch Dashboard Designer and ensure that *The Green Orange* Analysis Services data source is included in your workspace, as shown in Figure 7.6.

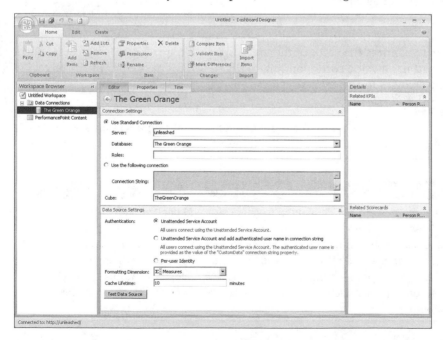

FIGURE 7.6   Include *The Green Orange* Analysis Services data source in your workspace.

2. Open the Create tab, and then click the KPI button to launch the Select a KPI Template Wizard.

3. Select Blank KPI on the Select a KPI Template page in the wizard, as shown in Figure 7.7, and then click OK. A KPI is created and the KPI editor appears in Dashboard Designer (see Figure 7.8).

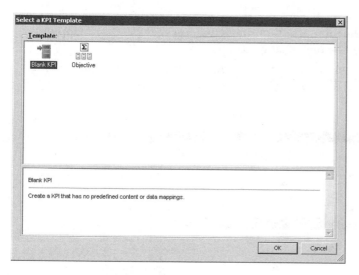

FIGURE 7.7   Select Blank KPI from the KPI Template Wizard.

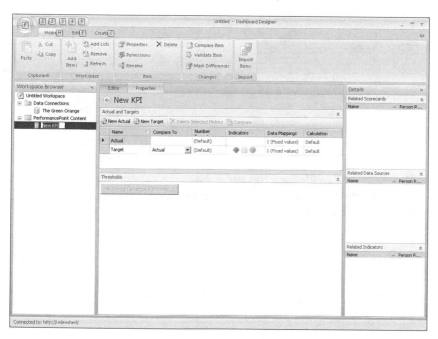

FIGURE 7.8   Use the KPI editor to map the data source.

NOTE

A Blank KPI template has no predefined content or data mappings. Data mappings will be added after the KPI is created in step 5.

4. To map the actual value of the data source to *The Green Orange* data source, click the 1 (Fixed Values) link at the intersection of the Actual row and the Data Mappings column. The Data Source Mapping dialog box appears.

5. Click the Change Source button at the bottom right of the Source Mapping dialog. The Select a Data Source dialog box appears, as shown in Figure 7.9.

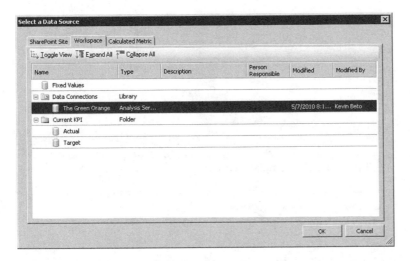

FIGURE 7.9   Select the data source from this dialog box.

6. From the Select a Data Source dialog box, find *The Green Orange* data source, and then click OK.

7. Now that *The Green Orange* Data Source has been selected, you need to select a measure that you want the KPI to display, as shown in Figure 7.10. To do this, select the Viewers measure, and then click OK.

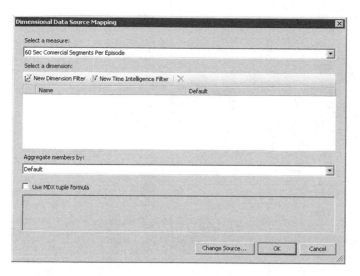

Dimensional Data Source Mapping

Select a measure:

60 Sec Comercial Segments Per Episode

Select a dimension:

New Dimension Filter   New Time Intelligence Filter   ✕

Name	Default

Aggregate members by:

Default

☐ Use MDX tuple formula

Change Source...   OK   Cancel

FIGURE 7.10   Select the measure to display for the KPI from this dialog box.

NOTE

There are other options you can select, such as adding dimension filters, adding time intelligence filters, and changing data source aggregation. You can also select a custom Multidimensional Expressions (MDX) formula to represent the KPI.

MDX is a query language used for online analytical processing (OLAP) databases. Within PPS, MDX is used primarily for querying multidimensional data for cases where the PPS dimension selection UI does not meet your needs.

MDX was more necessary in PPS 2007 because the product lacked features such as dynamic hierarchy selection that selects all children of a dimension member. For the most part, these functionality gaps have been closed in the SharePoint 2010 release. Therefore, the MDX feature remains primarily for backward-compatibility purposes.

8. At this point, you have mapped the actual value to the KPI. Notice that the Data Mappings field for the Actual row now displays your selections, as shown in Figure 7.11. Next you need to set an appropriate target by clicking the 1 (Fixed Values) link at the intersection of the Target row and the Data Mappings column.

9. In the Data Source Mapping dialog box, enter 30,000,000 as the fixed value you are going to target for the Viewer KPI, and then click OK.

NOTE

It is possible to map actual and target data to values that reside in different data sources. This is especially useful in scenarios where target data is not formally captured in a cube and it is necessary to provide target data from a separate data source, such as a SharePoint list or Excel Services.

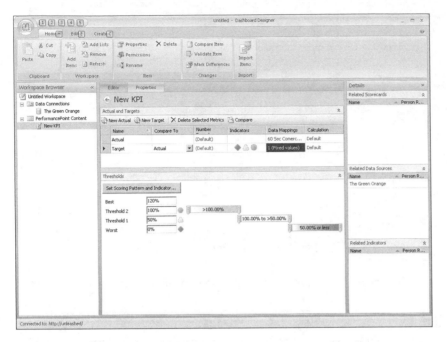

FIGURE 7.11   The Data Mappings selections appear for the actual.

This completes the process for configuring the KPI, shown in Figure 7.12. At this point, it is not possible to preview the rendered KPI within the KPI editor. You see the values displayed from the data source when the Viewer KPI is placed on a scorecard. This is discussed in the "Understanding and Working with Scorecards" section of this chapter.

> **NOTE**
>
> The Properties tab is a shared tab among all the different objects in the PPS world. From the Properties tab, you can rename the object, change the folder path, or define custom properties that can ultimately be displayed on a scorecard. See Chapter 5 for more information on how to use the Properties tab.

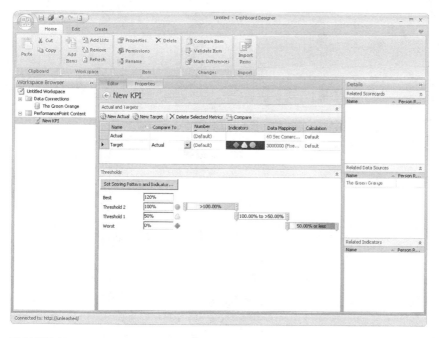

FIGURE 7.12   The data mappings selections appear for the target.

Understanding Multiple Targets and Actuals

With PPS 2010, you can define multiple metrics in a single KPI. Doing so proves particularly useful when defining KPIs that have multiple success factors associated with them. In *The Green Orange* example, the producers want to know both the popularity of the show, measured in viewers, and the revenue earned per viewer, shown in Figure 7.13. The producers also want to view this on the same scorecard, as shown in Figure 7.14.

- ▶ **Actual (Actual Viewers):** The total number of viewers that see each show. This metric comes directly from cube data.

- ▶ **Actual (License Fee):** A value contained within the cube that indicates how much incoming revenue comes from the affiliate stations broadcasting each episode. This metric is not shown on the final scorecard.

- ▶ **Actual (Revenue per Viewer):** A calculated metric determined by dividing the total number of viewers by the fees collected from the affiliates broadcasting the show.

- ▶ **Target (Potential Viewers):** A value contained within the data source indicating the total number of potential viewers for the show. This is compared to the Actual (Actual Viewers) metric.

- ▶ **Actual (Revenue per Viewer):** There is no metric in the cube for this value, so it is implemented as a fixed value with the goal of making about $85 per viewer. This is compared to the Actual (Revenue per Viewer) metric.

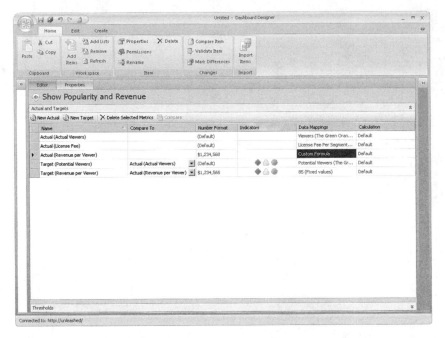

FIGURE 7.13   Multiple actuals and targets defined for a single KPI.

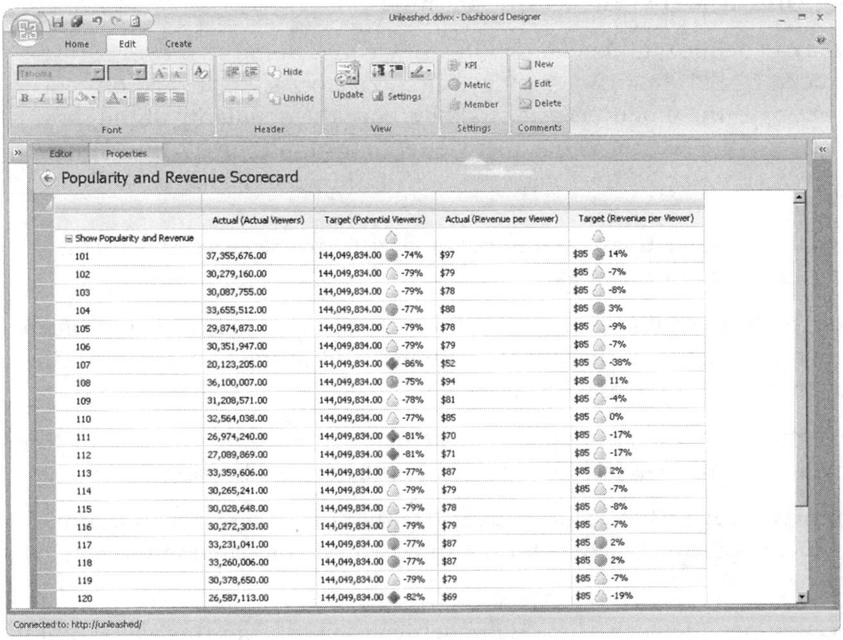

FIGURE 7.14   Scorecard with multiple actuals and targets shown.

With the KPI editor, you can create multiple metrics in a single KPI. This is useful when there is a KPI that may have multiple actual values such as products sold and products in inventory. These multiple values would be compared against multiple target values either on the same or different scorecards.

This functionality can be accessed by clicking the New Actual or New Target buttons in the KPI toolbar. The Compare To column for target metrics controls which actual metric will be used in scoring calculations for that target value.

Examining Data Mapping

Several different dialog boxes and options are available for selecting the data you want to use for a metric in a KPI, including the following:

▶ Fixed value

▶ Data sources

▶ Existing metrics

▶ Calculated metrics

Fixed Value

A fixed-value KPI is a hard-coded numeric value. This is used primarily for setting a target when you have a static target that is not stored in a data source.

For example, in *The Green Orange* scenario, a fixed value might be used to measure an average of critic rating of three stars or higher per show. The number three for a target will not change, so using a static or fixed value is appropriate.

This option always appears at the top of the Workspace tab in the Select a Data Source dialog box.

Data Sources

It is also possible to select any data source that PPS supports through the Date Source dialog box. All data sources currently in the workspace that is loaded in Dashboard Designer appear in the Workspace tab. If you want to pick a data source that is not yet loaded in the workspace, the SharePoint Site tab shows all data connection libraries that have been loaded in this workspace. Choosing a data source from the SharePoint Site tab automatically adds the selected data source to the current workspace.

The various options for data sources are discussed in-depth in Chapter 6.

Dimensional Data Source Mapping Dialog Box

The standard way to create a KPI involves mapping a measure from a data source to a KPI, as shown in Figure 7.15.

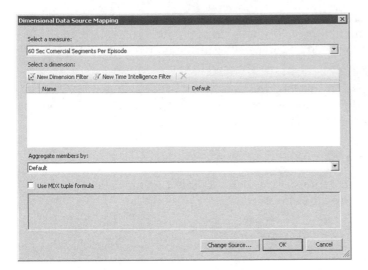

FIGURE 7.15   Use the Dimensional Data Source Mapping dialog box to map a measure from a data source to a KPI.

Listed here are the different options available when mapping data sources to metrics. Most likely, you will not need to use all of them on each data mapping that you do:

▶ **Select a Measure:** Enables you to select a measure to use from the cube or tabular data source. This is a required field.

▶ **New Dimension Filter:** Enables you to filter on a specific dimension. For example, in *The Green Orange* scenario, you can select to filter only on a particular season or a particular episode.

▶ **New Time Intelligence Filter:** Enables you to enter a time intelligence expression that will be used as a filter for the KPI.

▶ **Aggregate Members By:** Enables you to override the aggregation used in the cube for this metric. For example, you can change this option from Default to Sum if you want this KPI to represent the total number of 60-second commercial segments per episode rather than the default average.

▶ **Use MDX Tuple Formula:** This check box and associated edit box enable you to enter your own custom MDX to represent this KPI.

TIP

MDX refers to a language in which it is possible to select expressions from Analysis Services. Because this is a complex language, it is recommended that you refer to *Microsoft SQL Server 2008 Analysis Services Unleashed* (ISBN: 0672330016) for in-depth information on this topic.

Existing Metrics

It is possible to copy the settings from an existing metric from this KPI into the metric being edited. For example, doing so proves useful when making a series of similar metrics within a KPI. Instead of selecting all dimension filters from scratch each time, this will create an identical copy that can be edited independently of the source metric.

This option always appears at the bottom of the Workspace tab of the Select a Data Source dialog box, as shown in Figure 7.16. This option enables you to select any existing metric within the current KPI.

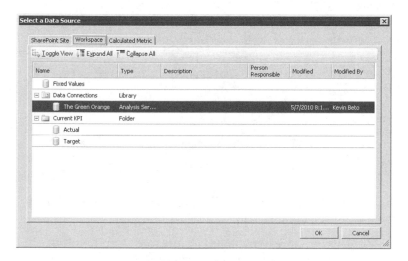

FIGURE 7.16   Selecting an existing metric to copy.

CAUTION

Keep in mind that the data is copied one time only. This means that if the source metric changes, the destination or copy of the metric will not automatically inherit changes made to the source version.

Calculated

PPS includes a sophisticated engine that allows for calculation and manipulation of data. This is particularly useful if the data source you are working with does not have the complete data set or structure required for your metrics.

To access the functionality for calculated metrics, open the Calculated Metric tab from the Select a Data Source dialog, and then select a calculation template. When you select a template, all the basic mathematical operations are supported as well as some special functions.

The Calculated Metrics Data Source Mapping dialog provides the following functionality (see Figure 7.17):

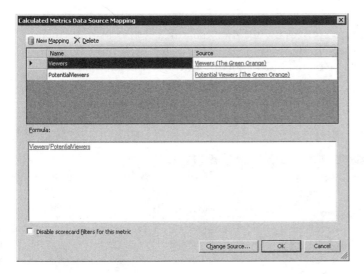

FIGURE 7.17   Use the Calculated Metrics Data Source Mapping dialog box to enhance the value of your data source.

▶ **New Mapping and Delete:** Use these buttons to add or remove mappings. Not all mappings need to be used in the formula field.

▶ **Mappings:** This grid displays the current mappings for the calculated KPI. It is possible to rename existing mappings here. Click the Source link to select a new mapping, which may include another calculated KPI.

▶ **Formula:** You can enter any mathematical formula you want for the calculated KPI in the Formula edit box. All standard mathematical functions (+, -, *, /) and parenthesis are accepted in this edit box. The special functions listed in Table 7.1 are also accepted in the Formula edit box.

▶ **Disable Scorecard Filters for this Metric:** Use this option to prevent filters from affecting any of the values mapped for the calculated KPI. This is useful if you do not want the metric to be affected by any filter settings that the user may set on the dashboard rendered in SharePoint.

▶ **Change Source:** This button offers the ability to change the KPI from a calculated metric to another type of data source, which, in effect, cancels the calculated metric functionality.

TABLE 7.1   Special Functions for Calculated Metrics

Function	Example Syntax	Description
Sum	Sum(val1,val2,val3)	Sums all the specified comma-delimited values.
Average	Average(val1,val2,val3)	Averages (via arithmetic mean) all the specified comma-delimited values.
Min	Min(val1,val2,val3)	Returns the minimum value of the collection of specified comma-delimited values.
Max	Max(val1,val2,val3)	Returns the maximum value of the collection of specified comma-delimited values.
Round	Round(20.333,1)	Rounds the number to the specified number of decimal places. Zero decimal places.
If	If(val1<=100,val2,100)	Similar in functionality to the If statement in Microsoft Excel. If the condition specified in the first part of the expression is true, the second parameter is used. Otherwise, the last parameter is used.
Abs	Abs(val1)	Returns the absolute value of the value specified.

Table 7.1 lists the special functions that can be entered in the Formula edit box when creating calculated metrics.

The following are examples of useful calculations:

```
If(value=null, 0, value)
```

▶ **Setting null values to 0:** This expression is useful when cleaning the data values of a data source. It is possible to take places in the data source where no data is specified and display a zero instead of an empty cell.

```
    If(value<1000, null, value)
```

▶ **Setting values under a certain amount to null:** This expression is helpful when filtering out values under a certain threshold. In this example, all values under 1,000 will be given a null value rather than their true value. If used in conjunction with the scorecard setting of filtering out null values, it has the effect of filtering out values below the specified threshold.

Number Formatting

The Format Numbers dialog box, shown in Figure 7.18, is accessible by clicking the link in the Number Formatting column on the KPI metric that you want to edit. The Format Numbers dialog box offers several self-explanatory options.

FIGURE 7.18   Use the Format Numbers dialog box to provide a uniform number display for all regional settings.

By default, PPS uses formatting from the data source and passes the current viewers regional settings down to the data source. For example, if the data source is Analysis Services and a scorecard viewer on an Italian browser views the scorecard, the number format will be represented in the European number format 1.000,00 rather than the U.S. number format 1,000.00. To homogenize the appearance for all scorecard viewers regardless of regional settings, set the values in the Format Number dialog box. Only change the settings in this dialog box if you want a uniform appearance for all other cultures that will be viewing the scorecard.

Calculation

The Calculation dialog box, shown in Figure 7.19, accessible by the link in the Calculation column, affects the rollup behavior of KPIs in a scorecard. Rollup behavior refers to how child KPIs are aggregated up to a parent level. For example, there might be one "show success" KPI that is a combination of several other KPIs such as popularity, revenue, and production cost. The calculation dialog controls how these child KPI values are aggregated up to the parent.

The settings in this dialog box do not apply if the KPI is leaf level on a scorecard. This means that the KPI has no child KPIs underneath it. If this is the case, all options except default and source data return empty results.

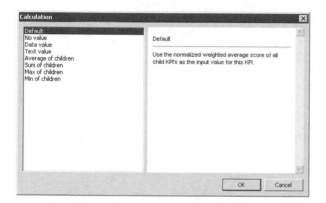

FIGURE 7.19   Calculation settings affect the rollup behavior of KPIs in a scorecard.

The settings in this dialog box do apply if the KPI is not at the leaf level of the scorecard, which means there is at least one KPI placed underneath it. This is useful in the case where you would like to compare the values of the child KPIs instead of the scores. It is important to note that in this case, the KPI will be ignored unless the aggregation is set to default or source data of the actual value.

The Use Calculated Values of Actual and Target to Compute Score check box appears only if the KPI metric calculation being edited is a target KPI. Clearing this check box creates an objective KPI. An objective KPI has no value. This is useful in the case where you would like to compare the scores of child KPIs rather than the values.

NOTE

The difference between an objective KPI and a standard or nonobjective KPI is that objective KPIs use only the calculated score of child KPIs, whereas standard KPIs operate over values of child KPIs. An example of this, shown in Figure 7.20, shows how two different measures, one on show viewers and the other on revenue, can be combined into a single metric.

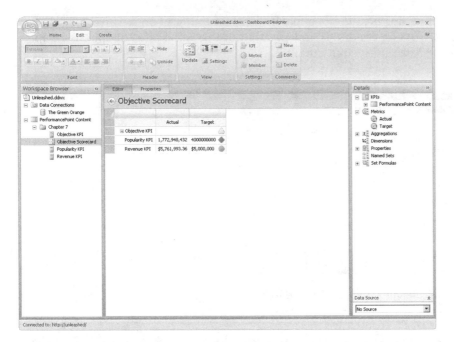

FIGURE 7.20   An example of an objective KPI with two child KPIs.

NOTE

Objective KPIs are useful in balanced scorecard scenarios when multiple and different types of metrics are compared. For example, if you want to reconcile your customer perspective and have several metrics from customer satisfaction, retention rate, and support costs per customer, an objective KPI will take the scores of each metrics and aggregate them to provide an overall perspective of how that segment of the business is running.

A standard KPI is useful when aggregating several of the same type of metrics such as an overall revenue amount for a division. If one KPI slightly outperforms against a large forecast, and one KPI grossly underperforms on a small forecast, the aggregate might be considered a good overall performance for that division. Aggregating this by score through an objective KPI will show that this division is performing poorly.

Understanding and Working with Scoring

Scoring is a complex concept that has been included in the PPS feature set. At a conceptual level, the score of a KPI is what is used to enable it to be compared to other KPIs that specifically have different metrics or thresholds.

Table 7.2 summarizes the terms unique to scoring that are used when discussing scoring concepts within PPS. These terms are all unique to PPS, but some of them do not apply to all types of scoring patterns.

TABLE 7.2   Scoring Definitions

Term	Definition
Score	A calculated value between 0 and 1 indicating the relative position, with 0 being worst and 1 being the best.
Scoring pattern	The definition of what is considered good or bad for the score. For example, Increasing Is Better means that a higher value is better, whereas Decreasing Is Better means that a lower value is better.
Threshold	A boundary where the indicator changes levels such as from yellow to green. There is one threshold per level available in the indicator being used.
Banding	The input type for the threshold boundaries. Normalized values are entered as percentages from the target, whereas numeric values are absolute values.
Normalize	In the case of parent/child KPI hierarchies, normalization is how the individual scores are combined to represent the parent or rollup score.
Best/worst value	Absolute values that represent the boundaries of possible values for the score. Any scores outside of this boundary are pegged at either 0 or 1.

Changing a Scoring Pattern

Scoring patterns for a KPI are stored within each target metric in the KPI. Scoring patterns can only be edited through the Edit Banding Settings Wizard. The user interface varies based on which scoring pattern is used. This example uses the default Increasing Is Better/Band by Normalized Value Pattern.

1. Click the Indicators column in the Target row, as shown in Figure 7.21.

2. Click the Set Scoring Pattern and Indicator button to display the Edit Banding Settings Wizard, as shown in Figure 7.22.

3. Choose the desired scoring pattern and banding method; then click Next. A brief explanation of the selected scoring pattern and banding method appears.

NOTE

This description shown in the Edit Banding Settings dialog is used to calculate the band by value, not the final score. See the discussion about scoring in the "Examining How a Score Is Calculated" section later in this chapter for details on how this works.

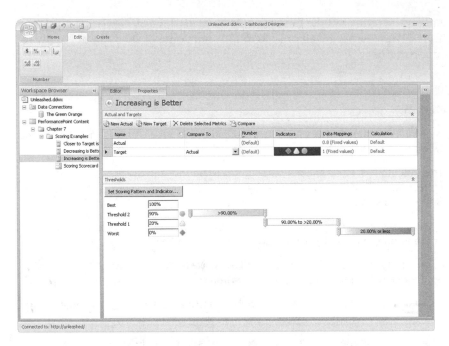

FIGURE 7.21   What you see will vary depending on the scoring pattern used.

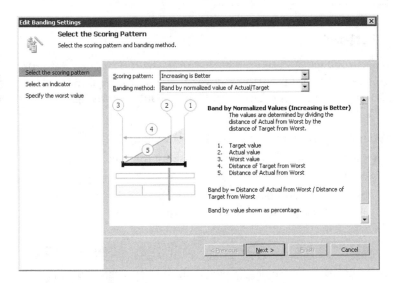

FIGURE 7.22   Use the Edit Banding Settings dialog to select your scoring pattern and banding method.

4. After choosing the scoring pattern and banding method, you need to select an indicator. User created indicators appear in the SharePoint Site or Workspace tabs, whereas default built-in indicators appear in the Available Indicators tab. Find the indicator that you want to use, select it, and then click Next.

> **NOTE**
>
> The indicators shown in Figure 7.23 match the scoring pattern. If Closer to Target Is Better is selected, only centered indicators will be shown. If the Increasing Is Better or the Decreasing Is Better scoring patterns are selected, standard indicators will be available for selection here.

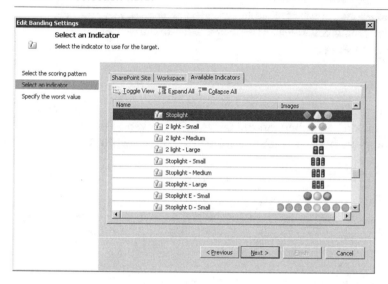

FIGURE 7.23   Next, choose the indicator.

5. The final screen of the wizard, shown in Figure 7.24, asks for the worst value that will be used in the calculation to determine the worst case for the actual value. If the score is below this threshold, the score will be pegged at zero.

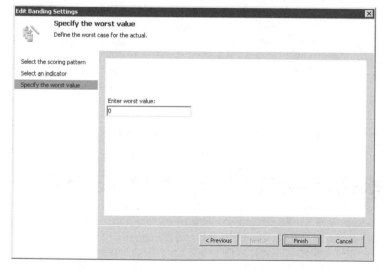

FIGURE 7.24   Specify the worst case for the actual value.

CAUTION

You may be tempted to put in an excessively large or small value for the worst value, especially in the Decreasing Is Better scenario. This value will directly affect the score generated, so setting an extreme worst value requires the creation of very tight and unnatural thresholds to ensure logical scoring behavior.

The score is capped at the worst value, so there is no benefit to setting an unrealistic worst value. Instead, make this the "best possible" worst value to make it easier to work with the threshold calculation.

Editing Thresholds

It is also possible to edit thresholds in the KPI editing user interface. You can access the Thresholds dialog box by clicking anywhere on the target metric row you want to edit. The threshold editing UI appears below the metrics for the KPI, as shown in Figure 7.25.

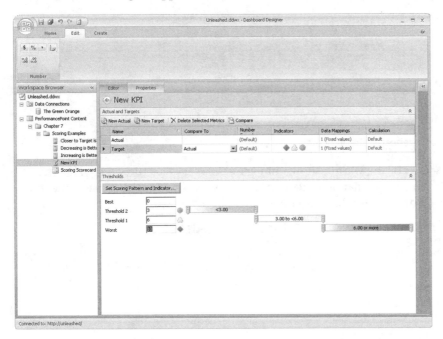

FIGURE 7.25   Click anywhere on the target metric row you want to edit to bring up the Thresholds user interface.

TIP

If you do not see the Thresholds user interface after selecting a target metric, it is probably collapsed. In this case, you can re-expand the view by clicking the expansion chevron on the Thresholds section at the bottom of Dashboard Designer.

The thresholds set in this example are dependent on the scoring pattern selected. The thresholds give a general impression of what color the indicators will be for various values.

CAUTION

Do not confuse this with the KPI score that can be displayed on the scorecard. This is actually the Band by Value number that the threshold editor is using. There is another step in the scoring process that normalizes the score based on the band. For more information, see the following section, "Examining How a Score Is Calculated."

Examining How a Score Is Calculated

This section discusses the steps involved in calculating the score that is ultimately used in the final scorecard.

Step 1: Calculate the Band by Value

The Band by Value number is calculated through the scoring mechanism called out in the scoring pattern selection screen. The available options are described next.

Band by Normalized Value

This option "normalizes" the score so that the thresholds can be dynamically compared. This is especially useful if both the target and actual values vary based on values coming from the data source. The formula varies depending on how the target value is to be used.

- **Increasing Is Better:** This scoring pattern is used when there is no upper bound on what is good, and when larger numbers are generally considered better than smaller numbers. One example of this is profits, where there is no such thing as having too much money.

$$\frac{Actual - Worst}{Target - Worst}$$

- **Decreasing Is Better:** This scoring pattern is used when there is no lower bound on what is considered good, and when smaller numbers are generally considered better than larger ones. One example of this is expenses where saving more money is usually better.

$$1 - \frac{Worst - Actual}{Worst - Target}$$

▶ **Closer to Target Is Better:** Headcount is an example where you might use this scoring pattern. When tracking headcount for a department or a project, it is possible to have too many or too few people. This means it is preferable to keep the actual count as close as possible to the target value.

$$\frac{Actual - Worst}{Target - Worst}$$

Band by Numeric Value of Actual

This option enables you to enter exact values for thresholds. This is the intended scoring pattern to use if there are static and absolute values that divide the indicator levels.

In *The Green Orange* business scenario, having a target number of commercials per episode is an example when this option might apply. It is not difficult to come up with worst and target values for number of commercials per episode. These values do not change across episodes, which means you can set the values once in Dashboard Designer and keep the values constant for future episodes.

This is also the easiest scoring pattern to understand since there is less math and calculations involved. Its simplicity makes it a good scoring pattern with which to begin.

Band by Stated Score

The Banding by Stated Score method enables you to bypass the calculation part of the score and directly select a Band by Value. It is possible to select a filtered data value directly from the data source or to author a custom MDX tuple expression.

This feature is tricky to use and is most applicable when dealing with Excel data sources where it is possible to do calculations in a data column and manually generate the Band by Value if you want more control over how the score is set.

The selection of the stated score query is only accessible through the Set Scoring Pattern and Indicator Wizard.

Step 2: Identify the In Band Value

When the Band by Value is calculated, the PPS scoring engine maps the Band by Value to a range defined by the Threshold settings, as shown in Figure 7.26.

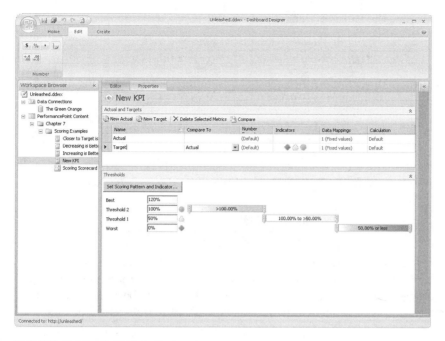

FIGURE 7.26   Define threshold settings here.

Step 3: Normalize the Score

When the appropriate threshold is identified, the true normalized score is calculated. This calculation varies based on the band in which the score was placed. The following points provide a high-level overview of this process:

▶ The bands are distributed evenly between zero, which is the worst score and one, which is the best score. All bands are given equal weight. This means that if there is a band that has a smaller percentage range, it is equivalent to a band that has a larger range.

▶ The relative range of the band that the Band by Value score falls in is determined.

▶ Final score is determined based on where that score falls within that range.

The technique used to accomplish this feat varies based on the scoring pattern and the banding method chosen. After the normalization takes place, this value can be compared side by side with other values.

Mathematically, the formula is a base adjustment for the band the value falls into, combined with the In Band Value, which is the relative position of that value within the specified thresholds. For example, if the value falls into the top band of a two-level indicator, the position will always be relative between the 50 percent and 100 percent marks, no matter how wide the range is for those values.

The formula to calculate the In Band Value is as follows:

$$\frac{Band\ By\ Value\ -\ Lower\ band\ threshold}{\#\ of\ Bands\ *\ (Upper\ band\ threshold\ -\ Lower\ band\ threshold)}$$

The formula to calculate the offset for the Increasing Is Better scoring pattern is shown here. This result is added to the In Band Value to get the final score:

$$\frac{Lower\ band\ index}{\#\ of\ Bands}$$

The formula to calculate the offset is similar for the Decreasing Is Better scoring pattern. It is flipped and when the calculation is done for the final score the In Band Value is subtracted from this:

$$\frac{Upper\ band\ index}{\#\ of\ Bands}$$

For the Closer to Target scoring pattern only, if the score is below the target value, it is subtracted from 1. If it is above the target, it is left alone. The value is then multiplied by 2. This is done to compensate as the range of possible values is doubled because conceptually this pattern is treated as two independent patterns, one above and one below the target.

TIP

If you want to understand more about how the score is calculated in PPS, it is helpful to experiment with fixed value KPIs while using an Excel spreadsheet with the calculations included that verify the outcome.

It is also helpful to show the score on a scorecard. To do this, right-click the target metric on the scorecard, select Metric Settings, and then set either the primary or the secondary value displayed to the score.

Examining a Scoring Walkthrough

The following example demonstrates Increasing Is Better scoring with normalized banding. This example walks you step by step through the scores that are applicable to the Increasing Is Better scoring type. You can use the same formulas and procedure with your own numbers to understand why PPS is giving you whatever scores it does.

The calculations relevant for this scoring pattern are the following:

$$Band\ by\ Value = \frac{Actual\ -\ Worst}{Target\ -\ Worst}$$

$$In\ Band\ Value = \frac{Band\ By\ Value\ -\ Lower\ band\ threshold}{\#\ of\ Bands\ \times\ (Upper\ band\ threshold\ -\ Lower\ band\ threshold)}$$

$$Score = \frac{Lower\ band\ index}{\#\ of\ Bands}\ +\ In\ Band\ Value$$

Consider the following thresholds as defined in Figure 7.27.

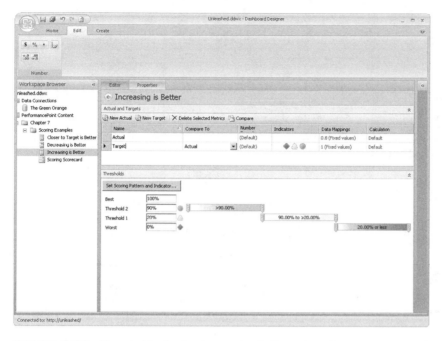

FIGURE 7.27   Thresholds for the Increasing Is Better scoring pattern example.

In this example, the worst value is 0, the actual value is .8, and the target value is 1.

The Band by Value would be (0.8 – 0) / (1 – 0), which is .8. This falls between Threshold 1 and Threshold 2. This means the indicator is yellow, which puts this score in the second band.

The In Band Value is calculated at (0.8 – 0.2) / (3*(0.9 – 0.2)), which gives a value of 0.285.

Adding in the band offset adds 1/3 to this value, which results in a normalized score of 0.619.

Decreasing Is Better Scoring with Numeric Value Banding Example

Because the Band by Value when using Numeric Values for banding is the actual, the calculation is only one step less:

$$In\ Band\ Value = \frac{Actual - Lower\ band\ threshold}{\#\ of\ Bands \times (Upper\ band\ threshold\ -\ Lower\ band\ threshold)}$$

$$Score = \frac{Lower\ band\ index}{\#\ of\ Bands} - In\ Band\ Value$$

Consider the following thresholds on a 10-level indicator as defined in Figure 7.28.

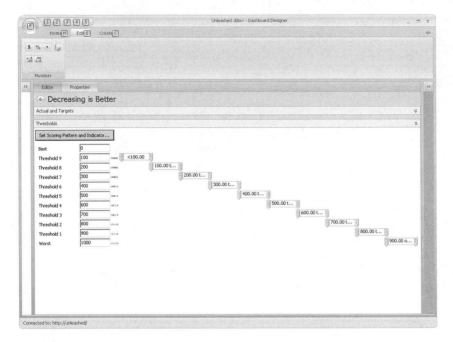

FIGURE 7.28   Thresholds for the Decreasing Is Better scoring pattern example.

In this example, the worst value is 1,000, the actual value is 170, and the target value is 0.

The Band by Value is the Actual (170), which is .8. This falls between Threshold 1 and Threshold 2, which means the indicator is yellow putting this score in the second band.

Normalizing the score with the previous formula gives you the following:

$$\frac{9}{10} - \frac{70 - 0}{10*(100 - 0)}$$

This results in a normalized score of 0.83.

Closer to Target Is Better Scoring with Normalized Banding Example

Listed here are the two calculations relevant for this scoring pattern:

$$Band\ by\ Value = \frac{Actual\ -\ Worst}{Target\ -\ Worst}$$

$$In\ Band\ Value = \frac{Actual - Lower\ band\ threshold}{\#\ of\ Bands \times (Upper\ band\ threshold\ -\ Lower\ band\ threshold)}$$

$$Score = \frac{Lower\ band\ index}{\#\ of\ Bands} + In\ Band\ Value$$

Consider the thresholds shown in Figure 7.29.

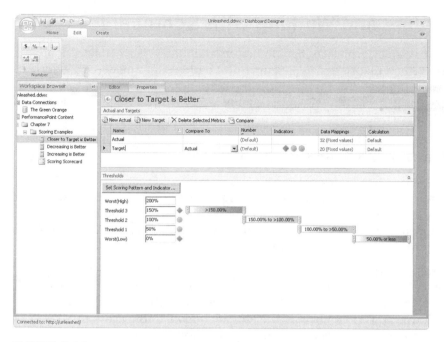

FIGURE 7.29   Thresholds for the Closer to Target Is Better scoring pattern example.

In this example, the worst value is 5, the actual value is 7, and the target value is 10.

The Band by Value would be $(7 - 5) / (10 - 5)$, which is 0.133. This falls between the Worst value and Threshold 1, which means the indicator is red putting this score in the bottom band.

As previously specified, because you are doing a Closer to Target Is Better scoring pattern, you need to multiply the In Band Value by 2 to compensate for the two halves to the scoring pattern. The In Band Value will be $2*(0.1333 - .0) / (4*(.5 - 0))$, which is 0.133.

Because it is in the bottom band, the band offset will be 0 / 2, resulting in a normalized score of 0.133, or 13.3%.

Examining Rollup Scoring

After the final scores have been calculated at a particular tree level in a scorecard, if there is an objective KPI above these scores, the score is "rolled up" to produce the value for the parent KPI.

The method to do this relies on the Calculation setting explained previously in the section "Understanding and working with KPIs" subsection, "Calculation," of this chapter. Some scores can be weighted more than others, which means they have larger influence over the rolled-up value. Weighting is a scorecard-level setting that can be done through the KPI settings dialog box. Note that weighting is used only if the default calculation is used on the parent KPI.

Understanding and Working with Scorecards

The scorecard is the display vehicle for both indicators and KPIs. It is a highly customizable presentation vehicle that is used to present critical business information. The scorecard is also the only PPS Web Part that can both receive parameters from and emit parameters to other Web Parts. This makes it a common "launch pad" around which most dashboards are constructed.

Creating KPIs with the Scorecard Wizard

The fastest and easiest way to create a scorecard is to create the KPIs directly from the data source that you want to use. The wizard creates both the scorecard and a set of associated KPIs with the scorecard. Though the wizard offers limited formatting options, it is possible to customize the scorecard and associated KPIs later. This means that it serves as a good tool to get up and running quickly with scorecards.

The following example demonstrates how to create a scorecard based on an Analysis Services data source. It is possible to import KPIs from Analysis, too, through the wizard. This assumes that you have KPIs stored in Analysis Services and that you want to use them. When importing KPIs from Analysis, the KPIs are imported using custom MDX as the KPI type. The example also imports any custom indicators that will be utilized.

> **NOTE**
>
> A SQL Analysis Services KPI is different from a PPS KPI. A SQL Analysis Services KPI is created using Business Intelligence Development Studio (BIDS), which comes with SQL Server; whereas a PPS KPI is stored in the SharePoint database.
>
> In essence, both KPIs do the same thing. However, the SQL Analysis Services KPI is aimed at an information technology worker or developer, whereas the PPS KPI is aimed toward the knowledge worker who might not have access to edit SQL objects directly.

> **TIP**
>
> The overall look and feel of the Scorecard Creation Wizard has not changed from PPS 2007 to PPS 2010. As a result, some of the new functionality, such as calculated KPIs, multiple actuals, and KPIs on columns cannot be created through this wizard. If you want to use these features, it is best to create a blank scorecard or create the KPIs you want from scratch.

1. To start the Scorecard Creation Wizard, right-click a PerformancePoint content list, select New, and then select Scorecard.
2. Select the Analysis Services template from the Select a Scorecard Template dialog, as shown in Figure 7.30, and then click Next.

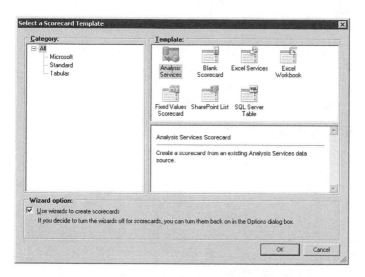

FIGURE 7.30   Start by selecting a scorecard template.

NOTE

There is an option to not use the Scorecard Creation Wizard when creating new score-cards on this page. Clearing this option automatically creates blank scorecards for the current user without presenting the wizard user interface. If the check box is accidentally cleared and you want to restore the Scorecard Creation Wizard, go to the Designer Options menu found under the Office jewel icon in the upper-left corner of Dashboard Designer.

3. Select an available Analysis Services data source in the Create an Analysis Services Scorecard dialog that contains KPIs to import (see Figure 7.31). An example of a sample data source that contains SQL KPIs is the Adventure Works Data Warehouse sample found at http://www.codeplex.com.

4. Accept the default option Create KPIs from SQL Server Analysis Services measure from the Select a KPI Source page in the wizard, and then click Next.

5. At this point, you see a blank list of KPIs. Click the Add button to create an entry in the grid, which enables you to choose from the available measures from the data source. You should also choose a banding method.

6. Select the KPIs you want to import from the Select KPIs to Import page in the dialog shown in Figure 7.32, and then click Next.

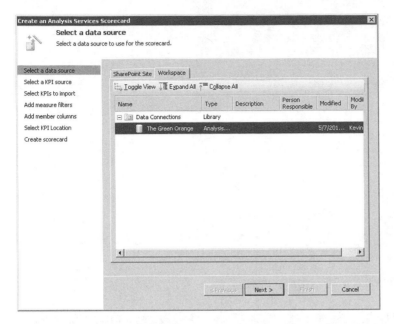

FIGURE 7.31   Select a data source.

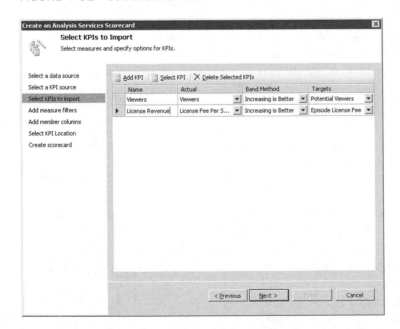

FIGURE 7.32   Select to add or import KPIs and select the band method.

NOTE

The Select KPI button allows inclusion of already created PPS KPIs into the scorecard you are creating.

7. The Add Measure Filters dialog page, shown in Figure 7.33, allows the addition of a single dimension filter to the data source. It is not necessary to make any changes to this screen. Click Next to continue.

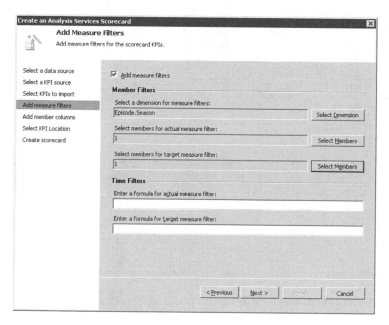

FIGURE 7.33   Select to add member or time filters.

NOTE

Filters added in this dialog will be placed on each KPI individually as a dimension filter. It is also possible to place time intelligence (TI) filters on the KPIs that are created by entering a TI formula in the Time Filters box.

---

8. The Add member columns page allows the addition of a dimension on the columns of the scorecard. There is no need to make any changes on this page. Click Next to continue.

NOTE

This performs the function of slicing the KPI across the dimension members selected to appear in the columns.

---

9. The Locations page enables you to create content in a specific PPS content list. Select the list in which you want to create the new scorecard and KPIs. Click Next.

At this point, the scorecard and all associated KPIs and indicators are created in Dashboard Designer and the scorecard is displayed, as shown in Figure 7.34. Do not forget to save the scorecard and associated KPIs to the server when you are pleased with them.

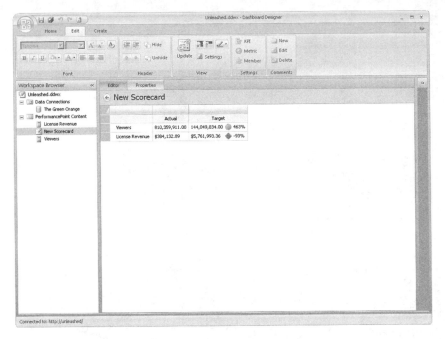

FIGURE 7.34   The scorecard appears in the Dashboard Designer Editor tab, where you can continue to work with it.

Adding a Dimension to a Scorecard

Slicing KPIs based on dimensions from the data source is a common need for scorecards. This is particularly useful for operational scorecards where specific details may be required. In *The Green Orange* scenario, an example of this would be to slice a Viewers KPI by each episode. This can be accomplished by dragging and dropping dimensions onto the scorecard. Follow these steps to do this:

1. Locate the dimension to be added to the scorecard by expanding the Dimension node in the Details pane.

TIP

Occasionally, no dimensions are displayed here. If you do not see dimensions, ensure that the scorecard contains a KPI and an associated metric with a valid data source and that the Data Sources drop-down box at the bottom of the Details pane has the data source with the dimension you want selected.

If you are working with multiple different data sources on a single scorecard, the Data Sources drop-down box allows toggling between the different data sources currently in use on the scorecard.

2. Drag and drop the dimension onto the columns of the scorecard, as shown in Figure 7.35. The member selector appears.

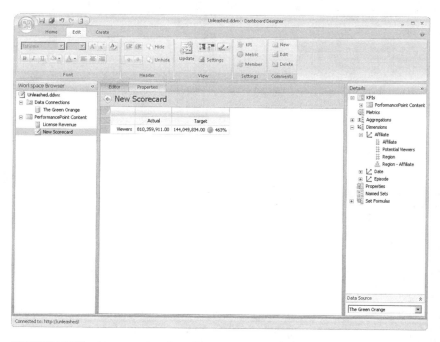

FIGURE 7.35   Expand the dimension to view the members.

NOTE

The UI is somewhat nonintuitive when dragging and dropping dimensions onto scorecards with multiple KPIs. To place a dimension underneath a single metric or KPI, press the Shift key while dragging the dimension around until the drop "hint" changes to show single placement.

This behavior, which is the reverse of behavior from PPS 2007, was changed in response to user feedback.

3. Select the desired members in the member selector, as shown in Figure 7.36, and then click OK. The dimensions are added to the scorecard.

4. Because the dimensions do not update automatically on the scorecard, click Update on the Edit tab to update the scorecard.

When the update is complete, a preview of the final scorecard appears on a dashboard, as shown in Figure 7.37.

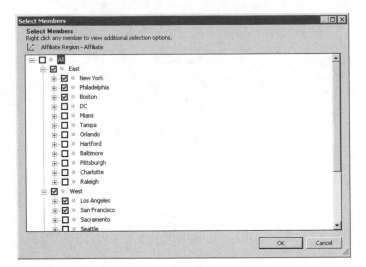

FIGURE 7.36   Select the members from this dialog box.

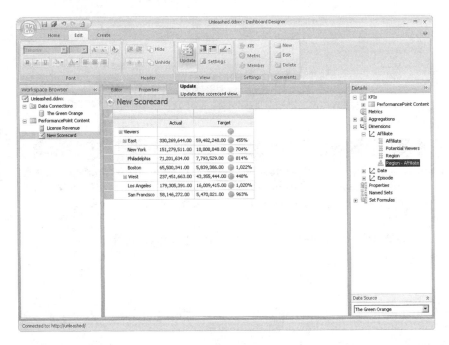

FIGURE 7.37   This is an example of a scorecard ready to appear on a dashboard.

Examining the Scorecard Editor

The scorecard appears in the center pane in the Editor tab. You will find all the functions you need to modify the scorecard either on the Edit tab or by right-clicking the scorecard to bring up context menus. The functions for editing the scorecard are identical, regardless of how you choose to access them. It is a matter of preference.

The Details pane on the right offers a palette to drag and drop items onto the scorecard. Many of these items are dynamically populated based on the current contents of the scorecard. Keep in mind that it is not possible to drag and drop items from the Workspace Browser pane on the left.

Updating Scorecards

Larger, more complex scorecards may take some time to render. In addition, they may involve several round trips to data sources, which means that automatic updating is disabled except in rare cases. If the scorecard does not update automatically or the data on the scorecard in Dashboard Designer is out-of-date, click the Update button on the Edit tab to update the data.

> **CAUTION**
>
> Do not confuse the Update button on the Edit tab with the Refresh button on the Home tab. The Update button, which is unique to scorecards, will trigger a refresh of the scorecard. The Refresh button does not update the scorecard. Instead, it connects with SharePoint and updates PPS content and Data Sources in the local copy of Dashboard Designer.

Designing Scorecards

Scorecards conceptually have two axes:

▶ Rows (the y-axis)

▶ Columns (the x-axis)

The scorecard editor is used by dragging and dropping items from the Details pane on the right onto the scorecard design surface.

Adding KPIs

To add a KPI to a scorecard, drag and drop the KPI from the Details pane onto the scorecard in the location you want. Only KPIs loaded in the local Dashboard Designer cache are available for you to add. KPIs can be placed on either the rows or the columns of a scorecard. When one KPI is placed, all other KPIs must be placed on the same axis.

Adding Metrics

Metrics can also be dragged and dropped onto the scorecard. Metrics must be placed on the opposite axis from all KPIs. The list of metrics available in the Details pane is dynamically populated from the KPIs currently placed on the scorecard.

Adding Aggregations

Aggregations on the scorecard serve as a tool to allow the summation of all metrics. It is used by adding the desired aggregation type above a metric column. Conceptually, this is used as a summation column. In this Figure 7.38, several actual metrics are aggregated and displayed in an Average column.

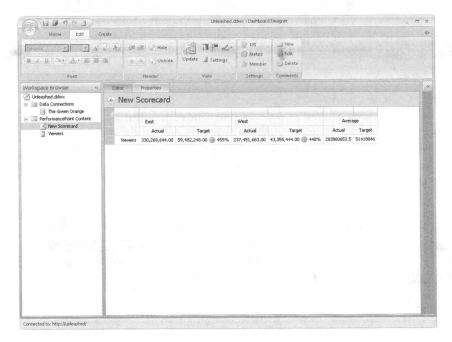

FIGURE 7.38   This is an example of aggregations on a scorecard.

There are several limitations to using aggregations on the scorecard:

▶ Aggregations are only done over columns. It is not possible to do an aggregation on row members.

▶ Aggregations are done by metric name. As long as all the columns to be aggregated have the same name, they will be aggregated together. There is no way to include or exclude other metrics.

▶ Trend aggregations are calculated based on the last two columns with matching metrics in the scorecard. If the number is decreasing, the arrow points down. If it is increasing, the arrow points up. Currently, there is no way to configure or tweak the trend calculation method.

Given some of these limitations, sometimes it is better to do aggregation manually by adding another KPI or metric to an existing KPI.

Adding Dimensions

Dimensions can be added by dragging and dropping the dimension to the appropriate place within a scorecard. These can be placed on rows, columns, or both if there are two dimensions that have an intersection. In addition, dimensions can be nested within each other.

Custom Properties

Custom Properties on KPIs can also be displayed. Creating and managing custom properties is covered in Chapter 5. It is important that the custom properties have the same property name.

Named Sets

Named sets from the cube can also be placed on a scorecard. These operate much like dimensions. However, they need to be placed in the appropriate spot.

Set Formulas

Set formulas represent the ability to add some advanced MDX or TI expressions to the scorecard.

The Time Set Formula option allows the entry of TI expressions that will be expanded on the scorecard. See the "Time Intelligence" section in Chapter 6 for more information about expressions that can be used here.

The Custom Set Formula option allows the entry of a MDX set expression that will be used within the scorecard. The usefulness of this feature has diminished somewhat with the new dynamic hierarchy selection capabilities included in PPS 2010. However, the Custom Set Formula feature does still have some value.

Summary

This chapter provided an overview of working with indicators and KPIs and how to integrate these objects in a scorecard. With a behind-the-scenes look at scoring calculations, patterns, methods, and thresholds, you should have gained a good understanding of how best to design and implement meaningful KPIs and scorecards for your organization.

With the information on data source mapping, you should understand how to select the data you want to use for a metric in a KPI. You should understand how to add dimensions and measures and use calculated metrics to create scorecards that provide refined and complex views into your organization's business information.

Best Practices

▶ When using standard indicators, decide whether it is better to increase or decrease when you create the KPI, not when you create the indicator.

▶ Use centered indicators for KPIs that aim for a specific target.

▶ Use custom indicators to add corporate branding or a personalized touch to scorecards.

▶ When using larger images for indicators, consider how many of those types of indicators you will have on a scorecard. A scorecard can quickly become crowded.

▶ Use the KPI editor to create multiple metrics in a single KPI for KPIs that may have multiple actual values.

▶ Use a fixed-value KPI for setting static targets.

▶ Placing filters at the KPI level is the least flexible option for filtering KPIs. Consider placing filters at the scorecard or dashboard level instead.

▸ Use the Calculated Metrics Data Source Mapping feature to create appropriate metrics if the data source you work with does not have the complete dataset or structure you require for your metrics.

▸ Change the settings in the Format Numbers dialog box only if you want a uniform appearance for all other cultures viewing the scorecard.

▸ Use objective KPIs in balanced scorecard scenarios when multiple and different types of metrics are compared.

▸ When editing banding settings, make sure to set the "best possible" worst value. There is no benefit to setting an unrealistic worst value, and this may even confuse the outcome of the threshold calculation.

▸ The fastest and easiest way to create a scorecard is to create the KPIs directly from the data source that you want to use.

CHAPTER 8

Reports

IN THIS CHAPTER

▶ Overview of Reports 165

▶ Examining Analytic Chart
  Reports 167

▶ Examining Analytic Grid
  Reports 175

▶ Examining Excel Services
  Reports 176

▶ Examining KPI Details
  Reports 180

▶ Examining ProClarity Analytics
  Server Page Reports 183

▶ Examining Reporting Services
  Reports 185

▶ Strategy Map 188

▶ Examining Web Page
  Reports 192

▶ Examining Decomposition Tree
  Reports 193

▶ Examining Show Details
  Reports 194

Reporting and visualization is an important aspect of any business intelligence (BI) system. PerformancePoint Services provides many different types of reports that enable business users to navigate and interact with data. Using these different report types, you can create a reporting structure that facilitates and enables timely business decisions and action across your organization.

In this chapter, you learn about the ten different types of reports provided by PPS. You also learn how to configure the various report types to consume data from different sources and how to visualize data in different ways. Each section includes information to explain the main features of the different report types you can use, as well as examples to illustrate implementation.

The following sections include in-depth information on the types of reports included in PPS.

Overview of Reports

Analytical reports enable you to analyze and investigate data that you monitor using KPIs and scorecards. PPS provides ten types of reports:

▶ Analytic chart

▶ Analytic grid

▶ Excel Services

▶ KPI details

▶ ProClarity Analytics Server Page

- ▶ Reporting Services
- ▶ Strategy map
- ▶ Web page
- ▶ Show details
- ▶ Decomposition tree

All these analytical reports are interactive and enable users to navigate data in a way that is intuitive and most useful to them. For example, the vice president of sales in a company might look at a scorecard and notice that the goal for Sales Profit Margin is not being met. The next question is, "Why?" It is often difficult to get an answer by simply looking at the scorecard. This is where an accompanying analytical report is most helpful. The vice president can browse the sales data and drill into different regions and products to compare sales over time. This may lead to the realization that a product line in a particular region costs too much to produce or is not selling well enough.

Some report types also enable changes while the user is browsing the report. For example, the default view of a report might be a grid, but the user can change the report view to a line, bar, or stacked bar chart. This is an important aspect of reporting because different data sets make more sense if the proper report view is used. For example, comparing different regions viewer contribution to overall total viewership makes more sense when a stacked bar chart is used (see Figure 8.1) whereas looking at viewers over time makes more sense when a line chart is used (see Figure 8.2).

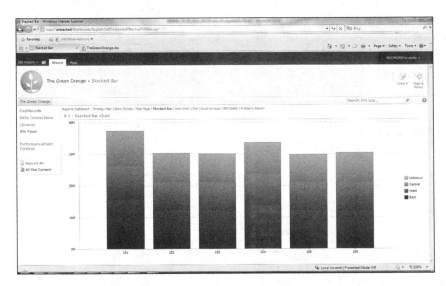

FIGURE 8.1   It is best to use a stacked bar chart when examining different regions viewer contribution to overall viewership.

For additional information on how you can display reports in a dashboard and apply filters, see Chapter 9, "Page Filters, Dashboards, and SharePoint Integration."

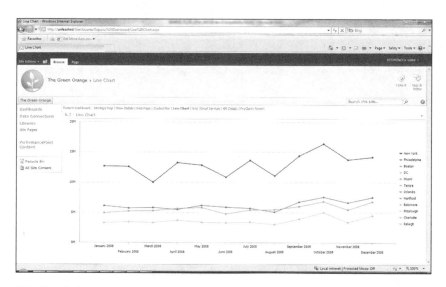

FIGURE 8.2   It is best to use a line chart when examining viewer trends.

Examining Analytic Chart Reports

An analytic chart is a highly interactive visualization that can be placed on a web page. The analytic chart enables deep analytics to be performed without the user installing any sort of client on their machine. The interactivity of the analytic chart enables the data to be displayed in many different ways and at different levels of detail so that users can view and look for trends in the data.

There are two ways to create an analytic chart. You can either select Analytic Chart from the Create tab in Dashboard Designer or you can right-click a PerformancePoint list in the Workspace Browser and then select Report from the pop-up menu and Analytic Chart from the dialog box (see Figure 8.3).

The next step is to select a data source. To do this, you can either select a data source that exists in your workspace or select a data source that has been deployed to SharePoint.

CAUTION

It is important to note that you can only use Analysis Services or PowerPivot data sources for these types of reports. You cannot select a tabular data source for these types of reports.

When you click Finish, the new report is added to your workspace. In this example, name the report Viewers per Season, as shown in Figure 8.4. Notice that the report appears in the Workspace Browser list under PerformancePoint Content.

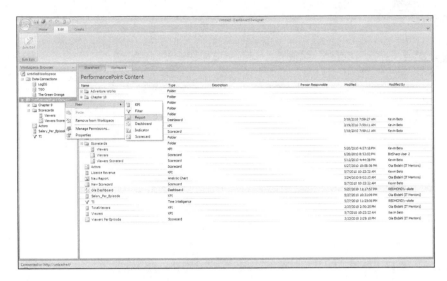

FIGURE 8.3   Right-click a PerformancePoint Content list to create an analytic report.

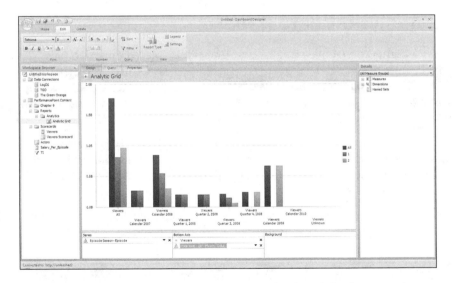

FIGURE 8.4   Viewers per Season is an example of analytic chart report.

You now have the ability to drag and drop measures, dimensions, and named sets and add these to the series (x-axis), bottom axis (y-axis), or background. The exact effect varies on the type of report, but in general, it is similar to the way Excel renders effects when data is added.

The analytic chart automatically appears as a bar chart. Even though this is the default setting, you can change the default analytic chart to any of the following chart types:

- ▶ Grid
- ▶ Stacked bar chart
- ▶ 100% stacked bar chart
- ▶ Line chart
- ▶ Line chart with markers
- ▶ Pie chart

Right-click anywhere on the report to change the report type. From the context menu that appears, select Report Type, and then select the type of report you want (see Figure 8.5).

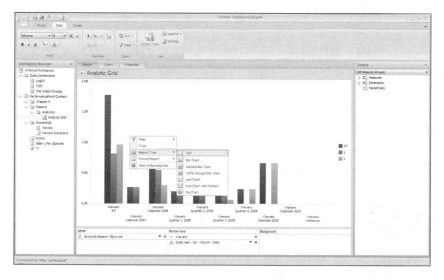

FIGURE 8.5   Use the context menu to change the report type.

Adding Data Elements

In this example, you modify a default report by adding data elements to break down viewers by season to illustrate how the interactivity of the analytic chart enables data to be displayed in many different ways and at different levels of detail.

Figure 8.6 shows you what the Design workspace looks like before any elements have been added.

The first step in this process is to add the Viewers measure to the Bottom Axis and the Season-Episode hierarchy from the Episode dimension to the Series axis. Add the measure and hierarchy by dragging the items from the Details pane on the right to the appropriate area in the Design workspace, as shown in Figure 8.7.

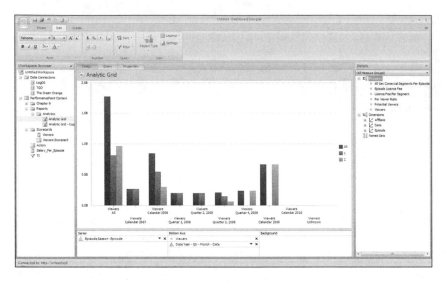

FIGURE 8.6   Drag the measures, dimensions, or named sets from the Details pane to the Design workspace.

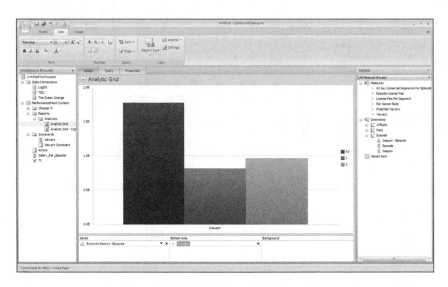

FIGURE 8.7   The report now displays viewers by season

Adding Additional Measures and Dimensions

Now you can continue to add additional measures, hierarchies, and attributes as necessary. One more attribute, Year, has been added to the report shown in Figure 8.8.

You can select the members you want to use in your chart. In this example, you added the Season-Episode hierarchy and all members of that hierarchy to the chart. You can also select individual members. Click the arrow next to the hierarchy name (Episode Season-Episode) to see the dialog box through which you can filter members. Figure 8.9 shows the dialog window that enables you to pick members.

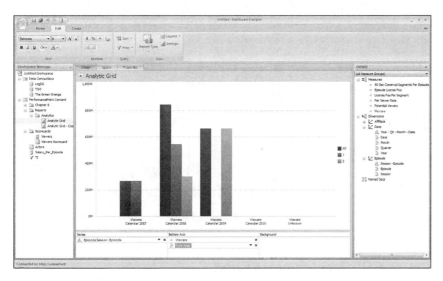

FIGURE 8.8   Including additional items enhances the informational value of your report.

FIGURE 8.9   Select Individual members from the hierarchy to customize your report further.

In this example, you selected episode 101, 102, and 103. Information for these episodes is now featured in the chart (see Figure 8.10).

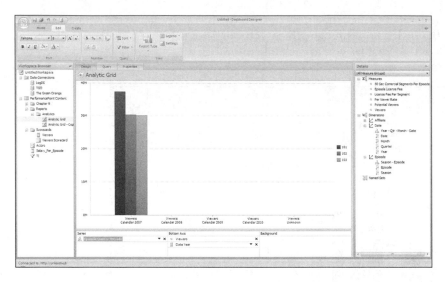

FIGURE 8.10   Additional items enhance the informational value of your report.

Using Measures and Dimensions as Filters

The background series enables you to add measures and dimensions that act as a filter. Continuing with this example, you add the Region-Affiliate hierarchy from the Affiliate dimension to the background series, and then you select the East region (see Figure 8.11).

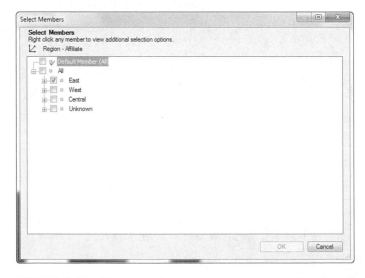

FIGURE 8.11   You can select to use measures as filters.

Notice that chart in Figure 8.12 has changed and now displays data for the East region only. By enabling the information bar, you can select to display the region in the upper-left corner of the report, underneath the report title.

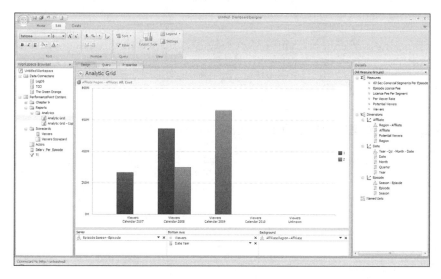

FIGURE 8.12   Using measures and dimensions as filters increases the informational value of your report.

Dimensions added to the background series are available when you add filters to your dashboard, too. For example, you can add a time hierarchy to the background series, configure it to use the All member, and then filter data based on year after the dashboard has been deployed. This topic is discussed in more detail in Chapter 9.

Using Interactivity Features and Context Menus

When you right-click an analytic chart, you expose interactive options that enable you to modify and refine the view on your data. Two context menus are available. One context menu is available by clicking a bar or line on the chart (see Figure 8.13.) The second context menu is available by clicking outside of a bar or line in a chart (see Figure 8.14).

With the context menu shown in Figure 8.13, you can do the following:

► Drill down to another dimension.

► Show only selected member.

► Show details (drill through).

► Remove the selected member.

► Remove all members but the selected one.

▶ See additional actions. These are actions defined in the cube such as drill through.

▶ Sort and filter data member such as Top 10, Largest to Smallest, Filter Empty series.

▶ Show or hide the information bar. This bar is displayed at the top of the chart.

▶ Pivot.

▶ Show a decomposition tree report. This report type is discussed in more detail in the Decomposition Tree section later in this chapter.

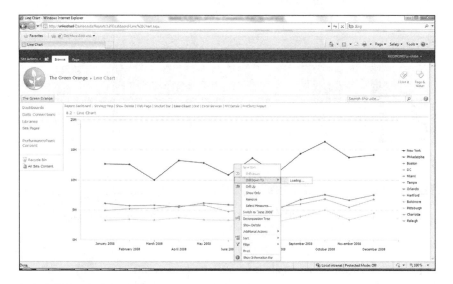

FIGURE 8.13   This context menu appears when you click a bar or line in a chart.

FIGURE 8.14   This context menu appears when you click outside of a bar or line in a chart.

With the context menu shown in Figure 8.14, you can do the following:

- ▶ Add or remove measures.

- ▶ Filter.

- ▶ Pivot.

- ▶ Change report type. For example, this context menu enables you to change from a bar chart to a grid, to a stacked bar chart, or to a pie chart.

Examining Analytic Grid Reports

The steps for creating an analytic grid chart are the same as for the analytic chart. You can create an analytic grid chart two ways. One method is to select Analytic Grid from the Create tab in Dashboard Designer. The second method is to right-click a PerformancePoint list in the Workspace Browser, select Report, and then select Analytic Grid from the dialog box.

Just as with the analytic chart, the analytic grid works only with Analysis Services cube and PowerPivot data sources.

> **NOTE**
>
> Notice that the design area for the analytic grid looks similar to the chart design area (see Figure 8.15).

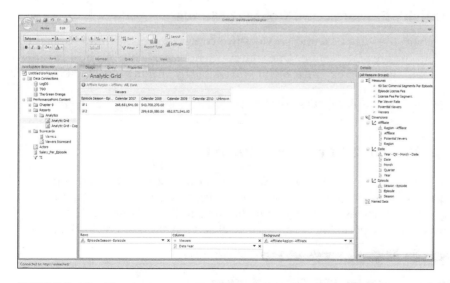

FIGURE 8.15   The design area for the analytic grid is similar to the chart design area.

With analytic grids, you can add measures and dimensions to rows, columns, and background. As shown in Figure 8.16, the measure Viewers and the attribute Year from the

Date dimension were added to columns. Next, you can add the Episode dimension to Rows to produce the report shown in Figure 8.16. The dimension members are expandable so that you can expand a parent to view its children.

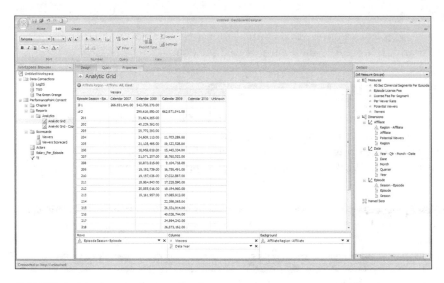

FIGURE 8.16   You can add measures to columns and rows to expand the view into your data.

Using Interactivity Features and Context Menus

Like the analytic chart, the analytical grid provides two context menus with the same options discussed in the previous section. One context menu is available by clicking the data on the chart, and the second context menu is available by clicking outside of the data in the chart (see Figure 8.17).

Examining Excel Services Reports

There are two ways to create an Excel Services report. You can select Other Reports from the Create tab in Dashboard Designer and then select Excel Services from the Report Template dialog box. Alternatively, you can right-click a PerformancePoint list in the Workspace Browser, select Report, and then select Excel Services from the dialog box.

There are two prerequisites for using an Excel Services report:

▶ You must deploy an Excel spreadsheet to SharePoint.

▶ You must have permissions to the location where you have deployed the spreadsheet.

FIGURE 8.17 The analytic grid also provides two context menus.

As shown in Figure 8.18, you start with an Excel workbook deployed with the following deployment properties:

▶ **Server:**http://unleashed

▶ **Document Library:**Documents

▶ **Excel Workbook:**TheGreenOrange.xlsx

FIGURE 8.18 This is an example of deployment properties for an Excel Services report.

To include this workbook into a dashboard, you need to create a new Excel Services report, as described earlier, and specify the deployment properties in the Report Settings, as shown in Figure 8.19.

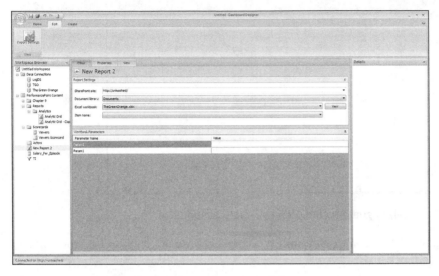

FIGURE 8.19   Specify the deployment properties in the Report Settings for your Excel Services report.

After the Excel Services report has been added to a dashboard, it will look like the report in Figure 8.20.

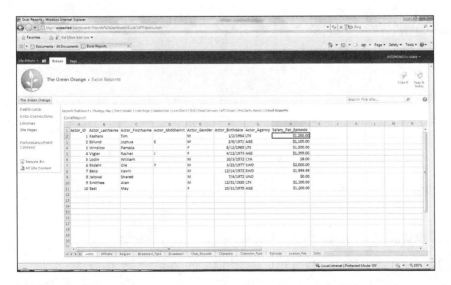

FIGURE 8.20   This is an example of an Excel Services report in a dashboard.

NOTE

Notice in Figure 8.20 that the entire workbook, including all the sheets, diagrams, and tables, is included. If you want to add only a specific item to the dashboard, you can specify the name of the item in the Excel Services Properties page (see Figure 8.21).

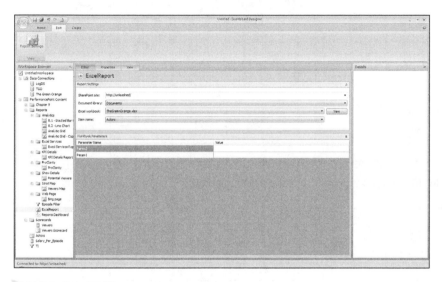

FIGURE 8.21 Use Item name on the Properties tab to show only a specific sheet, table, or chart.

After you add the report the dashboard, you only see the selected item, as shown in Figure 8.22.

If your workbook has one or more parameters defined, the names of these parameters appear in the Workbook Parameters section, and you can define default values (see Figure 8.23).

FIGURE 8.22   In this figure, the Excel Services report displays a single specified item.

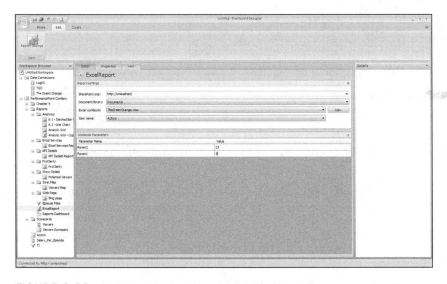

FIGURE 8.23   Define default values in the Workbook Parameters section.

Examining KPI Details Reports

A KPI details report enables you to click a key performance indicator (KPI) in a scorecard and display detailed properties about the KPI. This proves useful for conserving space on the screen while including available detailed information on indicators without displaying or printing this information for every single KPI. Figure 8.24 shows the available KPI properties for the KPI details report.

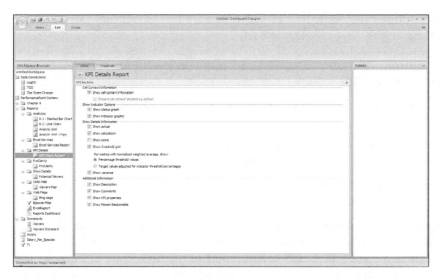

FIGURE 8.24   Properties that you can display in a KPI details report.

Show Cell Context Information is a KPI report that is available out of the box (OOTB). This type of KPI report shows information such as measures, filters, column, and row path information. For example, if a KPI has a filter applied to it, the report will indicate the active filter selections. You can use the PPS SDK to create additional types of KPI reports.

NOTE

There is an additional option available from the Show Cell Context Information called Expand Cell Context Sections by Default, as well as options for Show Status Graph and Show Indicator Graphic. These additional options are not yet fully implemented features. Look for this functionality to be completed at some point in the future.

▶ **Show Details Information:** Includes some additional numeric properties that might be of value to a scorecard viewer. They are only applicable when the metric selected is a Target metric and are especially useful when incomplete information is shown in the final scorecard such as when no actual column is displayed for space constraints.

▶ **Show Actual:** Shows the value of the actual metric against which this target metric is being compared.

▶ **Show Calculation:** Shows the scoring pattern used for this target metric.

▶ **Show Score:** The final calculated score for this target metric.

▶ **Show Threshold Grid:** A small chart showing all available indicator bands. It also shows where the thresholds are for this particular target metric. This grid is especially useful to help answer a question such as, "How close are we to green?"

▶ **Show Variance:** Shows the variance of the actual value from the target value.

Listed here are the Additional Information values, which are text values that can be displayed when the KPI is selected (see Figure 8.24).

▶ **Show Description:** This value comes directly from the Description text field in the Properties tab for the KPI.

▶ **Show Comments:** Shows a list of comments added to that cell in the KPI details report.

▶ **Show KPI Properties:** A series of values that come directly from the Custom Properties collection in the Properties tab for the KPI.

▶ **Show Person Responsible:** This value comes directly from the Person Responsible text field in the Properties tab for the KPI.

After you have specified the properties you want to display, you need to add the KPI report to a dashboard and create a connection from a scorecard KPI. In Figure 8.25, you see a scorecard in the left Zone 1 and a KPI details report in the right Zone 2. To create the connection, drag and drop the Cell - Context endpoint from the scorecard to the Drop fields to create the connections area on the KPI details report.

FIGURE 8.25   The KPI details report for the Viewers KPI.

TIP

This is a basic description on how to link these report types. See Chapter 9, for a more detailed explanation of these report types.

After the dashboard has been deployed, you can click any of the scorecard KPIs and see the details displayed in the KPI report.

Examining ProClarity Analytics Server Page Reports

There are two ways to create a ProClarity Analytics Server Page report. One method is to select Other Reports from the Create tab in Dashboard Designer and then select ProClarity Analytics Server Page from the Report Template dialog box. The second method is to right-click a PerformancePoint list in the Workspace Browser, select Report, and then select ProClarity Analytics Server Page from the dialog box.

There are two prerequisites for using a ProClarity Analytics Server Page report:

▶ You must deploy a ProClarity Analytics Server book to a ProClarity library.

▶ You must have access to the location where you have deployed the ProClarity Analytics Server book.

In Figure 8.26, a ProClarity Analytics report has been deployed showing how different affiliates contribute to overall viewership.

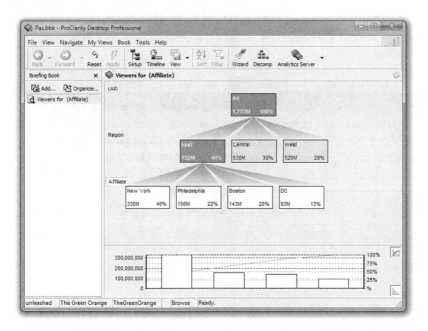

FIGURE 8.26   A ProClarity Analytics report that will be deployed for use in a PPS dashboard.

To add the report to a dashboard, after creating the report in ProClarity, you will configure the report in Dashboard Designer using the following properties: Server URL, Page, and Configuration options as seen in Figure 8.27. The Server URL option indicates the PAS server hosting the desired report, and the Page indicates the report to use.

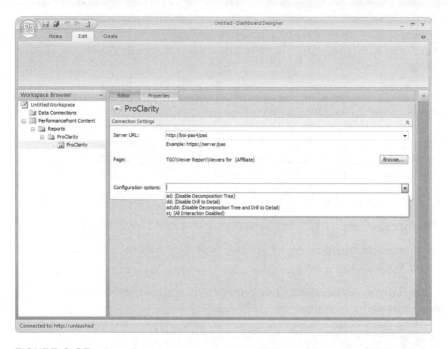

FIGURE 8.27   Specify the deployment properties in the Report Settings for your ProClarity Analytics Server Page report.

NOTE

The Configuration options enable you to restrict user interactivity. Some analytical operations can be performance-intensive. Restricting user interactivity can be useful to minimize the performance impact of PAS reports against the PAS or data source.

After the ProClarity Analytics Server Page report has been added to a dashboard, it should look like the report in Figure 8.28.

FIGURE 8.28   The ProClarity Analytics Server Page report has been added to a dashboard.

Examining Reporting Services Reports

There are two ways to create a Reporting Services report. One method is to select Reporting Services from the Create tab in Dashboard Designer. Alternatively, you can right-click a PerformancePoint list in the Workspace Browser, select Report and then Reporting Services from the dialog box.

Listed here are the three prerequisites for using Reporting Services report:

▶ Report Viewer 2008 must be installed on the machine running Dashboard Designer.

▶ You must deploy a Reporting Services report.

▶ You must have access to the location where you have deployed the Reporting Services report.

To fulfill the first prerequisite, you must first install Microsoft Report Viewer 2008, which is a free download from http://download.microsoft.com. If Microsoft Report Viewer is not installed, you receive the warning message shown in Figure 8.29. After you have installed this component, it is necessary to close and reopen Dashboard Designer for the changes to take effect.

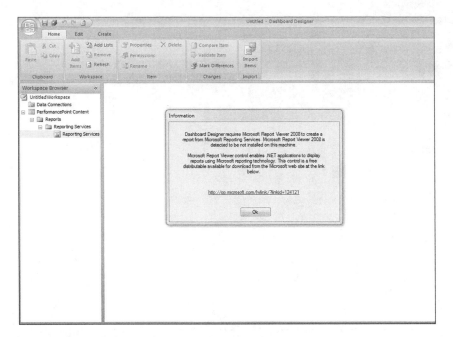

FIGURE 8.29   This warning message appears if Microsoft Report Viewer 2008 is not installed.

NOTE

Even if you are using reports hosted in Reporting Services 2005 or Report Services 2008 R2, you still need to install Report Viewer 2008. It is compatible with other versions of Reporting Services. Dashboard Designer is hard-coded to use only Report Viewer 2008.

Figure 8.30 shows a Reporting Services report displaying viewership for *The Green Orange*.

▶ **Server Mode:** Specify whether Reporting Services is integrated with SharePoint or a native installation. In this example, SharePoint Integrated mode is used.

▶ **Server Name:** Give the server a name, such as http://servername/ReportServer. The exact name you use depends on your actual installation.

▶ **Report:** Select a name for the report from the list of available reports on the server you selected.

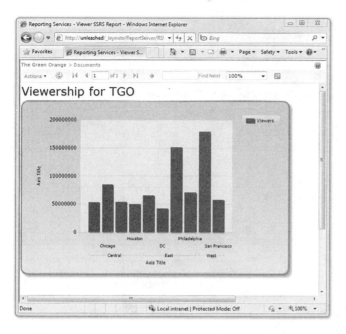

FIGURE 8.30   A Reporting Services report that will be deployed for use in a PPS dashboard.

TIP

If you are running in SharePoint integrated mode, the URLs can be tricky to set. It is important to know that the Server Name parameter turns into the Report Server URL parameter and the Report Parameter turns into the Report URL parameter. Therefore, both need to be set differently.

For example, in most scenarios the Report Server URL will be located on the same farm as SharePoint with a different port. It may look something like *http://servername:port/ReportServer*. If this is set correctly, the Report URL needs to be copied and pasted straight out of a browser viewing the report, usually something like *http://servername/reports/reportname.rdl*.

▶ **Show Toolbar:** Allows you to choose to hide or show the toolbar. The toolbar allows you to export the report, print, or zoom.

▶ **Show Parameters:** Toggles if the report parameters are shown to the user when the report is viewed on a deployed dashboard.

TIP

Remember that if the report has one or more parameters without default values, the user cannot set them if they are not visible.

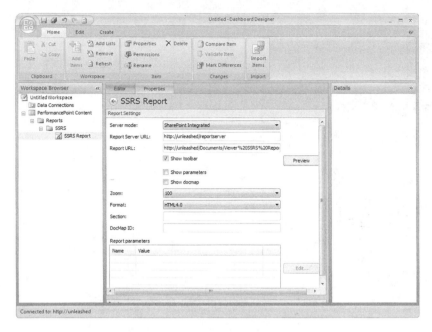

FIGURE 8.31   Specify the deployment properties in the Report Settings for your Reporting Services report.

▶ **Show Docmap:** A document map is a navigation pane that can be used to navigate through reports, pages, and sections.

▶ **Zoom:** Set the default zoom value.

▶ **Format:** Set the default display format. You can choose one of the following: HTML 4.0, MHTML, Image, Excel, CSV, PDF, or XML.

▶ **DocMap ID:** ID of document map to be used.

▶ **Report Parameters:** Use this property to set parameters to default values. Parameters displaying in this UI can also be connected through filters on the dashboard.

When the report parameters are complete and the object is saved to the SharePoint server, it is possible to use the Reporting Services report on a deployed dashboard.

Strategy Map

A strategy map enables you to connect scorecard data to Visio shapes. This provides a great opportunity to visualize data. For example, you can create Visio diagrams to illustrate the following:

▶ Sales pipeline

▶ Layout of a data center

▶ Layout of a factory floor

As a prerequisite for creating strategy maps, you must have Visio installed on the client machine running Dashboard Designer. A Visio installation is not required to view an already deployed strategy map.

In this example, the strategy map report will display the success of each show by region. To start, you need to create a new Visio diagram. You begin by creating a simple diagram with three rectangular shapes on top of a map of the United States (see Figure 8.32). The rectangular shapes have a default fill color of gray, and you have set the transparency of the fill color to 50 percent so that you can see the map underneath it. Later, you connect the KPI colors to the map to represent the success of each show. You call this diagram ViewerMap.VSD and use this diagram to map KPI data to the regions.

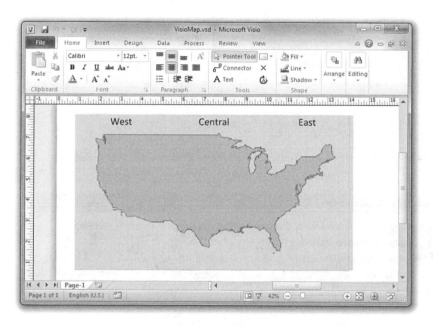

FIGURE 8.32   Begin by creating a Visio diagram.

Next, create a new strategy map from Dashboard Designer. At a conceptual level, a strategy map is just a view that sits on top of a scorecard. For this reason, the first step involves selecting a scorecard that will serve as the source for the colors and values that will be displayed on the strategy map.

Next, use the scorecard called Viewers Scorecard, which is a scorecard comparing viewers against potential viewers for each episode. Select the scorecard, and then click Finish. A gray area appears with a message that indicates you should select Edit Strategy Map from the Edit tab (see Figure 8.33).

This option opens the Strategy Map Editor, which allows you to import the Visio diagram created earlier.

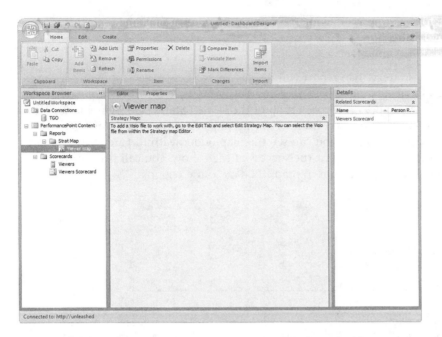

FIGURE 8.33   This message directs you to the Edit Strategy Map option on the Edit tab.

NOTE

The Visio diagram is imported and saved directly to the SharePoint content database. This means that any changes made to the Visio file after the import will not affect the strategy map. If you want to edit the strategy map after importing, you can either import the map again or edit it directly in the strategy map editor, which offers limited editing functionality. If you choose to import the map, you must re-connect all the shapes.

Next, choose the shape you want to connect to a KPI and click Connect Shape, as shown in Figure 8.34. This opens a dialog box from which you can choose the KPI you want to use.

Choose the KPI you want, click Connect, and then click Close. The shape displays the name and color of the KPI. The connection is dynamic, and the color of the shape changes when the KPI's actual to target ratio changes. You can also right-click the shape and select Insert Field to select additional meta data for display in the shape when editing a text field within Visio (see Figure 8.35).

TIP

The color selections for the strategy map come from the background color for the indicator that is being used for the KPI with which the shape is connected. If you want custom colors, you can create a custom indicator.

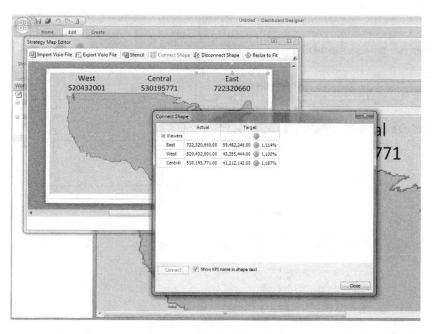

FIGURE 8.34   From the scorecard, choose the KPI you want to connect to the shape.

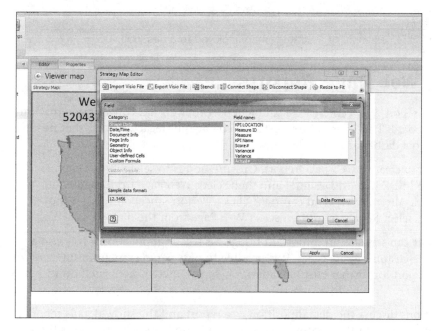

FIGURE 8.35   Select additional data to display in the shape on the strategy map.

As shown in Figure 8.36, the Actual value, which is in number of viewers, has been added to the shape and it has been deployed to a dashboard. The report has also been connected with a filter to filter the data per episode.

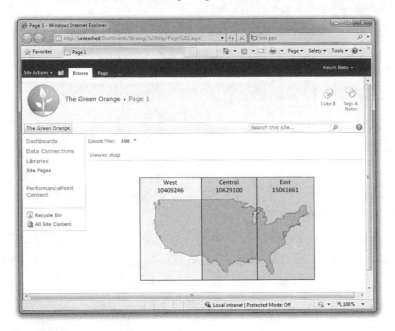

FIGURE 8.36   This is an example of a strategy map deployed to a dashboard.

Examining Web Page Reports

With the web page report, you can create a simple report that displays a web page that can be added to a dashboard. This is useful for custom web pages or legacy reports that need to be integrated into a dashboard.

There are two ways to create a web page report. One method is to select Other Reports from the Create tab in Dashboard Designer and then select Web Page from the Report Template dialog box. Alternatively, you can right-click a PerformancePoint list in the Workspace Browser, select Report, and then select Web Page from the dialog box.

The web page report can serve as an important bridge for legacy applications. It is also a simple way to create custom report types. It is possible to pass parameters from filters or scorecards to this report for further customization. These parameters are passed on the URL query string.

The following sections discuss the decomposition tree report and the show details report, which are both available from the context menu. You will also learn how to access these reports when browsing an analytical chart, grid, or scorecard.

Examining Decomposition Tree Reports

The decomposition tree (decomp tree) report enables you to visualize how child hierarchy members contribute to a parent. This is most useful when trying to understand the underlying data for a particular value. With the decomp tree, you can "decompose" the parent value into its constituent values and view them broken out by dimensions.

> **NOTE**
>
> Although this report is automatic in the analytic report types, some configuration is necessary to make this report available on a scorecard. The calculation for the KPI row needs to be set to Source Data. If the KPI row on the scorecard is configured in this way, the Show Details option will appear when you right-click the data cell.

The decomp tree report is only accessible from a context menu and will not show up with other report types in Dashboard Designer,

To access the context menu, begin with the Viewers and Potential Viewers Analytic Chart for Season 1, as shown in Figure 8.37. The high point in the graph is the data point for "episode 109. You can see more information about why this particular show was more successful than the other shows. To do this, right-click the point, and then select Decomposition Tree from the context menu that appears.

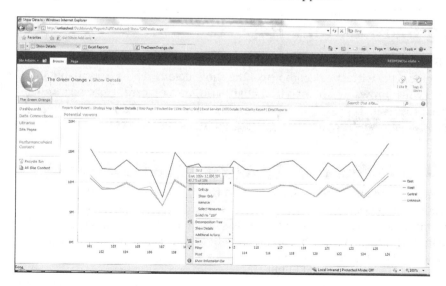

FIGURE 8.37   The Decomposition Tree option is available from the context menu on analytical charts, grids, or scorecards.

The decomp tree for this episode appears first with only "episode 109 (see Figure 8.38). To drill down and find out which region had the most viewers, left-click the 109 element, and then select Affiliate—Region. From here, it is possible to continue drilling down through to the Affiliate city and then into the Calendar to see the month. Eventually, you will locate the day with the highest number of viewers.

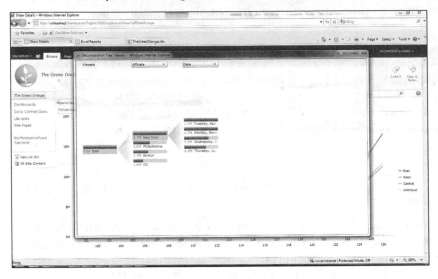

FIGURE 8.38   Browse the decomp tree for detail information.

Examining Show Details Reports

The show details feature is another report view that provides detailed row level information for a KPI or report. As with the decomp tree, the show details report is available from the context menu when browsing an analytical chart, grid, or scorecard. However, unlike the decomposition tree, which provides an interactive drill-down experience, the show details report provides a static display of data organized in a table format.

NOTE

Although this report is automatic in the analytic report types, some configuration is necessary to make this available on a scorecard. For example, the calculation for the KPI row needs to be set to Source Data. If the KPI row on the scorecard is configured in this way, right-clicking this data cell offers the Show Details option, which can be accessed by right–clicking the context menu.

Show details reports are most useful when you identify a value that seems interesting, but you would like more information on the exact data values that contribute to the data point of interest.

In The Green Orange example mentioned earlier that uses an analytic graph to compare viewers against potential viewers, you can see a dip in viewers for episode 107. You can right-click the data point for this episode to see the context menu for the show details report (see Figure 8.39).

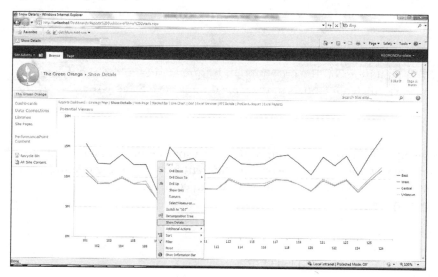

FIGURE 8.39   The Show Details option is also available from the context menu on analytical charts, grids, or scorecards.

When you select the Show Details option, the Details page appears in a separate browser window. The Details page shows all the database rows that contribute to the value calculated by Analysis Services (see Figure 8.40).

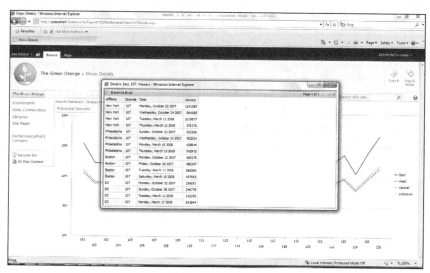

FIGURE 8.40   The Details page displays the databases rows that contribute to the value calculated by Analysis Services.

TIP

When the data is in the show details report, the data can be exported to Excel, where you can do a deeper analysis. Look for the Export to Excel icon in the upper-left corner of the report.

Under the covers, this report uses the SQL Server Analysis Services drill-through feature. This means that any limitations on the drill-through feature applies to the show details feature. For example, calculated members in the cube do not have a Show Details option.

Summary

This chapter provided an overview of how to configure various report types to consume data from different sources and to visualize data in different ways. After completing this chapter, you should have a good understanding of how to configure reports using the following PPS report types:

▶ Analytic chart

▶ Analytic grid

▶ Excel Services

▶ KPI details

▶ ProClarity Analytics Server Page

▶ Reporting Services

▶ Strategy map

▶ Web page

▶ Decomposition tree

▶ Show details

Using the information on report types and report options included in this chapter, you should select appropriate report types for your data. You should also understand how to enhance the value of a report by providing interactivity options and views into the underlying data in a report.

Best Practices

▶ Different datasets make more sense if the proper report view is used. Be sure you select an appropriate report type and view for the information you want to convey.

▶ Use the highly interactive analytic chart that allows deep analytics to be performed without the users installing any sort of client on their machine.

▶ Use the KPI details report to display detailed properties about the KPIs in a scorecard, including calculation, score, and threshold.

▶ If you use ProClarity, read the decomposition tree report, which is an enhancement inspired by ProClarity that was added to PPS 2010.

▶ If you are using reports hosted in Reporting Services 2005 or Report Services 2008 R2, be sure to install Report Viewer 2008.

▶ Use strategy maps to connect scorecard data to Visio shapes and provide a great opportunity to visualize data.

▶ Use the web page report for custom web pages or legacy reports that need to be integrated into a dashboard.

▶ Use the decomp tree report to visualize how children contribute to a parent and to understand the underlying data for a particular value.

∞

Page Filters, Dashboards, and SharePoint Integration

IN THIS CHAPTER

▶ Overview 199

▶ Creating Filters 200

▶ PPS Filters 200

▶ SharePoint 2010 Filters 204

▶ Creating Dashboards 207

▶ Web Part Connections 208

▶ Dashboards in Dashboard Designer 210

▶ Creating Dashboards in the Browser 227

After you create your key performance indicators (KPIs), scorecards, and reports, you are ready to use these elements to create dashboards that transform your organization's data into information. A well-designed dashboard uses these PerformancePoint Services (PPS) elements with filters to communicate key business information to key business users in a targeted, easily available manner.

You can create dashboards and connect filters in several ways. You can use Dashboard Designer, SharePoint Designer, or the browser on the SharePoint page. This chapter covers each of these ways of creating dashboards and how to connect filters to dashboards, including Time Intelligence and other typical filters. The chapter provides examples and illustrations and identifies the issues to consider when selecting a tool to create dashboards and connect filters.

At the end of this chapter, you have the information you need to create dashboards, apply filters, and integrate dashboards into SharePoint pages for access by your business community.

Overview

The preceding chapter discussed how to create various PPS elements such as KPIs, scorecards, and reports. Before you can deploy these elements to SharePoint, you need to assemble them in a dashboard. The dashboard is what you then deploy to SharePoint.

Typically, you also want to create filters to a dashboard to enable users to, for example, filter scorecard or report data to look at a specific region or a particular time period. It is common to have time-related filters on a dashboard because most analysis is done based on comparing what's going on today with what happened during a previous time period, or by reviewing revenue on a year-to-date basis.

This chapter explains how to create dashboards and filters and how to deploy dashboards to SharePoint.

Creating Filters

A filter is a Web Part object that will modify the data rendered on a dashboard in some way. Most dashboards have an associated filter. A time-related filter is a typical example of a filter. This type of filter enables users to examine values for a particular time period or for an aggregated value such as year-to-date. Another example is a filter that enables users to filter values based on a particular category for example products, regions, users, resellers, or episodes.

This chapter discusses in depth two main categories of filters:

▶ **PPS filters** are filters that can be created within Dashboard Designer. These filters are compatible with PPS objects.

▶ **SharePoint filters** are a wider set of filters that can be created either in the SharePoint Web Part page user interface (UI) or in SharePoint Designer. These filters are sometimes trickier to work with but do enable other options not available with PPS filters.

> **NOTE**
>
> In PPS 2007, filters were stored with specific dashboards. This meant that a filter could not be used between two different dashboards.
>
> In SharePoint 2010, filters have become their own objects independent of the dashboards that use them. This enables filters to be shared across different dashboards.

PPS Filters

Six different types of filters are available by default within PPS. It is also possible to create custom filters through the PPS software developer's kit (SDK):

▶ **Custom Table:** This template enables you to pick data values from a tabular data source (SQL table or SharePoint list, for example) and use the data values as filter values.

▶ **MDX Query:** This template enables you to retrieve a list of values from an Analysis Services cube using a Multidimensional Expressions (MDX) query.

▶ **Member Selection:** This template enables you to select members from an Analysis Services dimension and use the members in a filter.

► **Named Set:** This template enables you to select a member set that has been defined in an Analysis Services cube and use the member set values in a filter.

► **Time Intelligence:** This template enables you to specify Simple Time Period Specification (STPS) expressions and use the expressions for filter values. To use this template, you must have Time Intelligence configured on the data source.

► **Time Intelligence Connection Formula:** This template always shows a calendar control. From the calendar, the user specifies the date that should be considered as "today." PPS then uses this date and applies a connection formula. The formula is an STPS expression. For example, if you have a year-to-date (YTD) STPS expression defined and pick April 11, 2010 as "today," YTD is calculated based on April 11, 2010. To use this template you must have Time Intelligence configured on the data source.

Creating a PPS Filter in Dashboard Designer

Although you can create PPS filters through SharePoint Designer or through the browser, PPS filters are best created through Dashboard Designer. Follow these steps to create a PPS Member Selection filter:

1. Right-click a PPS Content List, and select New Filter.

2. After you do this you have the option to pick a filter template, as shown in Figure 9.1. Select Member Selection Filter, and then click OK.

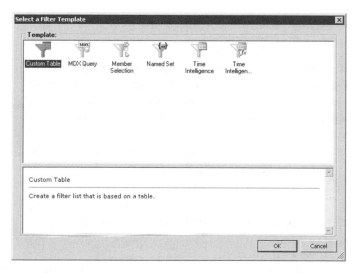

FIGURE 9.1   Choose a filter template from this dialog box.

3. The next step is to choose a data source. You can choose any data source, either a tabular data source such as SQL or a SharePoint list, or a dimensional data source such as Analysis Services. Pick an available data source, and then click OK.

4. The next step is to choose the dimension to use for the filter. Click the Select Dimension button shown in Figure 9.2, and then choose a dimension from the dimension selector that appears and click OK.

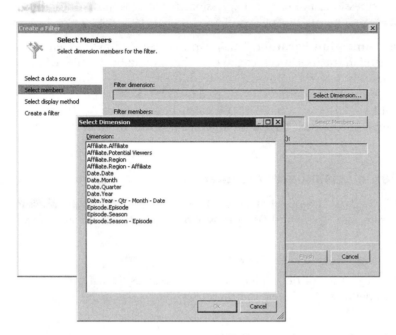

FIGURE 9.2   Choose the dimension to use for the filter from this dialog box.

5. The next step is to choose the members from the dimension that you want to have available in the filter. Clicking the Select Members button, as shown in Figure 9.3, brings up a member selector for the dimension selected in step 4. We can either explicitly check the members we want to include in the filter or do a dynamic selection (children or descendants, for example).

6. In this dialog, we can also specify if we want a different default member from the member defined on the dimension. To do this, right-click members and select Set as Default Selection. Doing so toggles the currently selected member as a default member on or off.

7. After you make your selections, click OK to confirm selections on the Select Member dialog. Then click Next from the wizard dialog to advance to the last step in the wizard.

8. In this last step, specify how you want to render the filter, as shown in Figure 9.4. Three different display options control the look and feel of the filter:

   ▶ **List:** Displays a flat list suitable for nonhierarchical data

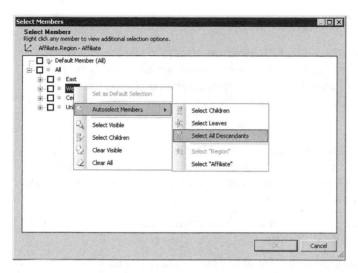

FIGURE 9.3 Choose the members to use for the filter from the Select Members dialog box.

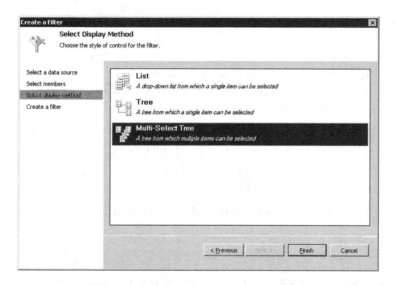

FIGURE 9.4 Choose a display option to set the look and feel of the filter.

▶ **Tree:** Displays the list in a tree view that enables users to navigate hierarchies

▶ **Multi-Select Tree:** Displays the list as a tree view but enables users to select multiple values

SharePoint 2010 Filters

SharePoint filters are filters not available for direct editing in PPS. They can be created either through SharePoint Designer or in the browser. Several types of filters are available by default with an installation of SharePoint, and others can be purchased from third-party vendors. The following list describes some of the filters you might use to connect to PPS objects.

▶ **Business Connectivity Services filter:** Enables filtering of a Business Connectivity Services (BCS) SharePoint list. The advantage of using this type of filter with BCS data is that the filter is applied before data is retrieved from the external data source, rather than after results have been returned.

▶ **Choice filter:** Enables users to pick a simple value from a drop-down menu and pass a specified value to other Web Parts.

▶ **Current User filter:** Passes the username of the current user to other Web Parts. This filter does not show any UI to the user (because it is intended to be used for personalization scenarios).

▶ **Date filter:** Enables users to select a specific date from a calendar control, which is then passed to other Web Parts.

▶ **Filter actions:** This Web Part is not a true filter. It disables dynamic filter application and replaces it with a button that applies filter selections when clicked. This is useful in scenarios when there are several other filters on a page and a user might want to change many of the filters before triggering a page refresh.

▶ **Query String filter:** Takes a value from the page query string and passes the value to specified Web Parts. This filter does not display a UI to the user.

▶ **SQL Server Analysis Services filter:** Brings up a simple dimension member picker and passes the specified value to other Web Parts.

▶ **Text filter:** Enables a user specified value to be passed to other Web Parts.

NOTE

You can create a PPS filter here natively in SharePoint as well, but you need to select a filter that was previously created with Dashboard Designer.

Creating a SharePoint Filter from SharePoint Designer

Although creating filters and working with Web Part pages is possible in the browser, it is a much better user experience to do this in SharePoint Designer, as follows:

CAUTION

The amount of configuration done with PPS Web Parts in SharePoint Designer is fairly limited. You cannot pass PPS values in the connections between Web Parts. Configuring other Web Parts or passing non-PPS-specific values works just fine, however. If you want to work with PPS Web Parts *and* pass PPS-specific values, it is best to use the browser rather than SharePoint Designer to create a filter.

---

1. Launch SharePoint Designer. Connect to a site by clicking the Open Site button or by clicking on a link in the Recent Sites section.

2. Create a new Web Part page by choosing Add Item – Web Part Page from the File menu.

3. Place the cursor selection on a Web Part field and select Web Parts – Web Part – More Web Parts from the Insert tab.

4. Type **Filter** in the Web Parts Picker UI, as shown in Figure 9.5, and choose the appropriate filter to be inserted.

FIGURE 9.5   Choose the appropriate filter to insert.

5. Choose a filter and click OK. In this example, we choose a Choice Filter Web Part.

6. At this point, you should see the filter added to the Web Part page, as shown in Figure 9.6. Double-click the filter to bring up the filter's Properties dialog.

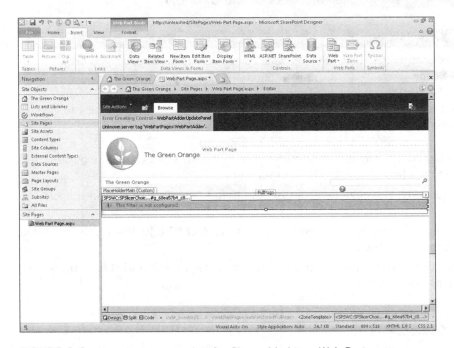

FIGURE 9.6   Here is an example of a filter added to a Web Part page.

7. In the filter's Properties dialog, as shown in Figure 9.7, enter a set of values and descriptions, and then click OK.

NOTE

For this particular type of filter (Choice Filter), the Value text is what is passed as a parameter to other Web Parts. The Description text is what is presented to the user.

At this point, the filter is ready to be connected to additional Web Parts.

This is discussed in detail later in this chapter in the "Creating Dashboards from the Browser" section.

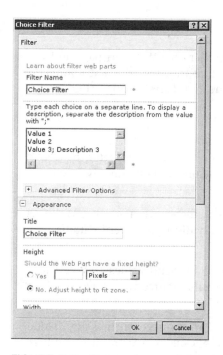

FIGURE 9.7   Enter values and descriptions in the Filter properties dialog box.

Creating Dashboards

Dashboards are the vehicle used to display PPS objects to end users. Dashboards do not require any special software on the client machine other than a browser and are implemented as Web Part pages. There are two different ways to create and configure dashboards:

▶ **Dashboard Designer:** This is the easiest way to configure a dashboard with just PPS objects on it. The design experience is optimized around creating connections between the Web Parts.

▶ **Browser:** After you browse to a SharePoint site, you can create and configure dashboards through your browser.

CAUTION

SharePoint Designer enables you to create Web Part pages using SharePoint 2010 filters, but unfortunately it does not support creating connections between PPS Web Parts. If you plan to do this, go ahead and do it in the browser.

Web Part Connections

Dashboards are implemented by putting Web Parts together on a Web Part page and configuring the connections between the Web Parts so that they interact. The connections function as a mechanism that passes values between the Web Parts, letting other Web Parts know what values to filter on.

A connection consists of four different pieces:

- ▶ **Get Values From:** This is the Web Part sending the specified parameter to another Web Part. Filters are usually source Web Parts as the user usually directly interacts with filters to select desired filter values.

- ▶ **Send Values To:** This is the Web Part receiving parameters from another Web Part. Reports are usually target Web Parts as they typically display different data based on what was selected in the Filter Value Web Part.

- ▶ **Source Value:** These are the types of values sent to the Send Values To Web Part. For instance, a member selection filter has two possible source values: Display Name and Member Unique Name

- ▶ **Connect To:** These are the ways in which a Web Part can receive the source values. For example, there are several different options applicable to a Scorecard Web Part, such dimensions on rows, columns, or page (both rows and columns).

NOTE

The terminology varies between Dashboard Designer, SharePoint Designer, and SharePoint in the browser. The terminology here is based on Dashboard Designer terminology. The concepts are the same for all three editors.

A connection must have all four of the pieces defined earlier to be valid. In addition, there is no error-checking on invalid-connection combinations. For instance, you will not receive an error when connecting a member selection filter's display name source value to a row dimension connect to value for an analytic report. After the Dashboard has been deployed, viewing this in the browser will result in an error.

NOTE

There is also a special type of connection available called Display Condition. This does not pass a value like the other connections; instead, it toggles this display of the Send Values to Web Part based on selections in the Get Values from Web Part. One typical configuration that takes advantage of this feature is a scorecard that, depending on which KPI is selected by the user, displays different reports in a stacked zone in the dashboard.

Source Values

This is a list of the major source values available in Get Values from Web Parts (see Table 9.1). The two typical Get Value from Web Parts are filters and scorecards.

TABLE 9.1   Source Values and Applicable PPS Objects

Source Values	Applicable PPS Objects	Description
Member unique name	Filters Scorecards	A fully qualified dimension member name. This is the source value to use when applying filters to scorecards or reports.
Display value	Filters Scorecards	The display text associated with the dimension member.
Time formula	TI filters	The Time Intelligence formula.
Date time	TI filters	The date and time.
Property value	Scorecard	Custom properties defined in Dashboard Designer for the KPI that was selected.
Cell context	Scorecard	An XML blob containing information on the KPI currently selected in a scorecard. Primarily useful when connecting to a KPI Details report.

Connect To Values

This is a list of the major Connect To values received by a Send Values to Web Part (see Table 9.2). Scorecards and reports are typical kinds of Send Values to Web Parts.

TABLE 9.2   Filter Source Values and Begin Points

Source Values	Begin Point	Description
Column	Member unique name	Applies the specified dimension filter to all dimensions on the columns of a scorecard.
Row	Member unique name	Applies the specified dimension filter to all dimensions on the rows of a scorecard.
Page/background	Member unique name	Applies the specified dimension filter to all dimensions on the entire scorecard, regardless of whether they have been placed on rows or columns.
Hierarchy	Member unique name	Replaces the dimension currently on the scorecard with the dimension selected in the filter. The dimension is completely replaced; so if an entirely different dimension is sent as a source value other than what it is connecting to, the original connect to value will no longer apply to the scorecard.

TABLE 9.2   Filter Source Values and Begin Points

Source Values	Begin Point	Description
Named value	Display name	This is a value that shows up in many different nonanalytic reports. Often, it is used for showing the currently selected filter values for SQL Server Reporting Services (SSRS) or Web page reports without incurring an extra round trip to the database.
Formula	Time formula	The Time Intelligence formula currently selected in the filter. Note that this uses the formula, not the member unique names returned by the formula, and the formula will then be reevaluated. This is especially useful when many members are returned in a TI formula and performance is a concern.
Date time	Date time	Sets the current date for Time Intelligence features. Used with the Time Intelligence Connection Formula filter.
Context	Cell Context	Accepts a cell context source value from a scorecard. Applies only to the KPI Details report.

Dashboards in Dashboard Designer

Dashboards are objects in Dashboard Designer just like other PPS objects such as scorecards and KPIs.

> **CAUTION**
>
> When deploying a dashboard, Dashboard Designer will overwrite the existing dashboard. Any modifications done after the initial deployment will be overwritten without warning.
>
> If you do accidentally overwrite a dashboard that has been modified, it is often possible to recover it by looking at previous revisions of the page and restoring a legacy version in SharePoint.

Creating and Deploying a Dashboard

> **CAUTION**
>
> Dashboards are ASPX pages. Because of this, standard contributor-level permissions in SharePoint are not enough to successfully create ASPX pages. Make sure your account has at least Designer-level permissions on the SharePoint site with the account deploying the dashboard.

In this example, we create a dashboard using the elements shown in Figure 9.8. Currently, we have two reports: one KPI and one scorecard.

Start the process of creating a new dashboard by clicking Dashboard on the Create tab. Alternatively, you can right-click the list, PerformancePoint Content in the Workspace Browser, and then select New, Dashboard, also shown in Figure 9.8.

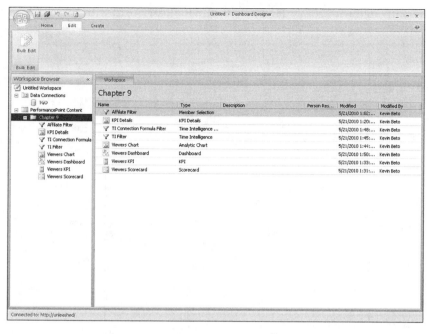

FIGURE 9.8   These are the elements available for the dashboard example.

When you do this, the Select a Dashboard Page Template dialog opens (see Figure 9.9). From here, you choose the initial layout of the dashboard. You can modify this layout after you create the dashboard.

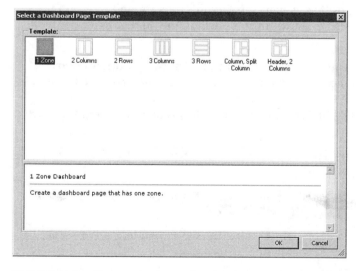

FIGURE 9.9   Choose the layout for the dashboards from this dialog box.

Each dashboard is configured with zones. Figure 9.10 shows a dashboard with three zones, one header, and two columns.

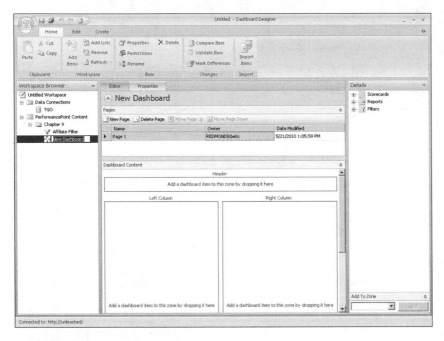

FIGURE 9.10   This is an example of a dashboard with three zones, one header, and two columns.

The zones define how you can position elements, scorecards, reports, and filters on the dashboard. The elements available are shown in the Details pane on the right side (see Figure 9.11).

There are two ways to add elements to a dashboard. In the first way, begin by choosing the item you want to add from the Details pane. Then choose the desired zone in the Add to Zone box at the bottom of the Details pane. Click Add to confirm your choice. Alternatively, you can simply drag the element from the Details pane and drop it in the desired zone.

In Figure 9.11, we have added the scorecard and one of the reports to the dashboard in the left and right columns, respectively.

Notice that we cannot preview the dashboard at this point. You must deploy the dashboard to SharePoint before you can see the final result.

Deploy the dashboard to SharePoint by right-clicking the dashboard in the Workspace Browser and then selecting Deploy to SharePoint, as shown in Figure 9.12.

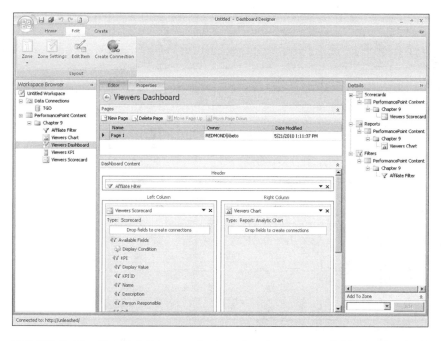

FIGURE 9.11   The Details pane displays the elements available for the dashboard.

> **NOTE**
>
> In PPS 2007, you had the option to preview the dashboard before deploying it to SharePoint. That option is not available in PPS 2010.

> **TIP**
>
> You will frequently use the deployment option. The shortcut key for deploying the dashboard to SharePoint is Control+D.

The next step is to pick the document library that will store the dashboard, as shown in Figure 9.13. You also need to choose the master page you want to use.

> **NOTE**
>
> Only master pages compatible with the version 4 SharePoint UI are available for selection here. If there is nothing available to select in this list, check that you have a master page with this compatibility available for this dashboard library.

The dialog shown in Figure 9.13 displays only the first time you deploy a dashboard. All subsequent deployments use those same settings. If you need to change the dashboard target location or master page, use the dashboard Deployment Properties, as shown in Figure 9.14.

FIGURE 9.12   When you are ready, Use Deploy to SharePoint from the Workspace Browser to deploy the dashboard.

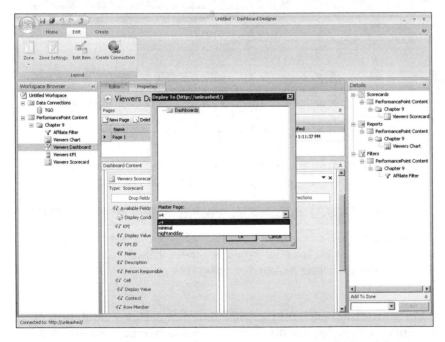

FIGURE 9.13   Choose the document library for the dashboard and the master page to use from this dialog.

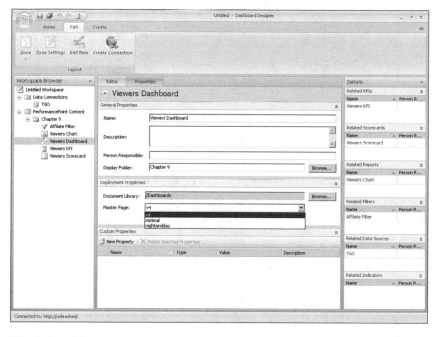

FIGURE 9.14   Use the dashboard Deployment Properties to modify the document library and master page settings.

A PPS dashboard is deployed as a folder in the document library with each page becoming an ASPX file within that folder. Figure 9.15 illustrates what the deployed dashboards looks like.

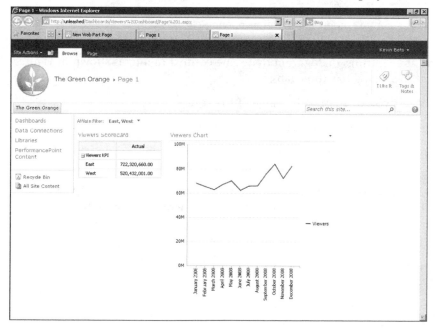

FIGURE 9.15   This is an example of dashboard deployed to SharePoint.

Dashboard Zones

You can add, remove, and split zones as necessary on a dashboard. To do this, right-click a zone, and then choose the appropriate selection from the context menu, as shown in Figure 9.16.

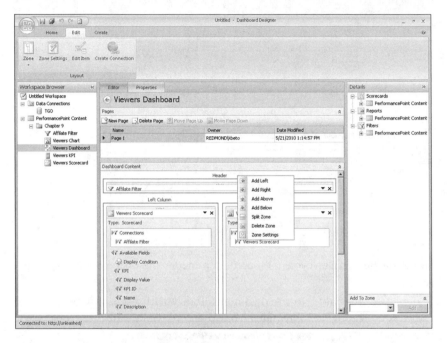

FIGURE 9.16   Use the context menu to add, remove, and split zones.

You can access the zone settings dialog from that same context menu, as shown in Figure 9.17. The Zone Settings dialog has three tabs:

▶ **General:** Enables you to change the name of the zone

▶ **Size:** Enables you to change the width and height of the zone

▶ **Orientation:** Enables you to specify whether the zone should be oriented vertical, horizontal, or stacked

The stacked option enables you to stack PPS elements on top of each other. In Figure 9.18, two reports have been added to the same zone, and the orientation option has been set to Stacked.

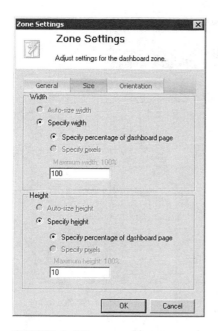

FIGURE 9.17   You can also use the Zone Settings dialog to adjust settings.

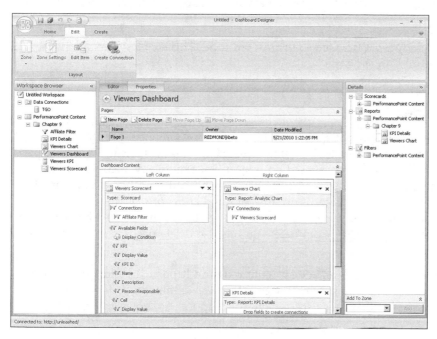

FIGURE 9.18   Use the Stacked option to stack PPS elements on top of each other.

Figure 9.19 shows the result when the dashboard has been deployed.

FIGURE 9.19   This is an example of a stacked setting as it appears on the dashboard in SharePoint.

Notice that a drop-down list is added to the stacked zone. This enables users to choose which report to display in the zone.

Dashboard Pages

In some scenarios, you might not want to place all scorecards, reports, or filters on the same dashboard page. For example, there might just be too many items to fit on one page, or perhaps you want to group items based on subject. For example, you could create a Sales, HR, and IT page, all available within the same dashboard. Another example might be that you want to place all scorecards on one page and all reports on another. To do this, you can create a new page by clicking the New Page button in the dashboard's Editor window, as shown in Figure 9.20. From here, you can also delete pages, change the order of pages, and name them.

In Figure 9.21, two pages have been added: Scorecards and Reports. To add a page list navigation that enables users to choose which page within the dashboard they want to view, you need to check the Include page list for navigation option, as shown in Figure 9.21.

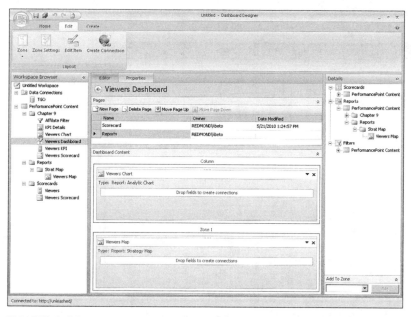

FIGURE 9.20   Use the Editor window from the dashboard to create new pages.

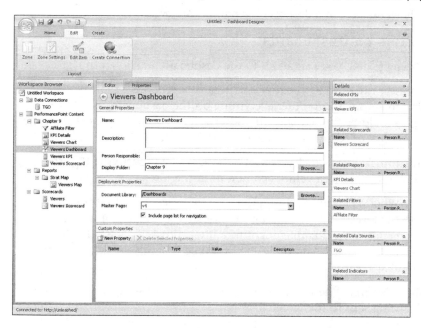

FIGURE 9.21   Be sure to check the Include page list for navigation option to enable users to choose the pages to view from the dashboard.

In Figure 9.22, you can see the navigation list that has been added at the top left (Viewers Dashboard: Scorecards | Reports). This allows you to switch between the Scorecards and the Reports pages.

FIGURE 9.22   This is an example of a dashboard with page list navigation.

Working with Filters on Dashboards

After the filter has been created, you can add it to the dashboard, as shown in Figure 9.23.

The last step is to connect the filter with either a scorecard or report on the dashboard. The filter is not going to automatically filter everything on the dashboard. You have to explicitly define what should be filtered and what filter values should be passed from the filter to its target, scorecard, or report. The available options are as follows:

▶ **Display Condition:** When you choose this option, you are specifying that the target will not be visible until a value is chosen from the filter.

▶ **Display Value:** When you choose this option, you are specifying that the value visible is sent to the target. A filter is going to have a name/value pair associated with each filter member. An example might be a filter showing dates. The display value would be April 11, 2010, and the value would be [Date].[Year - Qtr - Month - Date].[Date].&[1023].

▶ **Member Unique Name:** When you choose this option, you are specifying that the unique value is being sent to the target.

In our example, we want to send the unique episode value to the scorecard as a filter value. We accomplish this by dragging the Member Unique Name item to the Drop fields to the create connections area on the scorecard. When we do this, the dialog box in Figure 9.24 appears.

From here, we specify how we want the filter to target either a dimension or measure. These options are best explained with some visual examples.

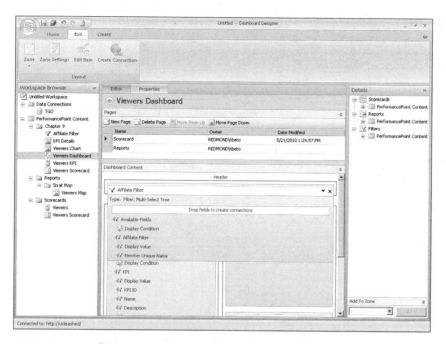

FIGURE 9.23   After a filter has been created, you can add it to a dashboard.

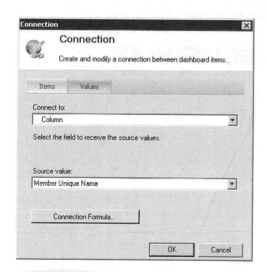

FIGURE 9.24   When you choose to create connections, you use the Connection dialog to specify connection settings.

In Figure 9.25 we selected the Column option. Notice that the filter options we select are shown on the columns.

In Figure 9.26, the option has been set to Row.

FIGURE 9.25   In this example, the field connection option has been set to Column.

FIGURE 9.26   In this example, the field connection option has been set to Row.

In Figure 9.27, the option has been set to Page. Notice that we are now looking at the aggregated value of the three episodes we selected in the filter.

The next example illustrates a filter based on the Time Intelligence filter template. We have started the filter creation and selected the data source already. The dialog shown in Figure 9.28 is where we add an STPS expression (which is more fully discussed in Chapter 6, "Data Sources")

FIGURE 9.27   In this example, the field connection option has been set to Page.

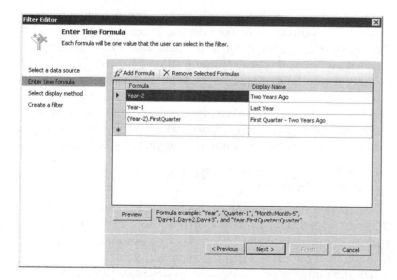

FIGURE 9.28   This is where you can add an STPS expression for a Time Intelligence filter.

In this example, we added two expressions: YTD and Yesterday. After the filter has been created, we must connect it to one or more targets. This time, we connect it to the two reports we have on the dashboard, as shown in Figure 9.29.

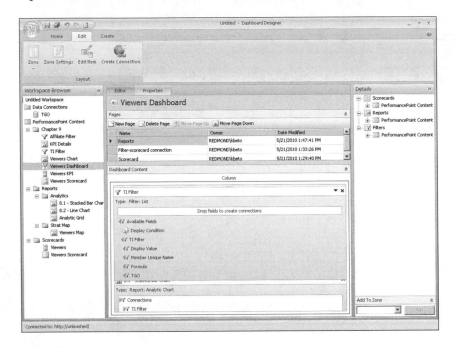

FIGURE 9.29   In this example, the filter connects to two reports.

Using the TheGreenOrange Data Source Option

Notice that we have two additional options available: Formula and TheGreenOrange. We will look at the Formula option later in this chapter. For now, we focus on the TheGreenOrange option. TheGreenOrange is the name of the data source used for this filter. If your data source is called MyDataSource, the option would be named MyDataSource. If you want to filter your target based on the STPS expressions you defined earlier, choose the data source option. In Figure 9.30, we have chosen TheGreenOrange and are about to connect the filter with the reports. When we connect a filter to a report, we get the option to select the dimension used in the report that we want to filter. Because we are working with Time Intelligence, we choose a dimension containing date data.

After the dashboard has been deployed, we can filter the reports using the Time Intelligence formula filter, as shown in Figure 9.31.

The Time Intelligence filter is based on the current day. If we have a YTD formula and today is April 11, 2010, YTD is calculated from January 1, 2010 to April 11, 2010 and so on. For more control over what date is considered to be "today," you can use a Time Intelligence Connection Formula filter template. With this template, you have the option to select a data source that has Time Intelligence configured, as described earlier, with the difference that there is only one filter display option, as shown in Figure 9.32.

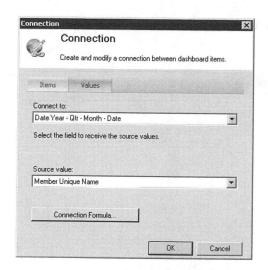

FIGURE 9.30   In this example the Time Intelligence filter connects to a dimension with date data.

FIGURE 9.31   In this example, reports can be filtered based on a Time Intelligence formula.

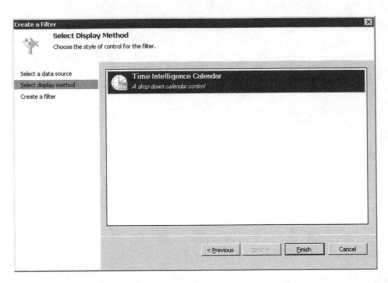

FIGURE 9.32   For more control over the "today" date, use a Time Intelligence Connection Formula filter template.

This template always shows a calendar control and allows users to choose the date that should be considered as "today."

In this example, we select the data source, TheGreenOrange. After we connect the data source with a target, we click the Connection Formula button. In the Connection Formula dialog, we specify the STPS expression that we want to use, as shown in Figure 9.33.

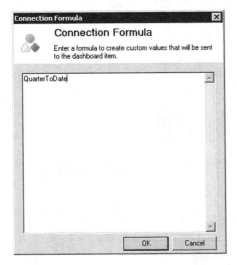

FIGURE 9.33   Specify the STPS expression to use in the Connection Formula dialog.

After we deploy the dashboard, we see a calendar control, and the STPS expression will be calculated based on the date that we pick from that control, as shown on Figure 9.34.

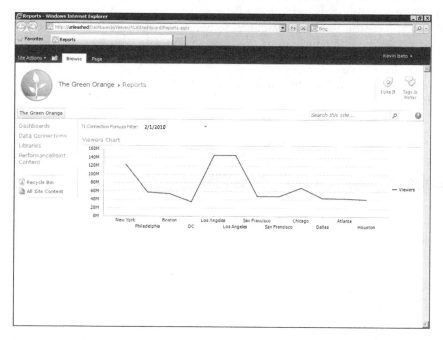

FIGURE 9.34   The deployed dashboard has a calendar control that enables users to pick a specific date.

Creating Dashboards in the Browser

It is also possible to create and edit dashboards when viewing a SharePoint site in the browser. Although there is more flexibility available in terms of Web Parts available and the overall look and feel of pages, configuring connections for PPS Web Parts is not as intuitive.

> **TIP**
>
> If you want the ease of connecting PPS objects in Dashboard Designer along with the flexibility of modifying the look and feel of pages in the browser, consider deploying the initial dashboard in Dashboard Designer, and then edit the newly deployed dashboard in the browser.

Create a Dashboard Using PPS Objects

Follow these steps to create a new dashboard using existing PPS objects. These steps walk through creating a simple dashboard containing a filter and a scorecard. A tremendous amount of flexibility and customization is available. So, while going through the steps, take some time to explore the different options available when using Web Parts within SharePoint.

1. In the Site Actions menu on the site you want to work with shown in Figure 9.35, select New Page.

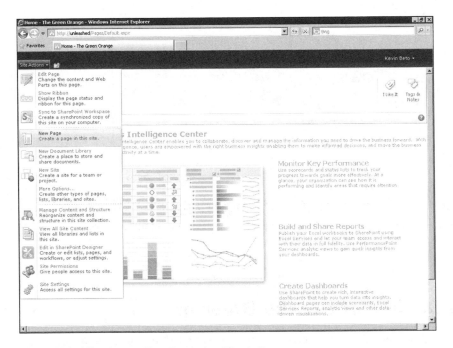

FIGURE 9.35   Select New Page the Site Actions menu.

2. Enter a name for the new dashboard page and click OK.

3. On the Insert tab, select Web Part.

4. Find the PerformancePoint Filter Web Part in the selection UI shown in Figure 9.36, and then click the Add button. Doing so adds a blank, not-yet-configured Filter Web Part to the page.

5. On the new PerformancePoint Filter Web Part that has been inserted, click the link labeled Click Here to Open in a New Tool Pane Link to open the Web Part Properties editing pane.

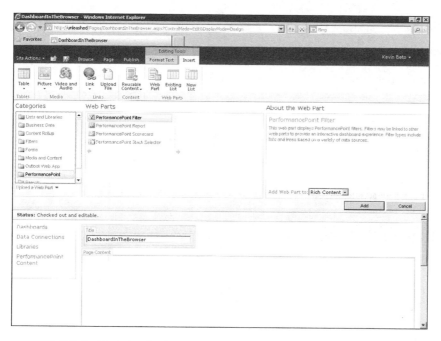

FIGURE 9.36   Find the PerformancePoint Filter Web Part in the selection UI.

TIP

This link is available only when the Web Part is not configured. If you need to return to this pane, you can find it by clicking the Web Part Properties button on the Web Part Tools – Options tab.

6. At the top of the Properties pane that appears on the right, you see a Location edit box. Click the Browse button to the right of this box.

7. Select a PPS Filter object from the SharePoint object selector, and then click OK.

CAUTION

There is little to no error checking here, so it is possible to select something other than a filter. It is even possible to select the entire list by just clicking OK. Neither is a valid selection, and either will result in errors later on, so make sure you have the right filter actually selected before clicking OK.

8. At this point, your screen should look like Figure 9.37. Click the OK button at the bottom of the tool pane on the right to apply the changes and dismiss the tool pane.

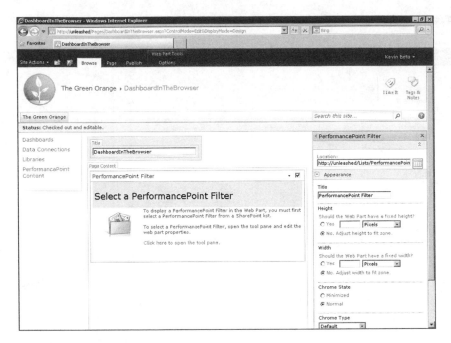

FIGURE 9.37   From here, you can select to apply the changes and dismiss the tool pane.

9. To insert the Scorecard Web Part, click the Web Part button under the Editing Tools –
Insert tab, and then find the PPS Scorecard Web Part and click Add.

TIP

If the Editing Tools – Insert tab does not appear here, make sure your cursor selection
is in the Page Content section of this page. If the Add button does not appear to work,
make sure you have dismissed the filter's Properties pane on the right by clicking the
OK button at the bottom of it.

10. Much like you did when configuring the filter, click the Click Here to Open the Tool
Pane link and select the scorecard you want to add to the dashboard here. Dismiss
the tool pane by clicking the OK button. The Web Parts should both render at this
point, as shown in Figure 9.38.

11. Both Web Parts work independently, but changing the filter does not affect the
values on the scorecard. Now we are going to create a connection between the Web
Parts. While hovering over the Scorecard Web Part with your mouse, you see a down
arrow appear in the upper-right corner of the Web Part. Select the down arrow, and
then select Connections, Get PerformancePoint Values From, PerformancePoint
Filter from the drop-down menu, as shown in Figure 9.39.

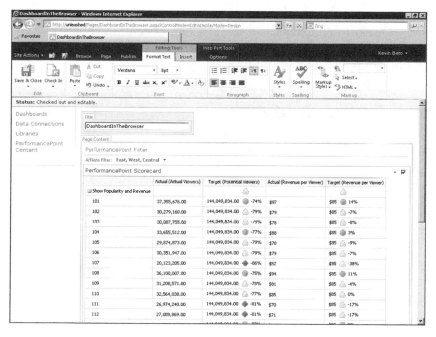

FIGURE 9.38   Select the scorecard you want to add to the dashboard here.

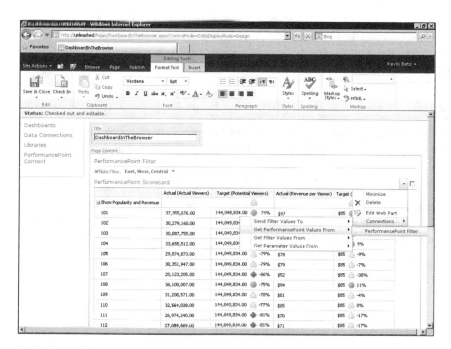

FIGURE 9.39   You create a connection between the Web Parts from here.

12. The Edit Connections dialog appears. Click the Add Connection button. Set the Source Value to Member Unique Name and set the Connect To the appropriate dimension or measure to filter. The dialog settings should appear the same as Figure 9.40. Click the OK button to confirm this connection.

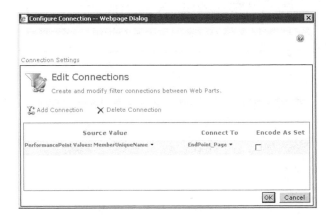

FIGURE 9.40   Create and modify filter connections between Web Parts from the Edit Connections dialog box.

13. At this point, the Web Parts on this page are connected, and changing the filter should adjust values in the scorecard. Click the Check In button in the Page tab to commit your changes and make the page available for other users of the SharePoint site.

Summary

With dashboards, you bring together and integrate key monitoring elements to create a flexible view into business performance. Deploying dashboards through SharePoint pages provides a straightforward and secure way of communicating this information across your business community and providing targeted information as required.

In this chapter, we discussed how to create, configure, and deploy PPS dashboards and filters using various tools. You learned about the issues to consider when selecting a tool to create dashboards and connect filters and saw examples of the different tools in action.

With this chapter, you have completed an important step in building your own performance-monitoring system.

Best Practices

► PPS filters are best created through Dashboard Designer; although, you can create PPS filters through SharePoint Designer or through the browser.

► Although creating filters and working with Web Part pages is possible in the browser, it is a much better user experience to do this in SharePoint Designer.

► Create new pages on the dashboard when there are too many items to fit on one page, or when you want to group items based on subject.

► For the ease of connecting PPS objects in Dashboard Designer along with the flexibility of modifying the look and feel of pages in the browser, consider deploying the initial dashboard in Dashboard Designer and then editing the newly deployed dashboard in the browser.

CHAPTER 10

Securing a PerformancePoint Installation

IN THIS CHAPTER

▶ Security Overview   235

▶ Applying Security to PPS Elements   236

▶ Applying Security to Data Connections   242

▶ Securing a Deployment with TLS   252

▶ Configuring Per-User Authentication with Kerberos   255

PerformancePoint Services (PPS) offers security capabilities to protect critical elements and data from attacks and data loss. If you manage or administer a PPS solution, you must know how to use PPS security functionality, features, and options to properly secure your PPS installation and data.

This chapter focuses on security that an organization can implement to protect information stored in a PPS solution. This includes PPS element security (that is, how to configure user access to scorecards, KPIs, data sources, and other objects); and PPS data security (that is, how to secure data that appears on the dashboard). A discussion of how to secure dashboards by applying Transport Layer Security (TLS) and how to use per-user authentication with Kerberos rounds out the information on security.

The chapter includes step-by-step instructions on how best to configure PPS security and discusses various things to consider when working through your security configuration

Security Overview

When discussing PPS security, we are talking about two types of security. The first type is *PPS element security*, which refers to how to configure user access to scorecards, KPIs, data sources, and other objects. For example, we can create a KPI and configure security for the KPI to ensure that it can be seen only by a particular user or group when they browse the SharePoint list where the KPI is stored.

The second type of security is *data security*, which refers to what data display when a user browses a dashboard. For example, we can configure security on the data source itself (an Analysis Services cube, for example) so that a user can see the sales numbers for a particular region only.

Both types of security are explained in this chapter.

Applying Security to PPS Elements

In PPS 2007, all elements were stored in a SQL Server database. Therefore, all element security was stored in that database, too. The security configuration was done using Dashboard Designer. When a user connected to a dashboard, SharePoint 2007 looked at the security information in the database and figured out which elements on the dashboard the user was allowed to access.

In PPS 2010, all elements are stored as items in SharePoint lists and libraries. Therefore, you now secure PPS elements by implementing SharePoint security.

All PPS elements have the same options available in the context menu when you right-click the element in Dashboard Designer. As shown in Figure 10.1, one of these options is called Manage Permissions.

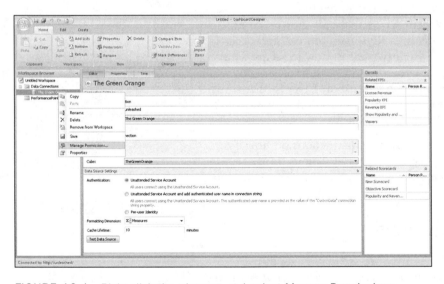

FIGURE 10.1   Right-click the element and select Manage Permissions.

> **TIP**
>
> The Manage Permissions option just loads up the SharePoint page that enables security permission configuration on the element selected. You can configure these permissions without using Dashboard Designer at all.

When you click this option, you are directed to a SharePoint page listing the current permissions for the selected element, as shown in Figure 10.2 (in this case, a data source).

You need to have full control permissions on the object in the SharePoint list to edit these permissions.

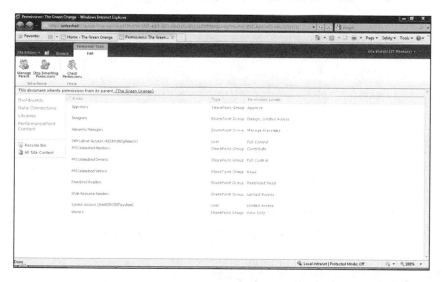

FIGURE 10.2   This is an example of the permission settings you see for a data source.

Notice the yellow status bar toward the top of the page: This Document Inherits Permissions from Its Parent (The Green Orange). All SharePoint security, not only for PPS, is configured on the topmost parent and then cascaded down to all children. Thus, by default, all security is defined on the site collection level and then applied to the site, list, and libraries, and last list and library items. The site collection used in this example is called The Green Orange. Clicking the The Green Orange link in the yellow status bar displays the security settings for the site collection, as shown in Figure 10.3.

From here, you can modify what access users will have to PPS elements by clicking Grant Permissions. From the Grant Permissions screen, you can select users or groups and add them to a SharePoint group, as shown in Figure 10.4. Users can be Lightweight Directory Access Protocol (LDAP; Active Directory) or local users.

You can also assign permissions directly. Therefore, you do not need to associate a user with a specific SharePoint group that has a set of predefined permissions. Instead, you may check specific permissions for a user. Figure 10.5 shows the available permissions.

FIGURE 10.3   This is an example of the permission settings you see for a site collection.

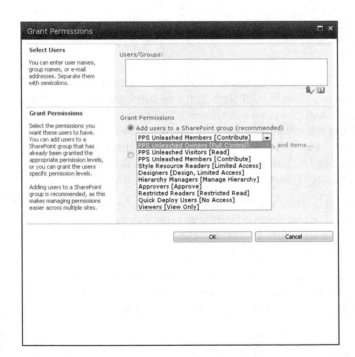

FIGURE 10.4   Use Grant Permissions to select users or groups and add them to a SharePoint group.

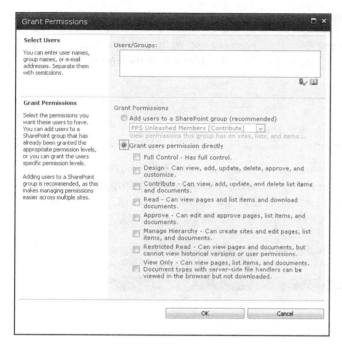

FIGURE 10.5   You can assign permissions directly for a specific user.

Defining Permissions Specific to an Element

Sometimes you might want to define permissions specific to an element. In other words, you might want to break the default security inheritance. To do this, open the Manage Permissions page, as shown in Figure 10.2, and then click Stop Inheriting Permissions. You see a dialog box, as shown in Figure 10.6, informing you that you are about to break inheritance for this specific document.

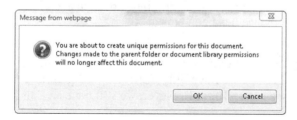

FIGURE 10.6   Use Stop Inheriting Permissions to break the default security inheritance.

NOTE

Notice that this is called a *document* even though we are still working with a data source. This is because all items stored in a document library are ultimately considered to be a document.

After you break the inheritance, the yellow status bar informs you that you are applying unique permissions to this document.

Here is what happens when we apply unique permissions on a data source. In this example, we work with a data source called The Green Orange. The permissions inheritance has been broken, as explained earlier. An account called BizSharp User 2 has been added with Restricted Read permissions only, as shown in Figure 10.7.

FIGURE 10.7   These are the permission settings for the The Green Orange data source example. In this example, the permissions inheritance has been broken.

If we log on to the site using the BizSharp User 2 account and open the The Green Orange data source context menu, we can see that because we have only restricted read permission, there is no option to edit properties (see Figure 10.8). However, we still have an Edit in Dashboard Designer option.

If we choose this option, the The Green Orange data source opens in Dashboard Designer. From there, we can look at all property settings, the connection string, comments, and other settings. If we try to make changes and then try to publish the data source back to SharePoint, by right-clicking the data source and then select Save, we get the error message shown in Figure 10.9.

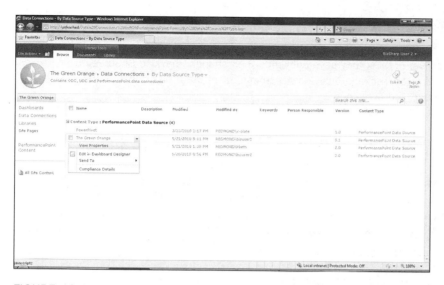

FIGURE 10.8   The Edit in Dashboard Designer option enables you to open the element in Dashboard Designer.

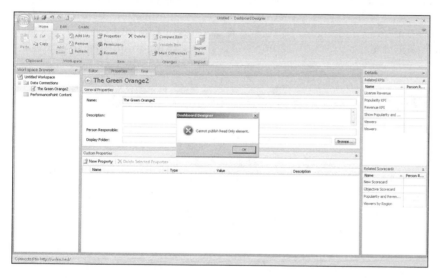

FIGURE 10.9   This is an example of the error message that occurs if users try to perform actions that exceed their security settings.

This error message occurs here because BizSharp User 2 has restricted read permission only.

CAUTION

Users can save any changes they make to a *local* workspace. This can sometimes be confusing when users think they have published their changes back to SharePoint. Even though the error message provides a warning, users must be educated about how changes are saved and published.

As demonstrated in this section, you can apply permissions on the top-level site collection or you can apply specific permissions on a list or list item. This allows the flexibility of assigning permissions and explicitly specifying what a user can do when creating and viewing PPS elements. Remember that even though this example worked with setting permissions on a data source, the same concept applies to any PPS element. Also remember that a child item will always inherit permissions from its parent unless the inheritance is explicitly broken.

Applying Security to Data Connections

First, data connections must be stored in a trusted location. This means that the document library must be registered with the PerformancePoint Services application. By default, all locations are trusted, as shown in Figure 10.10, but a user might run into issues if this setting has been changed and a user tries to use a data source from an untrusted location.

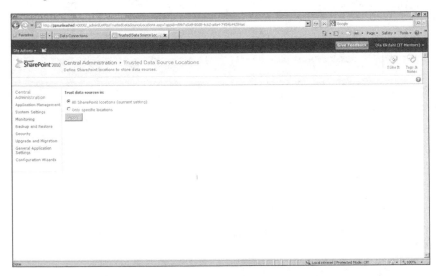

FIGURE 10.10   By default, all locations are trusted; although, this setting can be changed.

Chapter 6, "Data Sources," introduced the different ways that a user can be authenticated to a data source. To review, a user browsing a dashboard using tabular data sources is authenticated through one of two ways: the use of the Unattended Service Account or per-user identity, as shown in Figure 10.11.

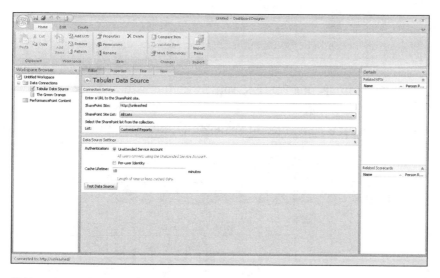

FIGURE 10.11   A user browsing a dashboard using tabular data sources is authenticated through the Unattended Service Account or per-user identity.

A user browsing a dashboard using an Analysis Services data source is authenticated through one of three ways (see Figure 10.12): the use of the Unattended Service Account, Unattended Service Account with the username added to the connection string, or per-user identity.

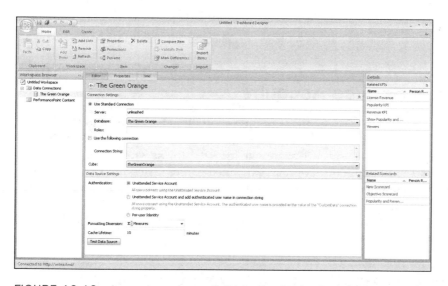

FIGURE 10.12   A user browsing a dashboard using an Analysis Services data source is authenticated through the Unattended Service Account, Unattended Service Account with the username added to the connection string, or per-user identity.

NOTE

For per-user identity to work properly, Kerberos authentication must be configured.

Kerberos is discussed in the "Configuring Per-User Authentication with Kerberos" section, later in this chapter.

The Unattended Service Account is configured in SharePoint Central Administration, as shown in Figure 10.13.

FIGURE 10.13   The Unattended Service Account is configured in SharePoint Central Administration.

Unattended Service Account

If you use the Unattended Service Account option, users will never connect to the data source, database table, or online analytical processing (OLAP) cube, for example, using their own identity. Instead, all users will share one identity; this is whatever identity has been configured in Central Administration, as explained earlier. Using this option enables SharePoint and the data source to cache a lot of information and data that can be reused by all users. This option provides the highest performance; however, if business users require more granular permissions on the data source, consider using one of the two additional options explained here.

Unattended Service Account with the Username Added to the Connection String

The Unattended Service Account with the username added to the connection string option works only with Analysis Services data sources. This option appends the specified user's identity (domain and username) to the information sent to Analysis Services. This information can then be extracted using the `CustomData()`Multidimensional Expressions (MDX) function and used as a lookup value. In other words, you can have a dimension that can be used to apply dynamic OLAP security. The following code sample shows how to use MDX and `CustomData()`:

```
Exists(  [Geography].[Country].[Country].Members,
Filter(Employee.Employee.Employee.Members,
Employee.Employee.CurrentMember.Properties("Login ID") = CustomData()),
"Reseller Sales")
```

Note that when using this option, the unattended service account will make the connection to the OLAP data source and that caching will be impacted since PPS and SSAS now have to cache per user.

Per-User Identity

The per-user identity option uses the user's actual identity to connect to the data source. This allows the database developer to apply security at the data level. For example, users might be restricted to viewing information for their region and location only.

To illustrate, we work with a simple scorecard shown in Figure 10.14, which filters data based on regions.

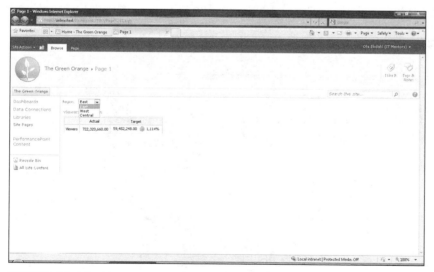

FIGURE 10.14 This simple scorecard filters data based on regions and is used to demonstrate setting security with per-user identity.

The current security setting is the default: Connect Using Unattended Service Account. We want to change this default to apply security at the data level so that a user sees data for a particular region only. The first step is to change the data source authentication setting to per-user identity, as shown in Figure 10.15.

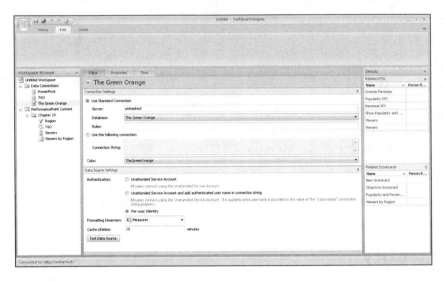

FIGURE 10.15   Start by changing the data source authentication setting to per-user identity.

The next step is to implement security on the data source. In this example, the data source is an Analysis Services cube, and we apply security using the SQL Server Management (SSMS) tool.

In SSMS, connect to the Analysis Services instance hosting the cube, expand the database, and open the Create Role dialog shown in Figure 10.16 by right-clicking the Roles folder. From here, select New Role.

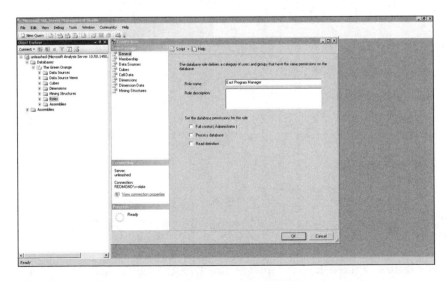

FIGURE 10.16   You can apply security using SSMS.

In this example, we name the role East Program Manager. The goal is to add program managers from the East region to the role and configure security on this role so that users can see viewer numbers in that region only.

In the next step, click Membership and add users and or groups to this role, as shown in Figure 10.17. In this example, we add just one user: BizSharp User 2.

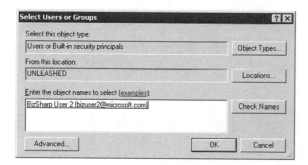

FIGURE 10.17   Use the Create Role dialog box to select users and groups.

The next step is to grant read access to the cube. Click Cubes and select the cube, as shown in Figure 10.18.

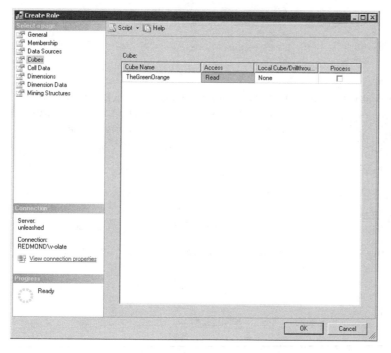

FIGURE 10.18   Next, grant read access to the cube.

By default, we have read access to all dimensions shown in Figure 10.19, and we leave those settings as is.

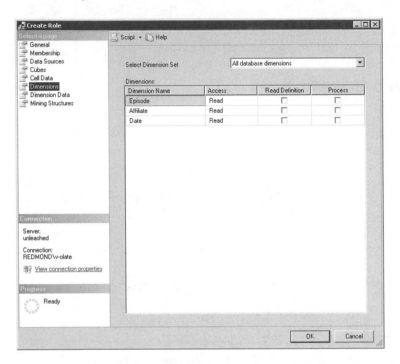

FIGURE 10.19   By default, there is read access to all dimensions.

To configure the regions that can be used later on in a dashboard, we click Dimension Data and select the dimension and attribute hierarchy we want to secure. In this example, it is Affiliate and Region, as shown in Figure 10.20. We finish by removing the selection for all regions except for East, and then click OK to complete the security setup.

You now see the new role under the Roles folder, as shown in Figure 10.21.

Before switching back to the dashboard to try the newly applied security, best practice is to verify that it has been applied correctly. Do this by browsing the cube in SSMS. Click the Change User button, as shown in Figure 10.22, to switch the role that is used.

Doing so opens the Security Context dialog, from where we can change the role that we want to use, as shown in Figure 10.23.

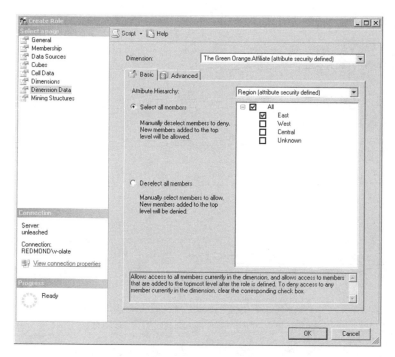

FIGURE 10.20   Select the members from this dialog box.

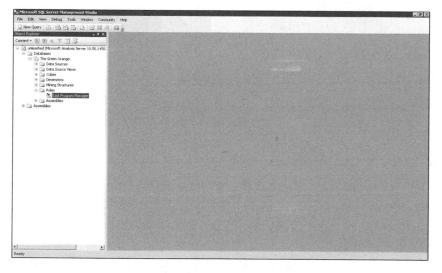

FIGURE 10.21   You can see the new role under the Roles folder.

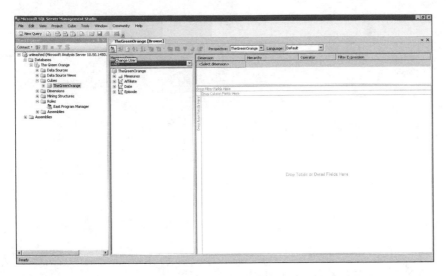

FIGURE 10.22   Verify the newly applied security by switching the role that is used.

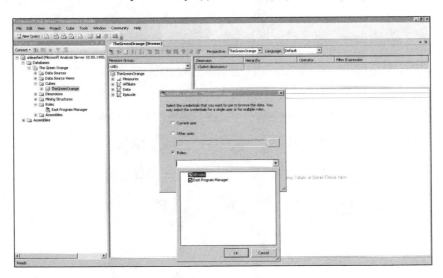

FIGURE 10.23   From this screen, you can change the role you want to use.

In Figure 10.24, we can see that only the East region is visible when browsing the cube using the East Program Manager role.

We are now ready to try this from the dashboard. The only change that we need to make is to the authentication setting on the data source, as demonstrated earlier. Everything else remains the same.

In Figure 10.25, we can now see that when BizSharp User 2 logs on and views the same dashboard as you saw in Figure 10.14, only the East region is visible.

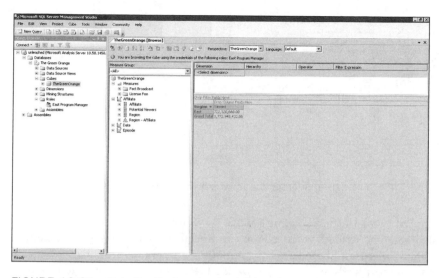

FIGURE 10.24   Only the East region is visible when browsing the cube from the East Program Manager role.

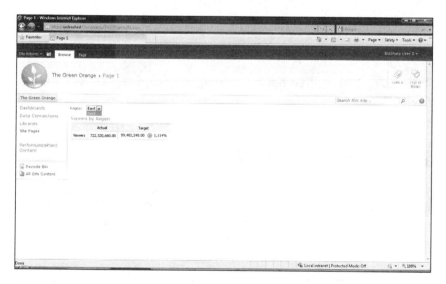

FIGURE 10.25   For this user, only the East region is visible from the dashboard.

Authentication Troubleshooting

If you change the authentication option for a data source to per-user identity and see the error message shown in Figure 10.26, you probably have not configured Kerberos properly.

Kerberos is discussed in the "Configuring Per-User Authentication with Kerberos" section, later in this chapter.

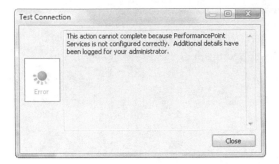

FIGURE 10.26   This error message appears if you have not configured Kerberos properly.

The log file mentioned is the Unified Logging Service (ULS) log. As the name implies, this is the log that all SharePoint services write to. You can find this log file in the %Program Files%\Common Files\Microsoft Shared\Web Server Extensions\14\LOGS directory. In this directory, you will most likely see a number of .log files. Sort the files by date modified and open the latest file. Search for UPN in the file and see whether you find a message similar to the one in the following example:

```
SPSecurityContext.WindowsIdentity: Could not retrieve a valid windows
identity for NTName='DOMAIN\user', UPN='user@domain'. UPN is required
when Kerberos constrained delegation is used.
```

If you find a similar message, Kerberos has not been configured properly; you need to configure Kerberos correctly.

Securing a Deployment with TLS

PPS uses three different legs to the communication to render a dashboard. All of them can be secured by applying Transport Layer Security (TLS). Securing them with TLS prevents information from being sent in clear text. (With clear text, a malicious user with a network packet monitor can see traffic sent between servers and potentially see confidential information.)

- ▶ Configuring TLS on web applications
- ▶ Configuring TLS on PPS web services
- ▶ Secure connections to data sources

TIP

TLS is also frequently referred to as Secure Sockets Layer (SSL) or Hypertext Transfer Protocol Secure (HTTPS).

CAUTION

Using SSL and secure connections to ensure that the data cannot be viewed by third parties comes at a cost to performance, however, so configure this only if the data is sensitive enough to warrant it. For instance, it makes sense to secure network traffic to a data source that contains employee Social Security numbers, but it might not make sense to secure network traffic to a data source that contains already publicly disclosed product information.

Configuring TLS on Web Applications

By configuring TLS for any SharePoint web applications hosting PPS content or dash-boards, all traffic between the end user and the SharePoint system will be encrypted. In most scenarios, securing traffic to and from web applications is sufficient. If the SharePoint servers, data source servers, and network switches and routers between them are all physically secure, firewalled, and using current information security best practices, it is unnecessary to apply security past this level.

Configuring TLS for SharePoint is a fairly straightforward and well-documented process. There are multiple ways to accomplish this. The following steps outline how to apply TLS to an existing SharePoint web application:

TIP

Don't forget to configure SharePoint Central Administration with TLS! Doing so will keep the Unattended Service Account password secure.

1. Obtain a certificate for all SharePoint servers in the farm.
2. Create a secure binding on the Internet Information Services (IIS) website for the web application.
3. Enable the Require SSL property for the IIS website.
4. Delete any non-SSL bindings.
5. Update alternative access mappings to reflect new HTTPS URL.

10

Configuring TLS on PPS Web Services

SharePoint service applications, such as PPS, frequently must communicate within the farm to retrieve information. This traffic never leaves the confines of the SharePoint farm. If you have a geographically dispersed farm with servers in multiple different locations, it might be a good idea to secure this chatter.

Changing from unsecure to secure traffic is a setting available in Central Administration for the service application.

1. Open SharePoint Central Administration.
2. Click the Manage Service Applications link under the Application Management heading.
3. Select the PerformancePoint service application, and click the Publish in the Sharing section of the Service Applications ribbon.

TIP

Make sure you do not click the name of the service application. Instead, click just next to it so that you highlight the row. Clicking the name opens the Manage PerformancePoint Services page, and this is not the page you want.

---

4. In the Publish Service Application dialog that appears, change the Connection Type from HTTP to HTTPS, as shown in Figure 10.27, and click OK.

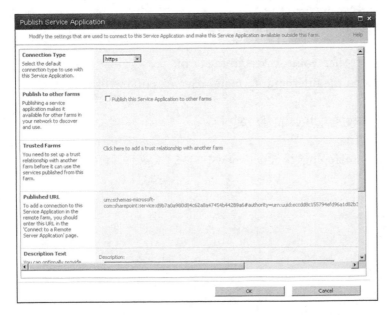

FIGURE 10.27   Change the connection type here.

Secure Connections to Data Sources

The final leg of communications that PPS performs is the connection to the data source. This is the PPS web service connecting directly to the data source either as the Unattended Service Account or the current user's credentials if per-user authentication is configured.

> **NOTE**
>
> The communication goes from the PPS web service to the data source, not from the end user's machine. At no point do users directly access the data source from their machine.

For data sources that require a URL, such as Excel services and SharePoint lists, this is done through configuring SSL to the web applications. If the web application the data source is connecting to has an HTTPS address, traffic will be secure.

For Analysis Services data sources, all communication is encrypted by default. This is a configurable setting disabled in scenarios in which high performance is required. The setting is configured in Analysis Services, and PPS respects the setting.

For SQL data sources, all communication is *not* encrypted by default. There are different ways to configure this, and the SQL online documentation on Microsoft TechNet has more information on how to accomplish this.

The Excel Workbook data source is all managed from within PPS, so no external connections are made when using the Excel Workbook data source.

Configuring Per-User Authentication with Kerberos

In PPS 2007, per-user authentication was configured per deployment. In PPS 2010, this setting is configured at a data source level, so it is possible to mix per-user data sources with data sources that use the Unattended Service Account.

Kerberos is a protocol used for authentication. It is used when there is a need for a server resource, such as PPS, to access another server resource, such as a database, on behalf of the user. In other words, the server needs to impersonate and pass along the identity of the calling user.

Before you start configuring Kerberos, be aware that you need to access the Active Directory domain controller for some configuration tasks. Therefore, you might need to involve other people to complete the setup. Make sure that you have access to all resources necessary before starting the configuration.

Also, consider configuring Kerberos in a test or demo environment before doing so in a production environment. Doing so allows you to get comfortable with the process. There are several steps involved, as described in the TechNet article referenced earlier, and if you configure a resource improperly, you risk impacting other non-SharePoint-related resources that are also using Kerberos.

CAUTION

Windows 2008 has some issues with Kerberos where it will periodically drop connections with Analysis Services. To avoid this problem, put Analysis Services on Windows 2003 or a Windows 2008 R2 machine or apply the hotfix from Microsoft KB article 969083.

As mentioned earlier, Kerberos has to be configured properly for per-user authentication to work properly. The following three steps need to be performed in this order for per-user authentication to work properly in farm scenarios:

1. Create service principal names (SPNs) for the farm and data sources.
2. Enable constrained delegation for computers and service accounts.
3. Configure and start the Claims to Windows Token service.

NOTE

If you have a farm installation, you need to configure Kerberos *even if* all components, SharePoint 2010, and data sources are installed on the same machine. The only scenario in which the default authentication scheme, NTLM, will work for per-user identity is if you do a standalone installation.

Create SPNs for the Farm and Data Sources

For Kerberos to function, the client and server need to mutually authenticate each other. Not only does the server verify that the client has access to resources, but the client also needs to verify that it is talking to the correct server. In the world of Kerberos, this is accomplished by creating SPNs. Each server service needs an SPN. Therefore, the SQL Server service needs an SPN, and SharePoint needs one, too.

Two SPNs need to be set for each service. One contains the NetBIOS name of the server. The other contains the fully qualified domain name (FQDN) of the server. This is necessary because Kerberos will authenticate as both the NetBIOS and FQDN. If one SPN cannot be found, the configuration is deemed invalid and will result in authentication errors.

You configure SPNs by either using a command-line utility called setspn.exe or the ADSIEDIT.msc snap-in. The following discussion looks at an example where we are registering an SPN for a SQL Server instance running on a server called Server1. The example assumes that the SQL Server service runs on the default port 1433.

The first SPN that needs to be set is on the SharePoint web application URLs. This enables the passing of user credentials between servers in the farm. This can also enable per-user authentication for Excel services and SharePoint list data sources if they are contained within the same farm:

- *<MOSS-NetBIOS>* is the NetBIOS name of the web front-end server that users will be accessing. For instance, if the SharePoint URL is http://mySite, the NetBIOS name would be mySite.

- *<MOSS-FQDN>* is the FQDN of the server. In the preceding example, the FQDN would be something like mySite.domain.companyname.com.

- *<AppPoolAccount>* is the account that the PPS service application is using for its application pool, specified as Domain\Username:

```
setspn -A HTTP/<MOSS-NetBIOS> <AppPoolAccount>
setspn -A HTTP/<MOSS-FQDN> <AppPoolAccount>
```

For per-user communication with Analysis Services data sources, the following two SPNs need to be set on all Analysis Services servers that will be accessible as data sources with per-user authentication:

- *<AS-NetBIOS>* is the NetBIOS name of the Analysis Services data source server that we will be accessing with per-user authentication.

- *<AS-FQDN>* is the FQDN of the Analysis Services server.

<ASAccount> is the account that the SQL Analysis Services Windows account is running under on the Analysis Services machine, specified as Domain\Username:

```
setspn -A MSOLAPSvc.3/<AS-NetBIOS> <ASAccount>
setspn -A MSOLAPSvc.3/<AS-FQDN> <ASAccount>
```

For per-user communication with SQL servers, the following two SPNs need to be set on all SQL servers to be accessible as data sources with per-user authentication. If SQL were configured to communicate on a different port, the port number should be changed from the default of 1433:

- <SQL-NetBIOS> is the NetBIOS name of the SQL database data source server that will be accessing with Per User authentication.

- <SQL-FQDN> is the FQDN of the SQL server.

<SQLAccount> is the account that the SQL Server windows service is running under on the SQL Server machine, specified as Domain\Username:

```
setspn -A MSSQLSvc/<NetBIOS>:1433 <SQLAccount>
setspn -A MSSQLSvc/<FQDN>:1433 <SQLAccount>
```

10

Enable Constrained Delegation for Computers and Service Accounts

After the SPNs have been set, the next step is to enable trust for delegation in Active Directory. You can do so in the Active Directory Users and Computers MMC snap-in. This usually requires domain administrator privileges because enabling it incorrectly could result in a malicious user "borrowing" credentials of other users. The first place that trust for delegation needs to be set is on the user account that the PPS service application uses for its application pool.

The user needs to be trusted for delegation to any SPNs configured in the previous step. For maximum security, select the Trust This User for Delegation to the Specified Services Only option and the Use Any Authentication Protocol option when enabling this, as shown in Figure 10.28. Doing so enables the user account to impersonate the user accessing the dashboard to the data source.

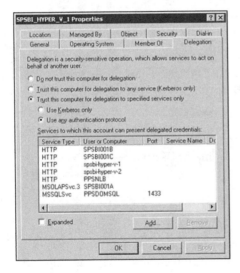

FIGURE 10.28   Set the delegation options here.

The other place where trust for delegation needs to be configured is for all servers in the farm hosting the PPS service. The steps are nearly identical to setting trust for the user account, except this is on the computer account. This enables the application server to impersonate the user accessing the dashboard to the data source.

TIP

If you do not see the Delegation tab when viewing the user or computer accounts in the Active Directory Users and Computers snap-in, check your SPNs. This tab appears only when SPNs are detected for the account being viewed.

Configure and Start the Claims to Windows Token Service

The last step in enabling per-user authentication is to configure and start the Claims to Windows Token service. This is a service included in the Microsoft Windows Identity Foundation that is new in SharePoint 2010. The service itself converts the user identity, which is handled inside the SharePoint farm as a Windows Claims identity, back into an impersonation-level Windows token that can then be presented to the data source. This needs to be performed on every SharePoint server in the farm.

The first step is to edit the C2WTSHost.exe.config configuration file. By default, the service is configured to deny any account on the box from using it. You can find this file at %ProgramFiles%\Windows Identity Foundation\v3.5, and the following highlighted line needs to be added into it:

```
<?xml version="1.0"?>
<configuration>
  <configSections>
    <section name="windowsTokenService" type="[assembly info]"/>
  </configSections>
  <windowsTokenService>
    <allowedCallers>
<add value="WSS_WPG" />
    </allowedCallers>
  </windowsTokenService>
</configuration>
```

After you have saved the file, the final step is to enable and start the Claims to Windows Token service. The service is disabled on installation of SharePoint. This can be done through the Server Manager. Set the service to Automatic start and then start the Claims to Windows Token service.

Summary

With PPS security functionality, features, and options, you can properly secure critical PPS elements and protect critical data. Further, properly configured security can enhance the business value of your PPS solution by allowing you to provide select data to select users based on business need.

By applying the various security settings and options as appropriate and by using TLS and per-user authentication options, you can apply layers of security to deployed PPS solutions and protect valuable organizational information.

10

Best Practices

▶ To avoid confusion, educate your users about how PPS saves and publishes changes.

▶ Secure PPS communication with TLS to protect information from malicious network packet attacks.

▶ Security can come at a cost to performance. Only configure security on data sensitive enough to warrant it.

▶ Consider configuring Kerberos in a test or demo environment before doing so in a production environment.

CHAPTER 11

Working with the Monitoring API

IN THIS CHAPTER

▶ Introduction: Extending PPS Functionality   261

▶ Installing SharePoint on a Client Operating System   262

▶ Setting Up Your Development Environment   265

▶ Working with PPS Objects   267

▶ Custom Objects and Editors   269

The native capabilities and functionality of PerformancePoint Services (PPS) will satisfy most business and technical requirements. In some cases, users might need to extend native PPS capabilities and functionality. The Monitoring application programming interface (API) included with PPS provides developers with tools and methods to extend PPS.

This chapter focuses on two primary ways of using the Monitoring API to extend PPS functionality: by creating custom objects and by creating editors or custom ASPX pages that are hosted inside of SharePoint.

The chapter begins by showing how to create a development environment, including the installation of SharePoint on a client operating system (OS). This is primarily useful for developers who do not have a server OS. It then steps you through the creation of a custom tabular data source and the creation of editor ASPX pages for a custom tabular data source.

Introduction: Extending PPS Functionality

The functionality included out-of-the-box in PPS 2010 should be enough to satisfy most needs. In some cases, it might be necessary to add custom written components to extend the functionality. You can extend PPS functionality in various ways to cover scenarios not included out-of-the-box, including the following:

▶ Creating custom objects

▶ Creating, reading, updating, and deleting PPS objects

- ▶ Modifying master pages to affect the look and feel of a dashboard
- ▶ Modifying CSS files to affect the look and feel of scorecards
- ▶ Adding in context menus for scorecards

This chapter covers the first two scenarios. For more information about the methods that apply to the other scenarios, consult the PPS software developer's kit (SDK) documentation or look for related blog entries.

TIP

At the time of this writing, the PPS team plans to publish several interesting and useful SDK samples on Codeplex.com. The PPS team also plans to interact with people through comments, so be sure to check the site frequently for new samples and techniques on how to accomplish customized scenarios with PPS 2010.

Installing SharePoint on a Client Operating System

With a few workarounds, you can install SharePoint on a client OS. This is primarily useful for developers who do not have a server OS. A SharePoint developer might use a client OS as the development environment if there is not a test server of SharePoint deployed and available for use.

This is not intended for production scenarios because the level of support you can receive from Microsoft is limited. However, because Windows client and server builds share the same code base, there is no technical reason why this should not work.

TIP

For more information, MSDN has a relevant topic "Setting Up the Development Environment for SharePoint Server" at http://msdn.microsoft.com/enus/library/ee554869(office.14).aspx.

NOTE

The only limitations that should exist are as follows:

A limit to the number of connections to IIS on the client OS. This is a hard-coded limit.

A limit to the number of processors and RAM that an instance of SQL handles at one time.

Installing Prerequisites

The Microsoft SharePoint 2010 Products Preparation Tool (PrerequisiteInstaller.exe) can not run unless it is on a server OS. To work around this, install the prerequisites for SharePoint manually. The following steps install all necessary prerequisites for SharePoint on a clean installation of a Windows 7 Enterprise x64 OS.

> **NOTE**
>
> The following steps are for installing on a Windows 7 OS. If you install on Vista, it is necessary to install Vista SP2, .NET Framework 3.5 SP1, PowerShell, and Microsoft Installer 4.5 separately before proceeding with these steps. Download locations for this software can be found on the http://download.microsoft.com website.

1. Install the Windows Process Activation service and required IIS features. You can accomplish this by using either the Turn Windows Features On or Off Wizard in the Programs and Features section of the Control Panel, or by executing the following command line:

```
start /w pkgmgr /iu:IIS-WebServerRole;IIS-WebServer;IIS-CommonHttpFeatures;
IIS-StaticContent;IIS-DefaultDocument;IIS-DirectoryBrowsing;IIS-HttpErrors;
IIS-HttpRedirect;IIS-ApplicationDevelopment;IIS-ASPNET;IIS-NetFxExtensibility;
IIS-ASP;IIS-CGI;IIS-ISAPIExtensions;IIS-ISAPIFilter;IIS-ServerSideIncludes;
IIS-HealthAndDiagnostics;IIS-HttpLogging;IIS-LoggingLibraries;
IIS-RequestMonitor;
IIS-HttpTracing;IIS-Security;IIS-BasicAuthentication;IIS-WindowsAuthentication;
IIS-DigestAuthentication;IIS-ClientCertificateMappingAuthentication;
IIS-IISCertificateMappingAuthentication;IIS-URLAuthorization;
IIS-RequestFiltering;
IIS-IPSecurity;IIS-Performance;IIS-HttpCompressionStatic;
IIS-HttpCompressionDynamic;
IIS-WebServerManagementTools;IIS-ManagementConsole;IIS-ManagementScriptingTools;
IIS-ManagementService;IIS-IIS6ManagementCompatibility;IIS-Metabase;
IIS-WMICompatibility;IIS-LegacyScripts;IIS-LegacySnapIn;
WAS-WindowsActivationService;
WAS-ProcessModel;WAS-NetFxEnvironment;WAS-ConfigurationAPI
```

2. Install the .NET Framework 3.5 SP1 and the Windows Communication Foundation services. You can accomplish this either by using the Turn Windows Features On or Off Wizard in the Programs and Features section of the Control Panel, or by executing the following command line:

```
start /w pkgmgr /iu:NetFx3;WCF-HTTP-Activation;WCF-NonHTTP-Activation
```

3. Install KB 976462 (KB 976394 on Vista), titled "A Hotfix for the .NET Framework 3.5 Service Pack 1 Is Available for Windows 7 and for Windows Server 2008 R2 as a Prerequisite for Microsoft Office SharePoint Server 2010." Reboot the system if the update requires a reboot.

NOTE

If you see an Update Does Not Apply to Your System error at this step, it can mean one of several things. Check to make sure that you have the right KB for the right OS and are running the RTM version of the OS. Check to make sure that you have the x64 version of the package, not the x86 version. Also check to make sure that the OS is not already installed. All these can trigger the same error.

4. To install the Microsoft Filter Pack 2.0, run the installer from your SharePoint installation point. The installer is located in the \PrerequisiteInstallerFiles\FilterPack\FilterPack.msi subdirectory.

5. Install the Microsoft Sync Framework 1.0. You can find it at http://download.microsoft.com.

6. Install KB 974405, titled "Windows Identity Foundation." You can find this by searching for KB Article 974405 and following the download links for your OS.

7. Install Microsoft Chart Controls for Microsoft .NET Framework 3.5. You can find this by searching http://download.microsoft.com.

8. Install SQL 2008 Native Client. You can find this by searching for "Microsoft SQL Server 2008 Feature Pack, April 2009" at http://download.microsoft.com.

Installing SharePoint 2010

After you install the correct prerequisite software, you can proceed with the installation of SharePoint 2010. If you attempt to install directly from an unmodified installation point, you get an error indicating that the client OS that you are on is not a supported OS. To work around that, it is necessary to edit a config.xml located within the installation files for SharePoint by following these steps:

1. Copy the entire installation folder to the local computer. This can be a network share, too, as long as you have read/write access to the files.

2. Edit the config.xml file located in the Files\Setup subdirectory in the local installation point and add the following entry into the Configuration xml:

```
<Setting Id="AllowWindowsClientInstall" Value="True"/>
```

The full file should look something like this with the line added in *italic*:

```
<Configuration>
<Package Id="sts">
<Setting Id="LAUNCHEDFROMSETUPSTS" Value="Yes"/>
</Package>
<Package Id="spswfe">
<Setting Id="SETUPCALLED" Value="1"/>
</Package>
<Logging Type="verbose" Path="%temp%" Template="SharePoint Server
Setup(*).log"/>
<!—<PIDKEY Value="Enter Product Key Here" />—>
```

```
<Setting Id="SERVERROLE" Value="SINGLESERVER"/>
<Setting Id="USINGUIINSTALLMODE" Value="1"/>
<Setting Id="SETUPTYPE" Value="CLEAN_INSTALL"/>
<Setting Id="SETUP_REBOOT" Value="Never"/>
<Setting Id="AllowWindowsClientInstall" Value="True"/>

</Configuration>
```

3. Save the config.xml file in place in the Files/Setup subdirectory in the local installation point.

4. Run PSConfig.exe to launch SharePoint setup, and continue through as you would on a server OS.

After the SharePoint 2010 Products Configuration Wizard completes, it is necessary to set the Secure Store key and set the Unattended Service Account for the PPS service application.

For more information about how to complete this task, see Chapter 4, "Installing Microsoft SharePoint Server 2010 and Configuring PerformancePoint Services."

Setting Up Your Development Environment

After installation has completed successfully, you can now use this installation as a development environment. After you develop your solution, you can port it over to a production server for use.

> **NOTE**
>
> This book assumes the use of Visual Studio 2010 as a development environment. If you use a different development environment, adjust the steps accordingly.

Copying PPS DLLs from the GAC

All SDK scenarios in PPS 2010 begin by using several dynamic link libraries (DLLs). You can find these DLLs in the Global Assembly Cache (GAC) after the Configuration Wizard has completed. You need to copy the DLL files out of the GAC and into a different file location before adding them to your Visual Studio project. Unfortunately, these files are not located in a convenient place, so getting them out of the GAC requires a little bit of work.

Copy the DLL files manually one by one from the GAC by browsing to %WinDir%\assembly\GAC_MSIL and opening each folder that contains the assembly you want. Then copy the DLL files to an intermediate location from which you can then add the necessary DLLs to your project as you need them.

Alternatively, you can run the following PowerShell command in the SharePoint 2010 Management Shell. This command can copy all PPS DLLs into a pre-created directory at C:\PPSFiles. You can then pick and choose which assemblies you need from the new folder location and add them to your project as you need them.

```
get-childitem $env:WINDIR\assembly * -Recurse -Include *performancepoint*.dll ¦
copy -dest C:\ppsfiles
```

Table 11.1 is a list of assemblies used for SDK development scenarios. Some other assemblies exist in the product, such as Microsoft.PerformancePoint.Scorecards.WebServer.dll and Microsoft.PerformancePoint.Scorecards.Upgrade.dll, but they handle internal server workings and are not designed for development scenarios.

TABLE 11.1   Use of DLL from SDK Perspective

DLL Name	Use from SDK Perspective
Microsoft.PerformancePoint.Scorecards.Client.dll	Contains classes for working with PPS objects found in the PPS Content List type, reports, scorecards, filters, dashboards, and indicators
Microsoft.PerformancePoint.Scorecards.Common.dll	Contains miscellaneous helper classes
Microsoft.PerformancePoint.Scorecards.DataSourceProviders.Standard.dll	Contains classes for working with data sources
Microsoft.PerformancePoint.ScorecardsScript.dll	Contains classes to help manage PPS Web Parts
Microsoft.PerformancePoint.Scorecards.Server.dll	Contains classes for creating custom filters and reports
Microsoft.PerformancePoint.Scorecards.ServerCommon.dll	Contains proxies to interact with the PPS service application
Microsoft.PerformancePoint.Scorecards.ServerRendering.dll	Contains classes for rendering controls on a dashboard page
Microsoft.PerformancePoint.Scorecards.Store.dll	Contains helper classes for working with repository items
Microsoft.PerformancePoint.Scorecards.WebControls.dll	Contains classes for supporting connection interfaces and for rendering Web Parts

Working with PPS Objects

You can create, read, update, and delete PPS objects through the SDK by calling into a web service, named the BIMonitoringAuthoringService, through a class available in the Microsoft.PerformancePoint.Scorecards.Client.dll named BIMonitoringAuthoringServiceProxy. This class contains static methods that can locate and instantiate an IBIMonitoringAuthoring object that enable interaction with the web service.

> **CAUTION**
>
> Technically you can call the web service directly without the help of the client-side assemblies, but the Web Service Description Language (WSDL) document that ships with PPS 2010 does not completely match the implementation. You need to either modify the WSDL or acquire an updated one from an alternative source.

To prepare your Visual Studio project, first add a reference to Microsoft.PerformancePoint.Scorecards.Client.dll. Then include the following using statement at the top of any file:

```
using Microsoft.PerformancePoint.Scorecards;
```

The web service calls are accomplished by creating an instance of a BIMonitoringAuthoringServiceProxy object and calling methods from the instance. In this code sample, we connect to the BIMonitoringAuthoringService from the root site collection. We then retrieve all the objects from a PPS Content list named PerformancePoint Content and print out their name and their content type designation:

```
string WebServiceUrl = "http://servername/_vti_bin/PPSAuthoringService.asmx";
string ListRelativeUrl = "/Lists/PerformancePoint Content";
IBIMonitoringAuthoring cService =
      BIMonitoringAuthoringServiceProxy.CreateInstance(WebServiceUrl);
FirstClassElementCollection allFCOs = cService.GetListItems(ListRelativeUrl);
foreach (FirstClassElement oneFCO in allFCOs)
    Console.WriteLine (oneFCO.Name + " of type " + oneFCO.ContentType);
```

This technique is useful when creating PPS objects, too. Often, it is not clear exactly what properties need to be set for an object to be usable in a dashboard or in Dashboard Designer. You can discover this information by creating objects through Dashboard Designer and then querying the object for properties in Visual Studio.

Creating Indicator Example

In the following example, we create an indicator that extends the built-in Stoplight indicator to change the default text color to purple:

- ▶ A GUID will be automatically assigned to the object upon saving to the SharePoint content list.

▶ Some indicator functionality is contained in a different namespace, so it is necessary to add this using a statement to the top of your coding file.

```
using Microsoft.PerformancePoint.Scorecards.Indicators;
```

▶ There is a special NoDataIndicatorBand that must be defined for each indicator created.

▶ In this example, we just copy the existing bands from a built-in indicator (the Stoplight pattern). You can create or customize your own indicator bands. The number of bands for an indicator is dynamically set by the number of bands added to the IndicatorBands collection of the Indicator object.

```
Indicator indicator = new Indicator();
indicator.Name.Text = "My Indicator";
indicator.IndicatorType = IndicatorType.Standard;
Indicator stoplightIndicator = Indicators.BuiltinIndicators.Indicators.
    First(s => s.Name.Text == "Stoplight");
indicator.NoDataIndicatorBand = stoplightIndicator.NoDataIndicatorBand;
foreach( IndicatorBand oneBand in stoplightIndicator.IndicatorBands )
{
    oneBand.Color = "#800080";
    indicator.IndicatorBands.Add(oneBand);
}
indicator.Validate();
IBIMonitoringAuthoring cService = BIMonitoringAuthoringService
Proxy.CreateInstance(WebServiceUrl);
cService.CreateIndicator(ListRelativeUrl, indicator);
```

Updating Custom Properties on KPIs

In the following example, we modify all KPIs in a specific content list to add a custom property that can then display on a scorecard. This code adds a single hyperlink property named Web Site Link to all KPIs and then saves the KPIs back to the server one by one:

```
IBIMonitoringAuthoring cService = BIMonitoringAuthoringService
Proxy.CreateInstance(WebServiceUrl);
FirstClassElementCollection allFCOs = cService.GetListItems(ListRelativeUrl);
foreach (Kpi kpi in allFCOs.Where(fco => fco.ContentType == FCOContentType.PpsKpi) )
{
    BpmPropertyHyperlink newHyperlinkProperty = new BpmPropertyHyperlink();
    newHyperlinkProperty.Hyperlink = "http://www.bing.com";
    newHyperlinkProperty.DisplayName = "Web site link";
    newHyperlinkProperty.UniqueName = Guid.NewGuid().ToString();
    kpi.Properties.Add(newHyperlinkProperty);
    cService.UpdateKpi(kpi);
}
```

Custom Objects and Editors

You can create customized objects that live within the PPS world, are available from within Dashboard Designer, and can interact with or supply data to other PPS objects. This proves useful in the following three cases, for example:

▸ Creating a custom tabular data source and having the data source used in KPIs, scorecards, and filters

▸ Creating a custom report type and linking it on a dashboard with a filter

▸ Creating a custom filter that does not depend on a data source like native PPS filters do

> **NOTE**
>
> In this book, we walk through the creation and deployment of a custom tabular data source solution. The data source we create for illustrative purposes simply enumerates files in a specified directory and represents filenames and extensions as dimension data and the file size as fact data. The steps to create and deploy custom reports and filters are similar. Refer to the PPS SDK documentation for more information on how to accomplish these scenarios.

Creating a Custom Tabular Data Source

You can create custom tabular data sources for data sources to be used in PPS filters, KPIs, and scorecards. The three steps to creating and using a custom tabular data source are as follows:

1. Create a signed class library for the custom tabular data source provider.

> **NOTE**
>
> The signing is necessary to generate a strongly named assembly and class that will later be used when deploying to SharePoint.

2. Create an editor for custom tabular data source objects.
3. Deploy the data source and its associated editor by modifying the web.config file, adding necessary files to the GAC, and deploying .aspx files to the layouts folder.

After you complete these steps, the custom tabular data source shows up as an available data source within Dashboard Designer and is usable just like tabular data sources that ship with PPS, such as SQL tables and SharePoint lists.

> **CAUTION**
>
> PPS supports only tabular custom data source providers. You cannot create a multidimensional or OLAP custom data source provider.

Creating a Class Library for the Custom Tabular Data Source Provider

Custom tabular data source providers must implement the
Microsoft.PerformancePoint.Scorecards.DataSourceProviders.TabularDataSourceProvider
abstract class. The first step to create a custom tabular data source provider is to create a
new class library project in Visual Studio. In this example, we create a simple example
custom tabular data source that reads files from a directory.

CAUTION

Make sure to set the Target framework of the project to .NET Framework 3.5 or lower. If
you set the target framework to .NET 4.0, PPS cannot discover this assembly in the
GAC at runtime.

You can have multiple custom tabular data sources or other custom objects defined in this
one assembly. Create a new CS class file with these using statements at the top.

```
using Microsoft.PerformancePoint.Scorecards;
using Microsoft.PerformancePoint.Scorecards.DataSourceProviders;
```

A friendly name set in the web.config file controls what the end user sees, so you can call
your class name whatever you would like. Ensure it inherits from the
TabularDataSourceProvider class:

```
public class FileSystemDataSource : TabularDataSourceProvider
```

Several methods need to be overridden. The order they appear in the class does not matter:

- ▶ GetId method
- ▶ IsConnectionStringSecure property
- ▶ Validate method
- ▶ SetDataSource method
- ▶ GetDataSet method
- ▶ GetDatabaseNames method
- ▶ GetCubeNames method
- ▶ GetCubeNameInfos method
- ▶ GetCubeMetadata method

GetId Method

The GetId method contains the unique identifier in a string format. The string value that
this method returns is used later when modifying the web.config file. In most cases, it is
sufficient to return a hardcoded string like this:

```
public override string GetId()
{
    return "FileSystemDataSource";
}
```

SetDataSource Method

The SetDataSource method defines the Dimensions and Fact columns available in this data source. This is roughly equivalent to the column definition user interface (UI) available when editing a PPS-supplied data source, such as a SQL table or SharePoint list, as the same options are available for each column. In this example, we define three columns: two dimension columns named Name and Type, which contain the filename and file extension, respectively, and a fact column that contains the file size:

> **NOTE**
>
> This method is called frequently. For great performance optimization, configure this method only if it is not already configured for the data source.

```
public override void SetDataSource(DataSource dataSource)
{
    base.SetDataSource(dataSource);

    // We only want to define column mappings if they haven't already been defined
    if (dataSource.DataTableMapping.ColumnMappings.Count <= 0)
    {
        dataSource.DataTableMapping.ColumnMappings.Add(new DataColumnMapping
        {
            SourceColumnName = "Name",
            FriendlyColumnName = "Name",
            UniqueName = "Name",
            ColumnType = MappedColumnTypes.Dimension,
            FactAggregation = FactAggregations.None,
            ColumnDataType = MappedColumnDataTypes.String
        });

        dataSource.DataTableMapping.ColumnMappings.Add(new DataColumnMapping
        {
            SourceColumnName = "Type",
            FriendlyColumnName = "Type",
            UniqueName = "Type",
            ColumnType = MappedColumnTypes.Dimension,
            FactAggregation = FactAggregations.None,
            ColumnDataType = MappedColumnDataTypes.String
        });
```

```
        dataSource.DataTableMapping.ColumnMappings.Add(new DataColumnMapping
        {
            SourceColumnName = "FileSize",
            FriendlyColumnName = "FileSize",
            UniqueName = "FileSize",
            ColumnType = MappedColumnTypes.Fact,
            FactAggregation = FactAggregations.Sum,
            ColumnDataType = MappedColumnDataTypes.Number
        });
    }
}
```

GetDataSet Method

The GetDataSet method is the method that actually does the work. We need to create a DataSet that matches the column schema that SetDataSource defines. After that DataSet object is created, it is necessary to fill the rows in the table with the correct data before finally returning the DataSet object:

TIP

This implementation uses a property inherited from the TabularDataSourceProvider base class named DataSource.CustomData. The CustomData field is the preferred mechanism to store user supplied data and is available as a field to change when implementing a custom tabular data source editor.

Depending on what type of data source you want to implement, it might be necessary to store data here in XML or otherwise delimited format if there are multiple values that a user would need to supply to the data source.

```
public override DataSet GetDataSet()
{
    DataSet myDataSet = new DataSet();
    DataTable myTable = myDataSet.Tables.Add();

    myTable.Columns.Add("Name", typeof(string));
    myTable.Columns.Add("Type", typeof(string));
    myTable.Columns.Add("FileSize", typeof(int));

    foreach (string filePath in Directory.GetFiles(DataSource.CustomData))
    {
        FileInfo oneFile = new FileInfo(filePath);
        DataRow oneRow = myTable.NewRow();
        oneRow["Name"] = oneFile.Name;
        oneRow["Type"] = oneFile.Extension;
        oneRow["FileSize"] = oneFile.Length;
```

```
        myTable.Rows.Add(oneRow);
    }

    return myDataSet;
}
```

Several other methods also need to be implemented to allow successful compilation. These methods are all not used in any fashion in PPS, so they can all throw NotImplementedExceptions:

TIP

The IsConnectionStringSecure method is a carryover from PPS 2007, and given the new extensibility model is deprecated.

The other methods are inherited from the CustomDataSourceProvider class, which is a base class for the TabularDataSourceProvider class. It is a bug in PPS where these methods should not be virtual methods in the TabularDataSourceProvider class. These methods would be called in the case of a custom multidimensional data source, which is not supported in PPS 2010.

```
public override bool IsConnectionStringSecure
{
    get { return false; }
}
public override void Validate()
{
    throw new NotImplementedException();
}

public override string[] GetDatabaseNames()
{
    throw new NotImplementedException();
}

public override string[] GetCubeNames()
{

    throw new NotImplementedException();
}

public override NameInfoCollection GetCubeNameInfos()
{
    throw new NotImplementedException();
}
```

```
public override Cube GetCubeMetaData(bool extendedMetadata)
{
    throw new NotImplementedException();
}
```

Signing the Assembly

If you use Visual Studio 2010, you can easily assign the assembly. View the properties of
the Class Library project, and in the Signing tab create a new strong name key file or
select an existing one from the list. Figure 11.1 shows what this looks like.

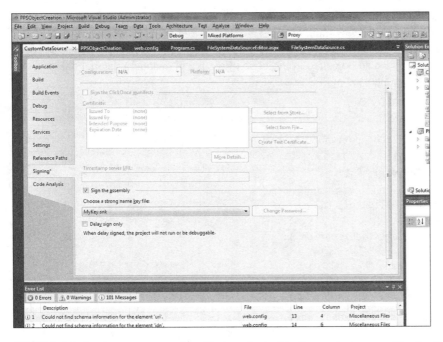

FIGURE 11.1   A strong name key file is selected in the project properties for the assembly
example.

Custom Object Editors

The next step to create a custom tabular data source is to create an editor. Editors are
custom ASPX web pages hosted inside of SharePoint. When a user attempts to use
Dashboard Designer to edit the custom tabular data source object, Dashboard Designer

launches a new browser instance to browse to the custom page and pass three parameters to the custom tabular data source object. The parameters are as follows:

- ▶ `Operation`: This is always set to `OpenItem`.
- ▶ `SiteCollection`: The URL to the root of the site collection containing the custom object.
- ▶ `ItemLocation`: The relative URL from the root of the site collection to the object being edited.

With these three parameters, you can retrieve the object using the `BIMonitoringServiceApplicationProxy` class and parse out any information you need to display on the ASPX page. When the user input is completed, use those same parameters to save the updated object back to SharePoint.

This step is necessary only if you want to have any user-defined parameters in your data source. If you want to just have a hard-coded data source that does not need to take any parameters, it is not necessary to create an editor.

NOTE

The method for creating custom object editors has changed from PPS 2007 to PPS 2010. In PPS 2007, it was necessary to create a custom WinForm plug-in that needed to be packaged with Dashboard Designer. Although this sounds easy in principle, it is difficult in implementation. Whenever Dashboard Designer's Click Once package is modified, it is necessary to regenerate manifest files and re-sign the whole package.

The new method of creating an ASPX page hosted in SharePoint is much easier to create and deploy. It has the added bonus of being directly accessible from SharePoint itself without using Dashboard Designer.

Creating a Custom Editor for the File System Data Source

Continuing with our example of a custom tabular data source, the next logical step is to develop a custom editor to allow the user to input the directory of files to enumerate. Following is the approach we take to develop this:

- ▶ Design an ASPX page layout
- ▶ Write the code-behind for the ASPX page

NOTE

Code-behind is a programming model used in ASPX development where the presentation, stored in an ASPX file, is separated from the functionality, stored in a CS file. When this book refers to code-behind, the reference is to the C# code written to implement the functionality exposed through the interface defined in ASPX.

Designing the page is a fairly straightforward task in Visual Studio 2010. In our example, Figure 11.2 shows the layout of a simple text box that enables the user to interact with an OK button that commits user changes to SharePoint.

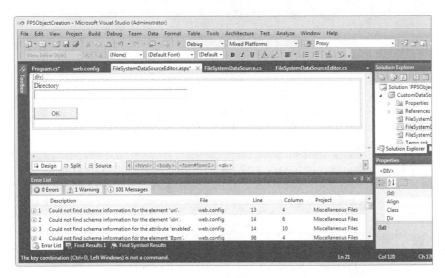

FIGURE 11.2   Design view for the custom tabular data source ASPX page.

The ASPX code that this generates looks like the following:

NOTE

As you can see in the Page Inherits directive, we include the code-behind the same assembly as the custom tabular data source provider for the sake of simplicity.

```
<%@ Page Inherits="CustomDataSource.FileSystemDataSourceEditor, CustomDataSource,
Version=1.0.0.0, Culture=neutral, PublicKeyToken=c0b442545fd021f3,
processorArchitecture=MSIL" %>
<!DOCTYPE html PUBLIC "-//W3C//DTD XHTML 1.0 Transitional//EN"
"http://www.w3.org/TR/xhtml1/DTD/xhtml1-transitional.dtd">
<html xmlns="http://www.w3.org/1999/xhtml">
<head runat="server">
    <title></title>
</head>
<body>
    <form id="form1" runat="server">
    <div>
        <asp:Label ID="labelURI" runat="server" Text="Directory"
```

```
            CssClass="ms-descriptiontext"></asp:Label>
        <br />
        <asp:TextBox ID="textboxDirectory" runat="server" Width="350px"
            CssClass="ms-input"></asp:TextBox>
        <br />
        <br />
        <asp:Button ID="buttonOK" runat="server" onclick="buttonOK_Click" Text="OK"
Width="100px" CssClass="ms-ButtonHeightWidth"/>
        <br />
        <br />
    </div>
    </form>
</body>
</html>
```

After the ASPX page has been created, the next step is to develop the code that will do the work of interfacing between the ASPX page and the SharePoint data store that contains our custom tabular data source object.

We need some using statements at the top of our code-behind. The System, System.Web.UI, and System.Web.UI.WebControls are necessary. The Microsoft.PerformancePoint.Scorecards namespace contains the BIMonitoringServiceApplicationProxy class and related classes that enable interacting with the SharePoint data store, and the Microsoft.PerformancePoint.Scorecards.DataSourceProviders namespace is necessary as we create a custom editor for a data source.

```
using System;
using System.Web.UI;
using System.Web.UI.WebControls; using Microsoft.PerformancePoint.Scorecards;
using Microsoft.PerformancePoint.Scorecards.DataSourceProviders;
```

We are going to name our class FileSystemDataSourceEditor and extend the System.Web.UI.Page class:

```
public class FileSystemDataSourceEditor : System.Web.UI.Page
```

We need to connect the HTML controls on the ASPX page to the code. We do so by overriding the CreateChildControls method and linking the textboxDirectory control to the textboxDirectory TextBox object that we have defined as a private variable in our class:

```
private TextBox textboxDirectory;
protected override void CreateChildControls()
{
    base.CreateChildControls();
```

```
    if (null == textboxDirectory )
        textboxDirectory = FindControl("textboxDirectory") as TextBox;
}
```

The next method we need to implement is the `Page_Load` method. This method gets called every time the page loads. In it, we retrieve the data source object from the query string and set the `CustomData` parameter. This parameter contains the directory to enumerate files from the data provider, and uses that information to fill the text box with a default value for the user. We are also going to cache the data source in the ASP.NET ViewState so that we can save a round trip to the server when we need to update the object after the user clicks the OK button.

> **TIP**
>
> Instead of creating a proxy object, we just use the default object offered here. There are no differences in functionality between the two methods, so use whichever method is most convenient for your purposes.

```
protected void Page_Load(object sender, EventArgs e)
{
    // initialization is only needed to be done once
    if (!IsPostBack)
    {
        EnsureChildControls();

        // Retrieve useful query string parameters
        string server = Request.QueryString[ClickOnceLaunchKeys.SiteCollectionUrl];
        string itemLocation = Request.QueryString[ClickOnceLaunchKeys.ItemLocation];

        // Retrieve the datasource
        DataSource datasource =
                BIMonitoringServiceApplicationProxy.Default.GetDataSource(
                    new RepositoryLocation(itemLocation));

        // Cache the data source object across page postbacks
        ViewState["datasource"] = datasource;

        // Fill in the text box with the current value
        if (null != datasource.CustomData)
            textboxDirectory.Text = datasource.CustomData;
    }
}
```

The last method we need to implement is the method for clicking the OK button. This method is called after the user updates the text box and clicks the OK button. All that needs to be done here is retrieve the data source from the cache, update the `CustomData` value, and then save the update to the server:

```
protected void buttonOK_Click(object sender, EventArgs e)
{
    EnsureChildControls();

    // Retrieve the data source from the ViewState;
    DataSource datasource = (DataSource)ViewState["datasource"];

    // Update the data source object with user changes
    datasource.CustomData = textboxDirectory.Text;

    // Commit changes to the server
    BIMonitoringServiceApplicationProxy.Default.UpdateDataSource(datasource);
}
```

Deploying the Data Source and Editor

When the custom tabular data source and its associated editor have been created, the final step is to deploy the data source and the editor to the server. This step has three parts:

1. Add the assembly to the GAC.
2. Deploy the editor file to SharePoint.
3. Update the web.config file.

Adding the Assembly to the GAC

You can add the custom tabular data source assembly to the GAC in several different ways. The simplest way is to drag and drop the built and signed assembly into the %windows%\Assembly directory. Other methods include using Gacutil.exe, which ships as part of the .NET Framework SDK, or developing an installer that can directly add the assembly to the GAC for you.

NOTE

In farms with multiple machines, it is necessary to register the assembly on all application servers in the farm running the PPS service.

When the assembly is in the GAC, as shown in Figure 11.3, note the assembly name, version, culture, public key token, and processor architecture. You need this information when you update the web.config file.

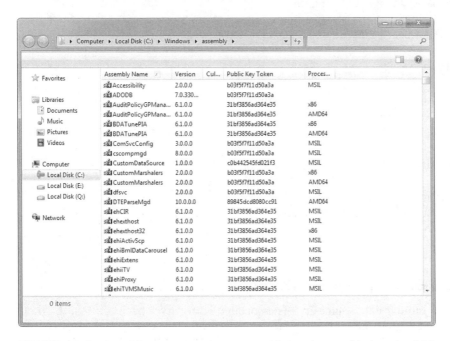

FIGURE 11.3   The CustomDataSource assembly has been added to the GAC.

Deploying the Editor File to SharePoint
If you have created an editor ASPX page, it is necessary to deploy the page to SharePoint. You can deploy custom pages to SharePoint in a few different ways. The easiest way is to copy the custom pages to the %ProgramFiles%\Common Files\Microsoft Shared\Web Server Extensions\14\TEMPLATE\LAYOUTS directory.

In our case, because we included the code-behind for the ASPX page as part of the assembly added to the GAC, it is not necessary to deploy the code-behind assembly again. If the code-behind is in a different assembly, make sure it is accessible by the ASPX page.

> **NOTE**
>
> In farms with multiple machines, it is necessary to copy the ASPX file and any support files to this directory on all SharePoint servers in the farm.

Updating the web.config File
After the custom tabular data source provider has been added to the GAC and the editor file has been deployed to SharePoint, the final step before using the object in Dashboard Designer is to update the PPS web service web.config file located at %ProgramFiles%\Microsoft Office Servers\14.0\WebServices\PpsMonitoringServer.

> **TIP**
>
> In our example, we make a number of changes to this file, and it is likely that you can make a number of changes to this file over time. It is a good practice to make a backup copy before making any changes.

1. Open the web.config file at C:\Program Files\Microsoft Office Servers\14.0\WebServices\PpsMonitoringServer\web.config.

2. In the configuration/configSections/sectionGroup node, add in the following entry:

```
<section name="CustomFCOGroup"
type="Microsoft.PerformancePoint.Scorecards.Common.Extensions.CustomFCOSection,
Microsoft.PerformancePoint.Scorecards.Common, Version=14.0.0.0, Culture=neutral,
PublicKeyToken=71e9bce111e9429c" allowLocation="true" allowDefinition=
"Everywhere" />
```

This enables the creation of an additional section later where we register our custom tabular data source.

3. In the configuration/Bpm node, add in a new child node named CustomFCOGroup that looks like this:

```
<CustomFCOGroup>
   <CustomFCO type="DataSource" subType="FileSystemDataSource" >
    <Resources
       FCOName="File System Custom Data Source"
       FCODescription="A custom data source for PPS Unleashed readers" />
     <EditorURI
uri="http://ppsunleashed/_layouts/FileSystemDataSourceEditor.aspx" />
   </CustomFCO>

   </CustomFCOGroup>
```

> **CAUTION**
>
> The subtype attribute on the CustomFCO node in this XML must match the value returned by the GetId method in your custom tabular data source.

This is not a minimal set of properties. The EditorURI node can be omitted and everything will still work fine with the exception that an editor will not be available for the custom object.

Several other properties are optionally available to add here. For example, you may add a property to control the icon used in Dashboard Designer and satellite resource assemblies. Refer to the PPS SDK documentation for more information on the other options available here.

4. In the configuration/Bpm/CustomDataSourceProviders node, add the following entry:

```
<add key="FileSystemDataSource" value="CustomDataSource.FileSystemDataSource,
CustomDataSource, Version=1.0.0.0, Culture=neutral, PublicKeyToken=
c0b442545fd021f3,
processorArchitecture=MSIL" />
```

CAUTION

The key attribute on the add node in this XML must match the value returned by the GetId method in your custom tabular data source.

This entry specifies the mapping between the object name and the class that implements the object loaded from the specified assembly from the GAC. Notice that the value attribute follows the format Namespace.ClassName, AssemblyName, AssemblyVersion, Culture, PublicKeyToken, ProcessorArchitecture.

Using the Custom Object

After the object has been created, Internet Information Services (IIS) should pick up the changes automatically, and the next time the user launches or refreshes Dashboard Designer, the updates should automatically take effect.

TIP

If something goes wrong with loading the custom object, you can usually find detailed error information in the application event log, usually after attempting to use the custom object in Dashboard Designer.

In the File System Data Source example, when you create a new data source in Dashboard Designer, as shown in Figure 11.4, you see an orange ball that represents the data source that was just registered. At this point, the data can be used just like any other tabular data source.

The only difference appears when editing the data source. When you open the data source in Dashboard Designer, as shown in Figure 11.5, you see a button to edit the data source instead of the usual data source configuration UI that appears for other data sources.

Clicking the Edit Data Source button brings you to the custom editor you created earlier in a new web page.

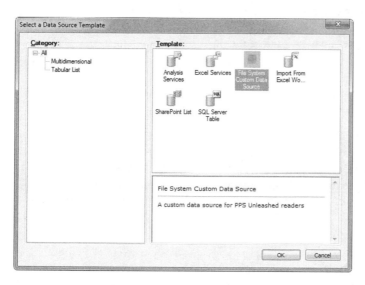

FIGURE 11.4   The File System Custom tabular data source is available as an option for data source creation in Dashboard Designer.

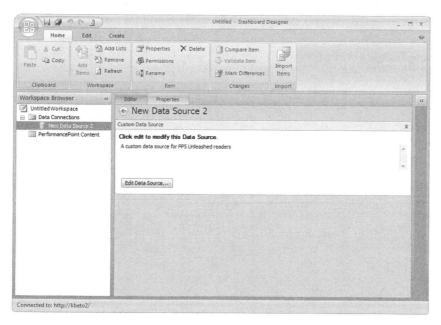

FIGURE 11.5   Editing a custom tabular data source in Dashboard Designer.

> **CAUTION**
>
> There is one bug you will likely run into when working with custom objects and their associated editors. After editing the data source, it is necessary to click the Refresh button on the Home tab of Dashboard Designer for the changes you just made to take effect in the Dashboard Designer session you are running.

Summary

With the Monitoring API, developers can extend native PPS capabilities and functionality as necessary. Developers can create a development environment to create custom objects, including custom tabular data sources, and editors or custom ASPX pages hosted inside of SharePoint and can be used to manage custom objects. The Monitoring API is a great way to take advantage of what PPS can offer for both out-of-the-box and customized business intelligence solutions.

Best Practices

- Best practice is to make a copy of the web.config file before making changes to this file.

- When adding the assembly to the GAC, note the assembly name, version, culture, public key token, and processor architecture. You need this information when you update the web.config file.

- If something goes wrong with loading a custom object in Dashboard Designer, look for detailed error information in the application event log.

CHAPTER 12

Maintaining a PPS Deployment

IN THIS CHAPTER

▶ Planning for High Availability   285

▶ Managing PPS   288

▶ Migrating from PPS 2007   299

▶ Using Windows PowerShell and Cmdlets   302

▶ Troubleshooting   312

As you know by now, PPS is integrated into SharePoint 2010, which means that maintaining SharePoint is part of maintaining PPS deployments. This chapter covers the tools SharePoint provides for monitoring and maintenance, including the PerformancePoint Service settings you can apply from the Manage PerformancePoint Services page in SharePoint. For the most part, these settings offer controls to limit the performance impact of various operations available to you through PPS, such as comments, cache, data sources, filters, select measure control, show details, and the decomposition tree.

This chapter also covers how to migrate content using the Import PerformancePoint Server 2007 Content functionality. A wizard steps you through the migration process, but the upgrade process does have significant points to watch for.

A discussion of managing deployments through PowerShell and cmdlets is also provided. This is a new concept in SharePoint 2010, and you can use a number of different commands to manage deployments in this way. The chapter closes with a brief discussion on troubleshooting and the error logs that may prove helpful when something goes wrong.

Planning for High Availability

High availability is an important topic for most server-based products. High availability is often expressed in terms of the percentage of "uptime." This refers to time when the server is accessible and functional for users versus time when it is not accessible.

SharePoint provides many mechanisms for achieving high availability. This section covers some of the more common tools and configurations you can implement to maximize and secure the operation of your installation.

Examining the Management Pack

There is a free download available for a SharePoint management pack for Microsoft's System Center Operations Manager (SCOM). The management pack is titled Microsoft SharePoint 2010 Products Management Pack and is available at http://download.microsoft.com.

This management pack needs to be installed on a SCOM server that is monitoring the SharePoint deployment. It deploys several rules that monitor all aspects of a SharePoint farm and enables you to attach custom actions or workflows when each rule is violated. There are three PPS specific triggers included that allow you to create notification rules when they are tripped, as follows:

▶ **Service Availability:** Monitors the PPS Service and triggers an action when the service stops running.

▶ **Database Availability:** Monitors the availability of PPS Service Application databases and triggers an action if the database becomes unavailable.

▶ **Unattended Service Account Status:** Monitors the validity of the Unattended Service Account and triggers an action if the account no longer authenticates for some reason. Often this catches expired passwords or domain connectivity problems.

TIP

SCOM used to be known as Microsoft Operations Manager (MOM) and is still frequently referred to as a MOM Pack.

Examining Network Load Balancing

SharePoint 2010 supports most standard network load-balancing schemes. *Load balancing* refers to distribution of the workload across multiple computers. A load-balancing scheme can be implemented either through a hardware or software solution. The configuration of the network load-balancing scheme is handled completely externally from SharePoint.

To use network load balancing effectively, it is important to configure Alternate Access Mappings (AAM) in SharePoint. AAMs are important because they allow SharePoint to properly recognize where users are coming from, especially in cases where there are multiple ways to access a SharePoint web application. In deployments involving reverse proxies or load balancing, the URL that the user enters could differ from the URL that is passed to SharePoint. Hence when SharePoint generates links, it needs to know both what possible public entry points exist for the site (Public URLs) and what potential URLs could be given by the load balancer (Internal URLs) and the mappings between them.

> **TIP**
>
> If you do not configure AAM for a web application, traffic may be diverted to one web front-end (WFE) server or you may experience Internet Information Services (IIS) or SharePoint errors.
>
> Go to a site collection in a web application browser and look at the URL. Does the address match what you are attempting to use as a hostname? If yes, your AAM configuration is correct. Does the address revert to the name of a web application? If yes, check your AAM settings again.
>
> For more information on configuring AAM, see *Microsoft SharePoint 2010 Unleashed* (0672333252).

Configuring Multiple Application Servers

SharePoint automatically configures multiple application servers. When requests come to the application servers, SharePoint applies a round-robin scheduling mechanism. With SharePoint 2010, round-robin scheduling is the only available load-balancing scheme. The scheme is implemented on a per service level, not at a machine level. For example, this means that Excel Services and PPS both have their own schedules. The first request to Excel Services will go to the first Excel Services service that was started, and the first request for PPS will go to the first PPS service that was started.

Round-Robin Scheduling

Round-robin scheduling is a simple form of scheduling that alternates requests between the available application servers that are running the PPS Monitoring Service.

Take a look at the server farm configuration in Figure 12.1, which includes one WFE server with three application servers.

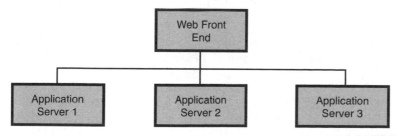

FIGURE 12.1   Round-robin scheduling alternates requests between available application servers.

The first request that requires a call to the application server will go to Application Server 1. The second request that requires a call to the application server will go to Application Server 2, and the third request will go to Application Server 3. When a fourth request comes in, this fourth request is routed to Application Server 1, and the cycle repeats.

Round-robin scheduling is one of the simplest forms of load balancing available. It works well in a SharePoint farm because the servers do not need to communicate detailed information about their current states. Often this detailed server information is outdated by the time an available application server has been identified to handle the call.

When a number of failures to a web service occur, SharePoint posts an error to the Unified Logging Service (ULS) trace logs and the Application event log. In addition, SharePoint stops the service and prevents it from servicing further requests. To resume its function, the service must be restarted.

Starting and stopping the PPS Monitoring Services is the best way to shape the load on the application servers in a farm. There should be no downtime when you do this.

Managing PPS

There are several settings available for the PPS service application. These settings apply to specific service applications so can only be applied at the web application level.

To access the PerformancePoint Service Settings section, follow these steps:

1. Browse to the SharePoint Central Administration site.
2. In the section called Application Management, click Manage Service Applications. This displays a list of SharePoint Service Applications, as shown in Figure 12.2.
3. Find the name of the service application you want to manage, and then click the link for the service application. This displays the Manage PerformancePoint Services page, as shown in Figure 12.3.

PerformancePoint Service Settings

The family of PerformancePoint Service settings can be accessed from the Manage PerformancePoint Services page by clicking the PerformancePoint Service Application Settings link.

For the most part, these settings offer controls to limit the performance impact of some of the more expensive operations available to you through PPS.

Secure Store and Unattended Service Account
Connection to the data source can occur through Per-User Authentication or, if this is not available, through the Unattended Service Account. The credentials for the Unattended Service Account are stored with a Secure Store Service Application, so they are not kept in plaintext within the SharePoint config database.

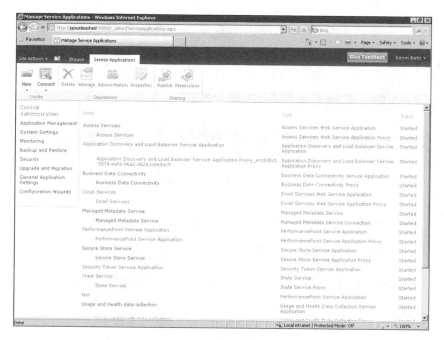

FIGURE 12.2 Select the service application you want to manage from the list.

FIGURE 12.3 You can manage the PerformancePoint Service Application Settings from here.

> **TIP**
>
> For all data sources that will be used by PPS, make sure that the Unattended Service Account is set to read-only access on any data sources it needs access to. Ensuring this account has minimum permissions on any data sources helps keep the data secure and minimize attack surface area for bad guys to attack.

> **NOTE**
>
> In PPS 2007, the Unattended Service Account was the identity of the application pool that SharePoint was running in IIS. In PPS 2010, the Unattended Service Account is a standalone configuration setting and is not inherited from the application pool under which the service is running.

Comments

The Comments section, shown in Figure 12.4, controls limitations on comments across all scorecards. These limitations help control the performance implications of comments in scorecards. In scorecards, comments add a hit to performance, whether or not the comment is displayed.

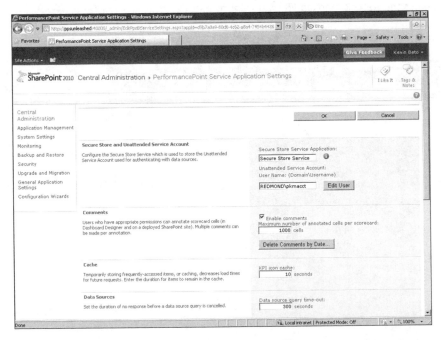

FIGURE 12.4   Configure the Comments settings in this section of the PerformancePoint Service Settings screen.

> **NOTE**
>
> PPS 2010 uses the terms *comments* and *annotations* interchangeably.

You can configure the following settings for comments:

▶ **Enable Comments:** If you do not intend to use comments, best practice is to disable Comments completely by clearing the check box.

▶ **Maximum Number of Annotated Cells per Scorecard:** This limits the number of comments that can be placed on a single cell in a scorecard. The default is set to 1,000, which is probably more than you will ever need. Best practice is to reduce the default value to a more reasonable number. Too many unnecessary comments may slow performance.

▶ **Delete Comments by Date:** Comments are never automatically deleted from scorecards. The performance of scorecards may be impacted if you have a large number of scorecards with many comments on each, even if the comments are not displayed. Deleting comments by date removes all comments older than the date you specify.

Cache

The values you enter for the KPI icon cache, shown in Figure 12.5, control how many seconds a particular custom indicator is cached. This applies only to custom indicators, as the default indicators are always cached.

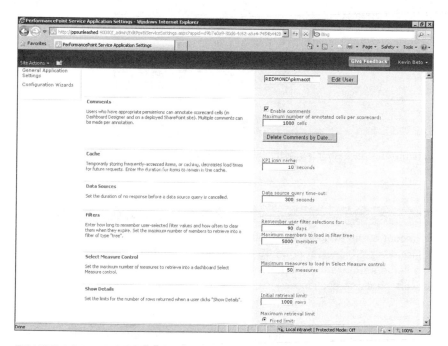

FIGURE 12.5   Configure the cache settings in this section of the PerformancePoint Service Settings screen.

You should never need to change this value as potential performance gains are minimal. However, you may want to change this value in a deployment where many large custom indicators are used in production. Increasing this value allows PPS to do a more aggressive job of caching the custom indicators and results in a slight performance improvement. The downside is that changes to the indicators result in a delay for the changes to the indicators to take effect.

Data Sources

The Data Sources setting, shown in Figure 12.6, is a PPS setting that determines how long a particular query may run before timing out.

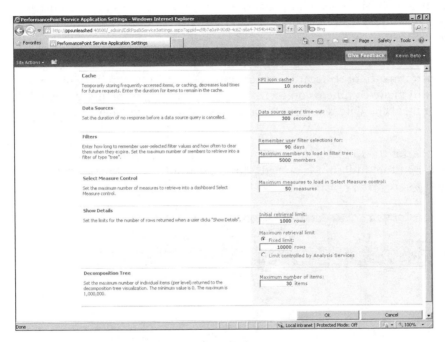

FIGURE 12.6   Configure the data sources settings in this section of the PerformancePoint Service Settings screen.

TIP

If you encounter timeout errors frequently, timeouts may be happening elsewhere. If your deployment includes a SQL server or an IIS server, the timeout error may be taking place on those servers. Remember to check timeouts on SQL servers, IIS servers, and any other network hardware appliances included in your deployment.

Filters

The family of settings for filters, shown in Figure 12.7, primarily applies to the user experience of filters on a deployed dashboard. The Remember User Filter Selections For setting specifies how long the filter settings apply when specified here.

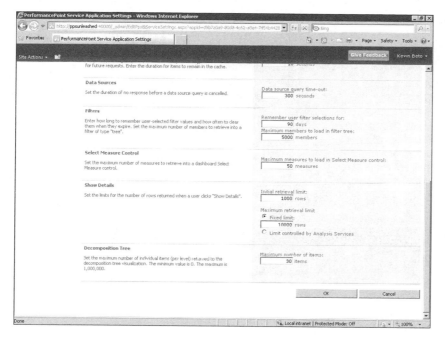

FIGURE 12.7   Configure the filters settings in this section of the PerformancePoint Service Settings screen.

In addition, it is possible to control the maximum number of members that will be returned in a filter. Doing so proves useful when users are working with large dimensions such as time. It is also useful if users select a flat dimension, which could have a significant performance impact on the server.

Select Measure Control

This setting, shown in Figure 12.8, limits the number of measures that can be returned when a user attempts to add more measures to an analytic chart or grid on a dashboard.

Analytic charts and grids are flexible enough that designing may occur on-the-fly. For example, while viewing an analytic line chart displaying viewers per episode, a user may also want to add an additional line to the chart displaying revenue per episode. If the data source has more than the maximum number of measures specified, it will truncate the number of measures displayed to this value.

Querying for measure information can be an expensive operation in terms of performance and will result in long loading times. This setting enables you to manage for performance. Change to a higher value if you have data sources with more than 1,000 measures. Change to a lower value if you have smaller cubes, but it is important to note that changing this value has no practical effect unless the number of measures in a cube crosses the limit you set. In addition, setting this value to 0 effectively disables the ability to add measures to analytic reports.

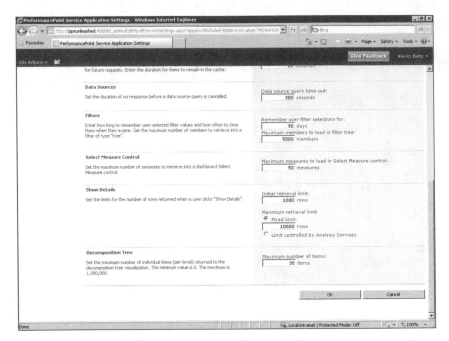

FIGURE 12.8   Configure the Select Measure Control setting in this section of the PerformancePoint Service Settings screen.

Show Details

There are two settings available under the Show Details heading, shown in Figure 12.9. The Initial Retrieval Limit setting governs how many rows are returned when a user first accesses the show details functionality. For example, if the retrieval limit is set to 10 rows, only 10 rows at a time display when a user requests a show details report, even if there are more than 10 rows to be returned overall.

After the completion of the initial retrieval, a user may retrieve more rows if the data is what is expected. In this case, the Fixed Limit setting controls how many rows will be returned in subsequent retrievals. There also is an option to have the limit controlled by Analysis Services, which uses the Analysis Services limit, which is controlled by the OLAP\Query\DefaultDrillthroughMaxRows server property.

Decomposition Tree

The decomposition tree visualization is a new feature in PPS 2010. If your users will be using the decomposition tree visualization frequently, best practice is to limit the number of items that can be returned, to help limit the performance impact on the data source. The setting for this is shown in Figure 12.10.

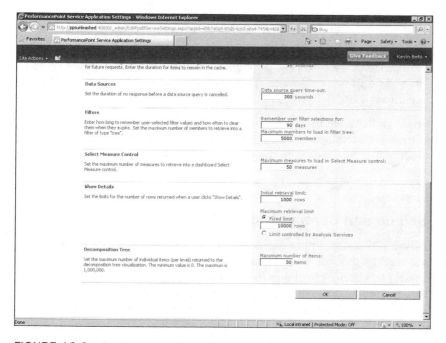

FIGURE 12.9   Configure the Show Details settings in this section of the PerformancePoint Service Settings screen.

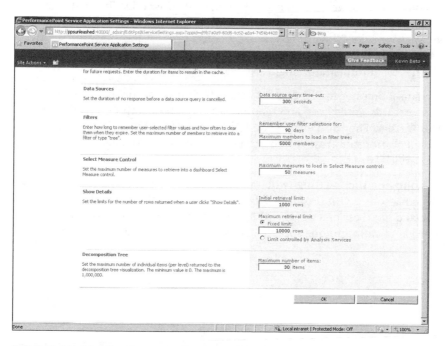

FIGURE 12.10   Configure the Decomposition Tree settings in this section of the PerformancePoint Service Settings screen.

If you drill down to a level of a decomposition tree that has more items than this setting, for example a date dimension with 1,000 members, PPS retrieves only the top 250 members of this dimension instead of retrieving and subsequently displaying all members of this dimension. This enables users to page through the top 249 members in the dimension. Other members will be shown as Bottom 751 as an aggregated value not directly accessible to the user through the decomposition tree visualization.

If in this same example you change this setting to 10, the user can see only the top 9 members, and the other 991 members will be aggregated as Bottom 991. If the user wants to see the smallest values first as opposed to the top values, the bottom 9 values will be shown as the Top 991.

Trusted Data Source and Content Locations

For enhanced security, a PPS service application can further lock down which objects are available for use by a user. In the case of data sources, a list of trusted data source locations enables an administrator to restrict the ability for PPS to use a data source that is not explicitly located in a trusted location. If a user does try, PPS denies access and gives an error message indicating that the administrator has denied a data source from that location. In the case of other PPS objects, access can be restricted in the same way with trusted content locations.

This feature mitigates against malicious user attacks that take advantage of the unattended service account to create their own data source list in a site or site collection that they have access to and where they can potentially elevate their privileges to view data that the unattended service account does have access to. For trusted content locations, the malicious user could use existing data sources and create their own KPIs that would expose some of that data that an administrator might not want exposed.

This can apply to data sources or to PPS content lists, which include key performance indicators (KPIs), scorecards, indicators, and reports. This family of settings enable you to secure data sources further. They also enable you to access content by clicking either Trusted Data Source Locations or Trusted Content Locations on the Manage PerformancePoint Services page.

Best practice is to configure these settings when you run the Unattended Service Account as a highly privileged account with broad access to sensitive data (for example, human resources or financial data). Best practice is also to restrict any data sources that can be used for that service application to one specific data source list with tightly controlled permissions.

You can grant trust to site collections, sites, or document libraries. This trust used in conjunction with restricting write access to these trusted locations through SharePoint security allows all users to take advantage of configured data sources while protecting data from inadvertent changes. It also takes advantage of elevated permissions through the Unattended Service Account.

TIP

The Trusted Data Source Locations and Trusted Content Locations options share similar concepts and user interfaces. The only difference is that the Trusted Data Sources Location settings take effect on a data sources list, whereas the Trusted Content Location settings take effect on a PerformancePoint Services content list. You often want to lock down data sources tighter than content locations. This is because the Unattended Service Account may be used to access data sources but is never used to access content locations.

Configuring a Trusted Data Source Location

When you configure a trusted data source location, lock the data source for the service application to one specific SharePoint list.

To configure a trusted data source location, follow these steps:

1. From the PerformancePoint Service Settings page, click Trusted Data Source Locations.

2. Change the radio selection from All SharePoint locations to Only Specific Locations, and then click Apply.

CAUTION

After you perform step 2, all data source locations will be inaccessible to PPS users until you configure all specific locations.

3. Click Add Trusted Data Source Location, as shown in Figure 12.11.

4. Enter the full URL of the data source document library that can be accessed by PPS users, and then click OK (see Figure 12.12).

When you complete this configuration, only data sources within the list of trusted locations will be available to users of Dashboard Designer and to previously deployed dashboards. Data sources outside the list of trusted locations will not be available to these users or to the dashboards.

FIGURE 12.11   Click Add Trusted Data Source Location from this screen.

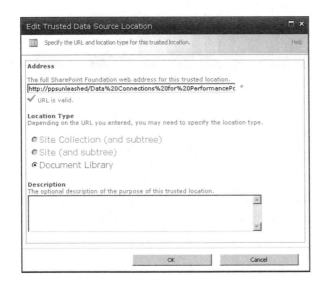

FIGURE 12.12   Enter the name of the data source document library on this screen.

Migrating from PPS 2007

There is no direct upgrade path from PPS 2007 to PPS 2010. For this reason, to migrate content, you need to use the Import PerformancePoint Server 2007 Content functionality provided in the PerformancePoint Service Settings page.

To accomplish this, connect to the PPS 2007 database and import the content into the SharePoint 2010 farm on which the wizard is currently being run.

The upgrade process does have some significant points to watch for:

- ▶ It is not possible to go backward in the wizard. If you make a mistake, you need to start the wizard over.

- ▶ All supported content is imported. Because of this, it is helpful to import content to a temporary empty PPS content list and then move the objects that you want to save to other content lists that are used.

- ▶ Several types of content not supported in SharePoint 2010 will not be imported, including the following:

  - ▶ Spreadsheets

  - ▶ Trend analysis charts

  - ▶ Pivot charts

  - ▶ Pivot tables

- ▶ Data sources and nondata source content are imported into separate locations. Data sources are imported into a document library and all other content is imported into a PPS content list.

- ▶ Dashboards need to be redeployed from Dashboard Designer. The dashboard objects are moved and should work successfully but will not be automatically deployed to SharePoint.

- ▶ Filters will be moved out of dashboards and become separate objects within PPS.

- ▶ Item-level permissions are also moved and are implemented at an item level. They are additive with the SharePoint permissions already set. Therefore, if a user has access to the content list, they will also have access to the object, even if they did not have access to the object in PPS 2007.

- ▶ Scorecard comments are migrated to the PPS Shared Service database.

- ▶ Errors and warnings that occur during upgrade are reported to the event log and to the Unified Logging Service (ULS) logs. Because the upgrade does not stop when an error occurs, the content will be incompletely imported. For example, you may receive a warning if permissions are missing or an error can occur when unsupported content types such as trend analysis charts are skipped. If you want to correct the problem and try again, it might make sense to delete all previously imported content; otherwise, it will create duplicates.

12

Step-by-Step Migration from PPS 2007

Before getting started with the upgrade, ensure that you have the following ready:

- ▶ Either a Windows or a SQL account with read access to the PPS 2007 database to be upgraded

- ▶ New and empty PPS content list

- ▶ New and empty data source for a PPS document library

When you have the correct account, lists, and data source ready, follow these steps to complete a successful import:

1. From the PerformancePoint Service Settings page, click Import PerformancePoint Server 2007 Content.

2. Click Next on the Welcome page of the Import Wizard.

3. In step 1 of the wizard, select the type of data source security that was enabled on the PPS 2007 server (see Figure 12.13).

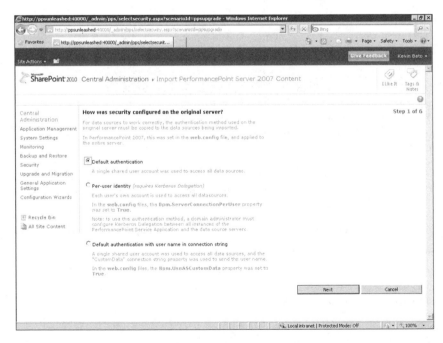

FIGURE 12.13   Copy the security settings from the original data source configuration.

NOTE

Step 3 is necessary because the data source configuration was done at the server level and the setting has moved to a data source level.

---

4. In step 2 of the wizard, enter the database server.

5. Enter Windows or SQL credentials for an account that has at least read access to the PPS 2007 database that you want to import on this server. Click Next.

6. In step 3 of the wizard, select the database to upgrade and click Next.

7. In step 4 of the wizard, select the content list where you want to move all non-data source content. Click Next.

8. In step 5 of the wizard, select the data source document library where you want to import all data source content. Click Next.

9. Step 6 is a confirmation page. Click Next to begin the import.

You now see an upgrade status page that refreshes periodically with current status information.

> **TIP**
>
> If you close this upgrade status page, the status is available as a timer job that can be accessed through the Monitoring—Job Status feature in Central Administration, as shown in Figure 12.14.

FIGURE 12.14　Monitor the status of the import process from this page.

When the upgrade completes, you see an Import Results page with detailed results on the success of the upgrade.

Using Windows PowerShell and Cmdlets

Managing deployments through Windows PowerShell is a new concept in SharePoint 2010. PowerShell is a scripting utility meant to enable server administrators to automate a wide range of administrative tasks. There are a number of different commands you can use to manage deployments in this way. For example, you can create, modify, and delete web applications and site collections through PowerShell and commandlets (cmdlets). You can also start and stop services or grant permissions through cmdlets.

STSADM, the command-line tool for managing SharePoint, is still included in SharePoint 2010 and retains SharePoint 2007 functionality. However, STSADM is being phased out, which means that none of the new SharePoint 2010 functions can be accessed by STSADM. However, all functions that are new to SharePoint 2010 are available through PowerShell. Because PPS is a new addition to SharePoint 2010, no supported features are available to manage PPS through STSADM.

> **TIP**
>
> Keep in mind that that STSADM may not be included in the next version of SharePoint. If you use or are developing solutions with STSADM, best practice is to switch over now to avoid future incompatibility problems.

Launching PowerShell

PowerShell can be launched using the Start menu on any server machine in the farm. It is located under the Microsoft SharePoint 2010 Products folder and is named SharePoint 2010 Management Shell. Launching from this location automatically loads SharePoint PowerShell objects and cmdlets.

If you create a script that is intended to run without the need to launch PowerShell from the SharePoint folder on the Start menu, this command loads all required SharePoint objects into the current PowerShell window or script:

```
Add-PsSnapin Microsoft.SharePoint.PowerShell
```

Cmdlet Reference

PPS cmdlets are the command-line style mechanism available to query information or to modify settings on various PPS system-level objects. PPS cmdlets are designed to integrate with the SharePoint cmdlet functionality. Cmdlets are divided into nouns and verbs. Nouns are types of objects to interact with, whereas verbs describe how to interact with types of objects. In addition, parameters are available for most objects depending on how you want to interact with an object. Nouns, verbs, and parameters are always combined in the following syntax:

```
Verb-Noun -ParameterName1 ParameterValue1 -ParameterName2 ParameterValue2
```

These are the generally available verbs that can be used when working with PPS objects:

- ▶ New

- ▶ Remove

- ▶ Get

- ▶ Set

These are the nouns that are implemented by PPS:

- ▶ SPPerformancePointServiceApplication

- ▶ SPPerformancePointServiceApplicationProxy

- ▶ SPPerformancePointServiceApplicationTrustedLocation

- ▶ SPPerformancePointSecureDataValues

NOTE

The SPPerformancePointServiceApplication and
SPPerformancePointServiceApplicationProxy cmdlets do not have a Remove verb.
This verb is covered by the SharePoint standard service application and application
proxy removal cmdlets of Remove-SPServiceApplication and Remove-
SPServiceApplicationProxy.

For example, to create a new service application, you would call the New verb with the
SPPerformancePointServiceApplication noun. The syntax would look like this:

```
New-SPPerformancePointServiceApplication -Name "MyFirstApplication" –AppPool "PPS
App Pool" New-SPIisWebServiceApplicationPool
```

CAUTION

For simplicity's sake, this example assumes there already is an application pool named
"PPS App Pool" that the code can use. The New-SPIisWebServiceApplicationPool
cmdlet can be used to create a new application pool. A more complete example that
also creates a new application pool at runtime is included in the Cmdlet Samples section later in this chapter.

Cmdlets Available Out of the Box

This section summarizes the cmdlets that are available out of the box. These tables
describe the parameters for each cmdlet.

The cmdlet in Table 12.1 creates a new PPS Service application with the specified parameters.

TIP

The `Administrators` property is a multivalue string property. To set multiple administrators for this service application, use this syntax:

`-Administrators {"domain\admin1","domain\admin2"}`

TABLE 12.1 **New-SPPerformancePointServiceApplication**

Property Name	Type	Description
`Name`	String	The name of the service application. This is a required parameter.
`Administrators`	String[]	The group of users who have permission to administer the service application. The default value is the SharePoint Farm Administrators group.
`ServiceAccount`	PSCredentials	The credentials of the Unattended Service Account. This is a required parameter.
`ApplicationPool`	String	The name of the application pool to use for this shared service. The application pool must be created prior to running this cmdlet. The `New-SPIisWebServiceApplicationPool` creates an application pool for you and can be used in conjunction with this cmdlet.

The cmdlet in Table 12.2 retrieves an existing PPS service application with the specified parameters.

TABLE 12.2 **Get-SPPerformancePointServiceApplication**

Property Name	Type	Description
`Identity`	String or GUID	The name or GUID of the service application to retrieve. If this parameter is not specified, a list of all service applications will be returned.

TIP

This cmdlet is most useful when querying for all service applications in a farm. It is also frequently used as an input to other cmdlets.

This cmdlet in Table 12.3 changes the settings of an existing PPS service application.

TABLE 12.3
Set-SPPerformancePointServiceApplication

Property Name	Type	Description
Identity	String	The name or GUID of the service application to set the properties of.
		This is a required parameter.
ServiceAccount	PSCredentials	The credentials of the Unattended Service Account.
		This is a required parameter.
ApplicationPool	String	The name of the application pool to use for this Shared Service. If the application pool does not exist, one will be created.
		The default value is the name of the service application.

There are a number of values that are applicable to most of the New, Get, and Set SPPerformancePointServiceApplication cmdlets. These shared values can be used by all the cmdlets discussed earlier. The shared values control various settings, most of which are available to set in the Shared Service Administrative user interface.

For example, if you want to pass a parameter to disable all comments on scorecards when creating a new PPS shared service application, all you need is this cmdlet with the CommentsDisabled shared value:

```
New-SPPerformancePointServiceApplication -name "MyFirstServiceApplication"
-CommentsDisabled true
```
This same syntax also works with the Set- SPPerformancePointServiceApplication cmdlet:

```
Set-SPPerformancePointServiceApplication -name "MyFirstServiceApplication"
-CommentsDisabled true
```
For retrieving the current value of this setting with the Get-SPPerformancePointServiceApplication cmdlet, you need to use this syntax:

```
(Get-SPPerformancePointServiceApplication –identity
"MyFirstServiceApplication").CommentsDisabled
```

Table 12.4 describes the shared values you can use with cmdlets.

TABLE 12.4   Shared Values for the **SPPerformancePointServiceApplication** Family of

Property Name	Type	Description
CommentsDisabled	Boolean	Allows users to add comments to scorecard cells.
CommentsScorecardMax	Integer	Maximum number of comments per scorecard.
IndicatorImageCacheSeconds	Integer	Seconds to cache KPI icons.
DataSourceQueryTimeoutSeconds	Integer	Seconds to time out for a data source query.
DecompositionTreeMaximum	Integer	Maximum number of items shown in a decomposition tree.
FilterRememberUserSelectionsDays	Integer	Days to remember user filter selections.
FilterTreeMembersMax	Integer	Maximum number of records to show in filter tree view control.
SelectMeasureMaximum	Integer	Maximum number of measures to show in a dashboard. Select measure control.
ShowDetailsInitialRows	Integer	Initial number of rows to retrieve for show details.
ShowDetailsMaxRowsDisabled	Boolean	Disable ShowDetailsInitialRows setting. If set to True, Analysis Services will control limit.
ShowDetailsMaxRows	Integer	Maximum number of rows to retrieve for show details.
MSMQEnabled	Boolean	Send notifications to Microsoft Message Queuing (MSMQ) on content change.
MSMQName	String	Queue name of the Microsoft Messaging Queue.
SessionHistoryHours	Integer	Hours to keep user navigation history.
AnalyticQueryLoggingEnabled	Boolean	Verbose logging of query events.

TABLE 12.4   Continued

Property Name	Type	Description
AnalyticQueryCellMax	Integer	The maximum number of values to return in an Analytic Chart or Grid. The default value is 100,000. If a user attempts to create an analytic grid that has 100 columns and 1001 rows, PPS will show an error rather than rendering such a large report.
TrustedContentLocationsRestricted	Boolean	When switched on, only trust specified locations. Default is to trust all content locations.
TrustedDataSourceLocationsRestricted	Boolean	When switched on, only trust specified locations. Default is to trust all data source locations.
DataSourceUnattendedServiceAccountUsername	String	The user name of the Unattended Service Account.
SettingsDatabase	String	The location of the database.

TIP

There are a few other properties available that are not listed in this table, such as some caching settings. They exist mainly for debugging caching scenarios during the development of the product and should remain untouched in all deployments.

Whenever you create a service application, best practice is to create a service application proxy to go with it. These go together like peanut butter and jelly; both are needed for each to work.

Table 12.5 describes a cmdlet that creates a new proxy for an existing service application.

TABLE 12.5   **New-SPPerformancePointServiceApplicationProxy**

Property Name	Type	Description
Name	String	The name of the service application proxy. This is a required parameter.
ServiceApplication	String or GUID	The name or GUID of the service identity with which to associate this proxy. The GUID is a system assigned identifier that can be queried. This is a required parameter.

TABLE 12.5   Continued

Property Name	Type	Description
Administrators	String[]	The group of users who have permission to administer the service application proxy. The default value is the SharePoint Farm Administrators group.

The cmdlet in Table 12.6 is used to remove service application proxies when they are no longer needed. Just like with creation, best practice is to delete the proxy at the same time you delete the service application.

TABLE 12.6   **Remove-SPPerformancePointServiceApplicationProxy**

Property Name	Type	Description
Identity	SPCmdletObjectId	The name of the service application proxy to delete. This is a required parameter.

The cmdlet in Table 12.7 adds a new entry to the trusted data source or trusted content locations.

TABLE 12.7
New-SPPerformancePointServiceApplicationTrustedLocation

Property Name	Type	Description
URL	String	The URL for the trusted location to add.
Type	Enumeration	The type of content at the URL specified in the URL parameter. Valid values are as follows: SiteCollection Site DocumentLibrary
ServiceApplication	GUID or String	Service application associated with this location.
TrustedLocationType	Enumeration	The type of content to trust in the specified location. Valid values are as follows: DataSource Content

NOTE

Use this cmdlet with the `TrustedDataSourceLocationsRestricted` or `TrustedContentLocationsRestricted` settings on the service application. By default, everything is trusted, which means that adding new locations to trust will not have any effect unless the service application has been set to trust nothing.

The cmdlet in Table 12.8 retrieves all trusted locations set for a specific service application.

TABLE 12.8 **Get-SPPerformancePointServiceApplicationTrustedLocation**

Property Name	Type	Description
ServiceApplication	GUID or String	Service application associated with this location

The cmdlet in Table 12.9 removes a single entry as a trusted location.

TABLE 12.9 **Remove-SPPerformancePointServiceApplicationTrustedLocation**

Property Name	Type	Description
Identity	String	ID property (GUID) of the trusted location to remove

Clear-SPPerformancePointServiceApplicationTrustedLocation
The cmdlet in Table 12.10 removes all trusted locations, including data source and content that have been set previously for a specific service application.

TABLE 12.10 **Clear-SPPerformancePointServiceApplicationTrustedLocation**

Property Name	Type	Description
ServiceApplication	GUID or String	Service application associated with this location

The cmdlet in Table 12.11 retrieves the status of the secure store target application and the name of the unattended service account.

TABLE 12.11
Get-SPPerformancePointSecureDataValues

Property Name	Type	Description
ServiceApplication	GUID or String	Service application associated with this location

The cmdlet in Table 12.12 sets the Unattended Service Account credentials.

TABLE 12.12
Set-SPPerformancePointSecureDataValues

Property Name	Type	Description
ServiceApplication	GUID or String	Service application associated with this location
DataSourceUnattendedServiceAccount	PSCredential	The identity to which to set the unattended service account

Cmdlet Samples

This section includes some useful scenarios that can be automated through cmdlets.

NOTE

Some of these samples use pipelining to send their output into other cmdlets. This is useful especially for properties such as GUIDs or SPCmdletObjectId parameters that are not easy to discover or type.

Pipelining is a concept from PowerShell. With pipelining, the output of one command can be directly sent to another command. Typically, this is seen when there is a Get command that retrieves a particular object and pipes the object to a Set command that sets a property on the object.

Creating a New Service Application

This cmdlet creates a new PPS service application with the specified name and using an already registered SharePoint managed account, such as the following:

```
New-SPPerformancePointServiceApplication -Name "MyServiceApplication"
-ApplicationPool (New-SPIisWebServiceApplicationPool "SharePoint Hosted Services"
-account "domain\SharePointManagedAccount")
```

Starting the Shared Service

This cmdlet starts the PPS shared service. You can run this cmdlet on any application server in the farm on which you would like to have this service started:

```
Get-SPServiceInstance ¦ Where{$_.TypeName -eq "PerformancePoint Service"} ¦
Start-SPServiceInstance Creating a New Web Application
```

This cmdlet creates a new web application at port 81 with the specified name, such as the following:

```
New-SPWebApplication -Name "MyWebApplication" -Port 81
```

Create a New Site Collection
This cmdlet creates a new site collection at the root of the web application at port 81, such as the following:

```
New-SPSite http://localhost:81 -owneralias domain\user
```

Changing PPS Service Settings
The cmdlets in this section change the Unattended Service Account. This proves especially useful for updating the unattended service account password after it has been changed.

This cmdlet displays a prompt for credentials and change the Unattended Service Account on the specified service application:

```
Set-SPPerformancePointSecureDataValues -ServiceApplication "MyServiceApplication"
-DataSourceUnattendedServiceAccount (Get-credential)
```
This cmdlet has the credentials for the Unattended Service Account stored in plain text in the command. By omitting the –name parameter from the `Get-SPPerformancePointServiceApplication` command, it executes on the default service application:

```
Get-SPPerformancePointServiceApplication ¦ Set-SPPerformancePointSecureDataValues
-DataSourceUnattendedServiceAccount (new-object
System.Management.Automation.PSCredential -argumentlist ("domain\serviceaccount"),
(ConvertTo-SecureString "password" -asPlainText -force))
```

Adding a Trusted Data Source Location
This cmdlet switches the trusted data source locations from trusting all locations to trusting specific locations:

```
Get-SPerformancePointMonitoringServiceApplication ¦
Set-SPPerformancePointServiceApplication -TrustedDataSourceLocationsRestricted 1
```

Next, this cmdlet adds a single document library trusted location for data sources for the default service application:

```
Get-SPPerformancePointServiceApplication ¦ New-
SPPerformancePointServiceApplicationTrustedLocation -url
http://SharePointServer/Data%20Source -Type DocumentLibrary -TrustedLocation Data
Source
```

Retrieving All Configured Trusted Locations

This cmdlet retrieves a collection of all configured trusted locations for the default service application:

```
Get-SPerformancePointMonitoringServiceApplication ¦
Get-SPPerformancePointServiceApplicationTrustedLocation
```

Troubleshooting

In a system as complex as SharePoint, there are many points of failure. Troubleshooting can be a difficult task when something goes wrong.

To assist with troubleshooting, error information is logged in two main places:

- ▶ Windows Application Event log
- ▶ ULS Trace log

Normally errors are logged to both logs. General information and activity are also logged to the ULS Trace logs.

Errors communicated through Dashboard Designer and the SharePoint Web Parts are not very descriptive and are not intended to be used for security purposes. Sometimes they contain an error code that is helpful when searching the event logs or the ULS logs for more detailed error information.

Unfortunately, PPS is fairly chatty when it comes to error messages. Errors can be logged for mundane reasons such as when a user types an invalid server name for a data source or an invalid MDX when authoring an analytic report.

This makes it tricky to monitor the PPS components of SharePoint aggressively for uptime. The best way to monitor for uptime is by using a tool such as Microsoft System Center. This tool is capable of monitoring the rendered dashboards for uptime from the user perspective as opposed to monitoring failures in logging locations.

Event Viewer

The most severe errors are logged to the Event log. When troubleshooting a system down error, the Event log will most likely contain the most useful information.

In most cases, the errors are logged with the Source of "PerformancePoint Service." This allows you to view PPS errors only by filtering on Source in the Windows Event Log Viewer.

Sometimes the errors displayed through the PerformancePoint Service source paint an incomplete picture of the problem. If this is the case, it is helpful to look for log events that occurred immediately before or after the PPS error.

Trace Log Files

The trace log files are located at %ProgramFiles%\Common Files\Microsoft Shared\Web Server Extensions\14\LOGS and contain a wealth of information on SharePoint activities, perhaps too much information! The abundance of information can make these log files tricky to read. Several free tools are available to help parse the ULS logs. One of the best tools is an open source tool named ULSViewer that is available as a free download at http://ulsviewer.codeplex.com/.

Trace log files are a good second level of detail to examine when the error messages in the Event Viewer do not shed light on the problem you are experiencing.

Summary

Planning for high availability and optimizing performance are important considerations in SharePoint and PPS deployments. When you understand the tools SharePoint provides for monitoring and maintenance, including the PerformancePoint Service Settings, you will be better equipped to maintain reliable and stable deployments. In addition to these tools, command-line administration using PowerShell and cmdlets is available to provide additional administrative functionality. Learning how to migrate from PPS 2007 and understanding troubleshooting tips adds to your knowledge of administering and maintaining a PPS deployment.

Best Practices

► If you do not intend to use comments on a scorecard, best practice is to disable comments completely.

► Best practice is to reduce the default number of annotated cells per scorecard to a reasonable number. Too many unnecessary comments may slow performance.

► In a decomposition tree, best practice is to limit the number of items that can be returned, to help limit the performance impact on the data source.

► Best practice is to configure settings for trusted data source and content locations when you run the Unattended Service Account as a highly privileged account with broad access to sensitive data.

► If you use or develop solutions with STSADM, best practice is to switch over now to avoid future incompatibility problems.

► Whenever you create a service application, best practice is to create a service application proxy to go with it.

► Best practice is to delete a service application proxy at the same time you delete the service application.

Index

A

Abs function, 139

actuals, KPIs, 133-135

Add Items option (Workspace section), 79

Add Lists option (Workspace section), 79

ADOMD.NET 2008, 41

aggregation types, data sources, 100

aggregations, scorecards, adding, 161-162

Agile Management, 9

Analysis Services data source

    creating, 92-95

    time intelligence, configuring, 109-110

Analysis Services KPIs, creating, 128-132

analytic chart reports, 167-175

    additional measures, adding, 170-172

    context menus, 173-175

    data elements, adding, 169-170

    dimensions, adding, 170-172

    filters, 172-173

    interactivity features, 173-175

analytic grid reports, 176-177

APIs, Monitoring API, 261

    custom editors, 269-274

    custom objects, 269-274

    development environment setup, 265-266

    extending PPS functionality, 261-262

    PPS objects, 267-268

Apples and Oranges Productions case study, 19-21, 38

    architecture roadmap, 25-26

    business situation, 21-24

    dashboards, 22

        designing, 34-36

    data analysis, 29

    dimensional data warehouse, building, 27-28

    expansion strategies, 24-25

    gathering data, 26-27

    KPIs, designing, 30-33

    market extensions, 22-24

    measures, identifying, 29

    project plan, 26-36

    reports, designing, 32-34

    requirements, 21-24

    scorecards, 22

        designing, 30-33

Application Server Role, 41

application servers, multiple application servers, configuring, 287-288

architecture, Apples and Oranges Productions case study, 25-26

authentication

    Analysis Services data source, 93-94

    Kerberos, PPS, 255-256

    PPS, troubleshooting, 251-252

Average function, 139

B

Balanced Scorecard, 9

best practices

    Dashboard Designer, 87

    dashboards, 233

    data sources, 119

    high availability, 313

    indicators, 163-164

    KPIs, 163-164

    performance optimization, 313

    PPS, security, 260

    PPS (PerformancePoint Service) installation, 68-69

    reports, 197

    scorecards, 163-164

BI (business intelligence), 5-7, 12, 19-20

    Apples and Oranges Productions case study, 19-21

        business situation, 21-24

        requirements, 21-24

    as discipline, 5-9

    as enhancer, 9-10

    integrated business planning, 10-12

    operational decisions, 6

    performance management methodologies, 9

    strategic decisions, 6

    tactical decisions, 6

Blank Indicator template, 125

Browning, Elizabeth Barrett, 1

browsers, dashboards, creating in, 227-232

Bulk Edit section (Dashboard Designer Edit tab), 81-82

Business Connectivity Services filter, 204

business intelligence (BI). See BI (Business Intelligence)

C

cache intervals, Analysis Services data source, 95

cache settings (PPS), 291-292

Calculated Metrics Data Source Mapping dialog box, 138

calculating scoring, KPIs, 146-150

calculating metrics, KPI data mapping, 138-139

Calculation dialog box, 140-142

case studies, Apples and Oranges Productions case study, 19-21, 26-38

    architecture, 25-26

    business situation, 21-24

    expansion strategies, 24-25

    requirements, 21-24

centered indicators (PPS), 122

Changes section (Dashboard Designer Home tab), 80

Chart Controls for .NET 3.5, 41

choice filters, 204

claims, Windows Token service, configuring, 259

class libraries, custom tabular data source, creating for, 270-274

ClearSPPerformancePointServiceApplication-TrustedLocation cmdlet, 309

ClickOnce Applications, Dashboard Designer, 72-73

client operating systems, SharePoint Server 2010, installing on, 262-265

cmdlets (PPS), 302-312

    ClearSPPerformancePointServiceApplication TrustedLocation, 309

    GetSPPerformancePointSecureDataValues, 310

    GetSPPerformancePointServiceApplication-TrustedLocation, 309

    NewSPPerformancePointServiceApplication, 304

    NewSPPerformancePointServiceApplication-Proxy, 307

    NewSPPerformancePointServiceApplication-TrustedLocation, 308

    RemoveSPPerformancePointService-ApplicationProxy, 308

    RemoveSPPerformancePointService-ApplicationTrustedLocation, 309

    service applications, creating, 310

    SetSPPerformancePointSecureDataValues, 310

    SetSPPerformancePointServiceApplication, 305

    shared services, creating, 310

    SPPerformancePointServiceApplication, 304, 307

CMMI (Capability Maturity Model Integration), 9

Colon operator (STPS), 113

column types, tabular data sources, 100

Comma operator (STPS), 113

Comments section (PPS Settings screen), 290-291

Compare Item option (Changes section), 80

computer accounts, constrained delegation, 258

configuration

    Analysis Services data source, time intelligence, 109-110

    multiple application servers, 287-288

    PPS (PerformancePoint Service), 39, 53-67

        Secure Store Service, 53-56

        service application creation, 56-57

    tabular data sources, time intelligence, 110-111

    TLS, web applications, 253

    WFE (web front-end) servers, 58

    Windows Token service, claims, 259

Configuration Wizard, server farm installation, 47-53

Connect To values (Web Parts), 209-210

Connect To Web Part connection, 208

connection strings, Unattended Service Account, username added to, 245

constrained delegation, computer and service accounts, 258

content migration, Dashboard Designer, 84-86

context menus
  analytic chart reports, 173-175
  analytic grid reports, 176-177

Create tab (Dashboard Designer), 82

CRM (Customer Relationship Management), 9

current user filters, 204

custom indicators
  creating, 123-126
  editing, 126-127

custom object editors, 275-283
  deploying, 279-282
  file system data source, creating for, 275-279

custom properties
  KPIs, updating on, 268
  scorecards, 162

Custom Properties section (Dashboard Designer Properties pane), 84

Custom Table filter (PPS), 200

custom tabular data source
  class libraries, creating for, 270-274
  creating, 269

Customer Experience Improvement Program, 51

D

Dashboard Designer, 71, 86
  best practices, 87
  content migration, 84-86
  Create tab, 82
  custom indicators, creating, 123-126

dashboards, 232
  best practices, 233
  creating, 207, 210-215
  deploying, 210-215
  filters, 220-224
  pages, 218-220
  zones, 216-218

Details pane, 77

Edit tab, 81-82

examining, 76-79-84

first class objects, 78

GreenOrange data source option, 224-227

Home tab, 79-80
  Changes section, 80
  Import section, 80
  Item section, 80
  Workspace section, 79

installing, 73-75

launching from FireFox, 75

main screen, 77

PPS filters, creating, 201-203

prerequisites, 72-73

Properties pane, 83-84

uninstalling, 75

Workspace Browser, 77

dashboards, 1, 78, 199-200, 232
  Apples and Oranges Productions case study, 22
  best practices, 233
  creating, 207, 210-215
    browsers, 227-232
    PPS objects, 228-232
  deploying, 210-215
  designing, 34-36
  filters, 220-224
  GreenOrange data source option, 224-227
  pages, 218-220

Web Part connections, 208-210

zones, 216-218

data analysis, Apples and Oranges Productions case study, 29

data connections, PPS, security, 242-244

data elements, analytic chart reports, adding to, 169-170

data gathering, Apples and Oranges Productions case study, 26-27

data mapping, KPIs, 135-142

calculating metrics, 138-139

data sources, 135

fixed values, 135

metrics, 137

number formatting, 140

data sources, 78, 89-92, 118

aggregation types, 100

Analysis Services data source, creating, 92-95

best practices, 119

custom tabular data source, creating, 269

Excel Services data sources, creating, 97-101

Import from Excel Workbook data source option, 102-104

KPI data mapping, 135

multidimensional data sources, 90-91

OLAP (online analytical processing) data sources, 91

PowerPivot data sources, creating, 95-96

PPS, secure connections, 255

SharePoint list data source, 105-106

SPNs, creating for, 256-257

SQL Server Table data source, 107-108

tabular data sources, 91

column types, 100

time intelligence, 108-118

Analysis Services data source, 109-110

STPS syntax, 111-118

tabular data sources, 110-111

trusted data sources, PPS, 296-297

trusted locations, 92

Data Sources settings (PPS), 292-293

date filter, 204

decomposition tree reports, 193-194

Decomposition Tree settings, 294-296

Delete option (Item section), 80

deleting, Dashboard Designer, 75

deploying PPS

maintaining, 285

TLS, 252-253

designing

dashboards, 34-36

KPIs, 30-33

reports, 32-34

scorecards, 30-33, 161-163

Details pane, Dashboard Designer, 77

development environment, Monitoring API, setting up, 265-266

dialog boxes

Calculated Metrics Data Source Mapping dialog, 138

Calculation, 140-142

Dimensional Data Source, 135-137

Edit Banding Settings, 144

Dickenson, Emily, 2

dimension intervals, Analysis Services data source, formatting, 95

Dimensional Data Source dialog box, 135-137

dimensional data warehouse, building, 27-28

dimensions

analytic chart reports

adding to, 170-172

filters, 172-173

scorecards, adding, 158-160, 162

disciplines, BI (Business Intelligence), 5-9

DLLs, PPS, copying from GAC, 265-266

Drucker, Peter, 19

E

Edit Banding Settings dialog box, 144

Edit tab (Dashboard Designer), 81-82

editing

custom indicators, 126-127

scoring thresholds, 146

elements (PPS), security, 236-242

permissions, 236-239

enhancers, BI (Business Intelligence), 9-10

Event Viewer, SharePoint Server 2010, troubleshooting, 312

examining, Dashboard Designer, 76-84

Excel, Import from Excel Workbook data source option, 102-104

Excel Services data sources

best practices, 119

creating, 97-101

Excel Services reports, 176-180

expansion strategies, Apples and Oranges Productions case study, 24-25

F

farm sources, SPNs, creating for, 256-257

file system data source, custom object editors, creating for, 275-279

filters, 78, 199-200

analytic chart reports, 172-173

Business Connectivity Services filter, 204

choice filters, 204

creating, 200

current user filters, 204

dashboards, 220-224

date filter, 204

PPS filters, creating, 200-203

query string filters, 204

SharePoint Server 2010 filters, creating, 204-206

SQL Server Analysis Services filters, 204

text filters, 204

filters settings (PPS), 292-293

FireFox, Dashboard Designer, launching from, 75

first class objects, Dashboard Designer, 78

First<Member> function (STPS), 114

FirstChild function (STPS), 114

fixed values, KPI data mapping, 135

Full<Member> function (STPS), 115

functions

calculated metrics, 139

STPS syntax, 113-115

G

General Properties section (Dashboard Designer Properties pane), 83

Geneva Framework Runtime, 41

Get Values From Web Part connection, 208

GetDataSet method, 272-274

GetSPPerformancePointSecureDataValues cmdlet, 310

GetSPPerformancePointServiceApplication, 304

GetSPPerformancePointServiceApplicationTrust
edLocation cmdlet, 309

GreenOrange data source option, dashboards,
224-227

H

hardware prerequisites, PPS (PerformancePoint
Service), 39-40

high availability

best practices, 313

PPS, planning for, 285-288

Home tab (Dashboard Designer), 79-80

Changes section, 80

Import section, 80

Item section, 80

Workspace section, 79

I

If function, 139

Import from Excel Workbook data source
option, creating, 102-104

Import section (Dashboard Designer Home tab),
80

importing content to Dashboard Designer,
84-86

Indicator Template Wizard, custom indicators,
creating, 123-126

indicators, 78, 121-122, 163. *See also* KPIs
(key performance indicators)

best practices, 163-164

creating, 267-268

custom indicators

creating, 123-126

editing, 126-127

KPIs, 128

actuals, 133-135

Analysis Services KPIs, 128-132

data mapping, 135-142

multiple targets, 133-135

scorecards, 154

sources, 122-123

styles, 122

installation

Dashboard Designer, 73-75

best practices, 87

PPS, security, 235

PPS (PerformancePoint Service), 68-69

best practices, 68-69

prerequisites, 39-40

validating, 67

SharePoint Server 2010, 39, 44, 45-53

client operating systems, 262-265

minimum requirements, 39-43

server farm installation, 47-53

standalone installation, 44, 45-47

integrated business planning, BI (Business
Intelligence), 10-12

interactivity features

analytic chart reports, 173-175

analytic grid reports, 176-177

Item section (Dashboard Designer Home
tab), 80

K

Kaplan, Robert S., 19, 22

Kerberos, per-user authentication, PPS, 255-256

KPI details reports, 180-182

KPIs (key performance indicators), 8, 78, 89, 121, 128, 163

  actuals, 133-135

  Analysis Services KPIs, creating, 128-132

  best practices, 163-164

  creating, Scorecard Wizard, 154-158

  custom properties, updating on, 268

  data mapping, 135-142

    calculating metrics, 138-139

    data sources, 135

    fixed values, 135

    metrics, 137

    number formatting, 140

  data sources, 89-92

    Analysis Services data source, 92-95

    Excel Services data sources, 97-101

    multidimensional data sources, 90-91

    PowerPivot data sources, 95-96

    SharePoint list data source, 105-106

    SQL Server Table data source, 107-108

    tabular data sources, 91, 100

    time intelligence, 108-118

    trusted locations, 92

  designing, 30-33

  multiple targets, 133-135

  scorecards, 154

    adding dimensions, 158-160

    designing, 161-163

    rollup, 140-142

    Scorecard Editor, 160-161

    updating, 161

  scoring, 142-153

    calculating, 146-150

    editing thresholds, 146

    walkthrough, 150-153

  scoring patterns, changing, 143-145

L

language form, STPS syntax, 112

Last<Member> function (STPS), 114

LastChild function (STPS), 114

launching

  Dashboard Designer from FireFox, 75

  PowerShell, 302

M

management pack, 286

managing, PPS, 288-297

Mark Differences option (Changes section), 80

market extensions, Apples and Oranges Productions case study, 22-24

Max function, 139

MDX, 137

MDX Query filter (PPS), 200

measures

  analytic chart reports

    adding to, 170-172

    filters, 172-173

  Apples and Oranges Productions case study, identifying, 29

Member Selection filter (PPS), 200

<Member>ToDate function (STPS),

methods, GetDataSet, 272-274

metrics

  KPI data mapping, 137

    calculating, 138-139

  scorecards, adding, 161

Microsoft Filter Pack 2.0, 41

Microsoft Operations Manager (MOM), 286

migration, PPS 2007, 299-301

Min function, 139

minimum requirements

Dashboard Designer, 72-73

SharePoint Server 2010, installation, 39-43

MOM (Microsoft Operations Manager), 286

Monitoring API, 261

custom editors, 269-274

custom object editors, 275-283

creating for file system data source, 275-279

custom objects, 269-274

custom tabular data source

class libraries, 270-274

creating, 269

development environment, setting up, 265-266

PPS, extending functionality, 261-262

PPS objects, 267-268

SharePoint, installing on client operating systems, 262-265

multidimensional data sources, 90-91

multiple application servers, configuring, 287-288

multiple targets, KPIs (key performance indicators), 133-135

N

Named Set filter (PPS), 201

named sets, scorecards, 163

.NET Framework, ClickOnce Applications, 72-73

.NET Framework 3.5 SP1, 41

network load balancing, 286-287

NewSPPerformancePointServiceApplication cmdlet, 304

NewSPPerformancePointServiceApplication Proxy cmdlet, 307

NewSPPerformancePointServiceApplication TrustedLocation cmdlet, 308

normalized banding, scoring, 146-153

Norton, David P., 19, 22

number formatting, KPI data mapping, 140

O

object editors (custom), 275-283

creating for file system data source, 275-279

deploying, 279-282

OLAP (online analytical processing) data sources, 8, 91

operators, STPS syntax, 113

P

pages, dashboards, 218-220

Parent function (STPS), 114

performance management methodologies, BI (Business Intelligence), 9

performance optimization, best practices, 313

Performance Point Content lists, analytic chart reports, creating, 168

PerformancePoint Dashboard Designer. See Dashboard Designer

permissions, PPS elements, 236-239

Permissions option (Item section), 80

per-user authentication, PPS, Kerberos, 255-256

per-user identity, PPS, 245-251

PowerPivot data sources, creating, 95-96

PowerShell, launching, 302

PPS (PerformancePoint Services), 13, 19-20, 39

Apples and Oranges Productions case study, 19-21

architecture, 25-26

business situation, 21-24

requirements, 21-24

application
    activating features, 64-67
    creating, 58-67
architecture, 13-15
cmdlets, 302-312
configuring, 39, 53-67
    Secure Store Service, 53-56
    service application creation, 56-57
Data Sources setting, 292-293
Decomposition Tree settings, 294-296
deployment, maintaining, 285
discontinued features, 17
DLLs, copying from GAC, 265-266
elements, permissions, 236-239
extending functionality, 261-262
filters, creating, 200-203
filters settings, 292-293
high availability, planning for, 285-288
indicators, 122
    sources, 122-123
installing, 68-69
    best practices, 68-69
    prerequisites, 39-40
    security, 235
    validating, 67
KPIs, scoring, 142-153
management pack, 286
managing, 288-297
multiple application servers, configuring, 287-288
network load balancing, 286-287
new features, 15-16
objects, 267-268
overlapping features, 16-17
PowerShell, 302
PPS 2007, migrating from, 299-301

reports, 165-166, 196
    analytic chart reports, 167-175
    analytic grid reports, 175-177
    best practices, 197
    decomposition tree reports, 193-194
    Excel Services reports, 176-180
    KPI details reports, 180-182
    ProClarity Analytics Server Page reports, 183-185
    Reporting Services report, 185-188
    show details reports, 194-196
    strategy maps, 188-192
    web page reports, 192
security, 235-236, 259
    authentication, 251-252
    best practices, 260
    constrained delegation, 258
    data connections, 242-244
    data source connections, 255
    deployment with TLS, 252-253
    elements, 236-242
    per-user authentication with Kerberos, 255-256
    per-user identity, 245-251
    SPNs, 256-257
    Windows Token service, 259
Select Measure Control setting, 293
service settings, changing, 311
settings, accessing, 288-296
Settings screen
    cache settings, 291-292
    Comments section, 290-291
Show Details settings, 294
starting, 57-58
trusted data sources, 296-297
Unattended Service Account
    security, 242-244
    setting, 61-62

PPS objects, dashboards, creating with, 228-232

Prerequisite tool, 42-43

running, 42-43

prerequisites

Dashboard Designer, 72-73

SharePoint Server 2010 installation, 39-43

ProClarity Analytics Server Page reports, 183-185

project plan, Apples and Oranges Productions case study, 26-36

Properties option (Item section), 80

Properties pane (Dashboard Designer), 83-84

proxy groups, service application proxy, associating with, 63

analytic grid reports, 175-177

best practices, 197

decomposition tree reports, 193-194

designing, 32-34

Excel Services reports, 176-180

KPI details reports, 180-182

ProClarity Analytics Server Page reports, 183-185

Reporting Services report, 185-188

show details reports, 194-196

strategy maps, 188-192

web page reports, 192

requirements, SharePoint Server 2010 installation, 39-43

rollup, KPIs, scorecards, 140-142

Round function, 139

Q

query string filters, 204

R

Refresh option (Workspace section), 79

RemoveSPPerformancePointServiceApplicationProxy cmdlet, 308

Report Viewer 2008, SQL Server Reporting Services reports, 87

Reporting Services report, 185-188

reports, 78, 165-166, 196

analytic chart reports, 167-175

adding additional measures, 170-172

adding data elements, 169-170

adding dimensions, 170-172

context menus, 173-175

filters, 172-173

interactivity features, 173-175

S

SCOM (System Center Operations Manager), 286

Scorecard Editor, 160-161

Scorecard Wizard, KPIs, creating, 154-158

scorecards, 78, 121, 154, 163

aggregations, adding, 161-162

Apples and Oranges Productions case study, 22

best practices, 163-164

custom properties, 162

designing, 30-33, 161-163

dimensions, adding, 158-160, 162

KPIs

creating, 154-158

rollup, 140-142

metrics, adding, 161

named sets, 163

Scorecard Editor, 160-161

set formulas, 163

updating, 161

scoring

definitions, 143

KPIs, 142-153

calculating, 146-150

walkthrough, 150-153

thresholds, editing, 146

scoring patterns, KPIs, changing, 143-145

Secure Store Service (PPS), configuring, 53-56

security (PPS), 235-236, 259

authentication, 251-252

best practices, 260

constrained delegation, 258

data connections, 242-244

data source connections, 255

deployment with TLS, 252-253

elements, 236-242

per-user authentication with Kerberos, 255-256

per-user identity, 245-251

SPNs, 256-257

Unattended Service Account, 242-245

Windows Token service, 259

Select Measure Control setting (PPS), 293

Send Values To Web Part connection, 208

server farm installation, SharePoint Server 2010, 47-53

server requirements, PowerPivot data sources, 95

service accounts, constrained delegation, 258

service applications, creating, 56-57, 310

services settings (PPS), changing, 311

set formulas, scorecards, 163

SetSPPerformancePointSecureDataValues cmdlet, 310

SetSPPerformancePointServiceApplication cmdlet, 305

Settings screen (PPS)

cache settings, 291-292

Comments section, 290-291

Data Sources setting, 292-293

Decomposition Tree settings, 294-296

filters settings, 292-293

Select Measure Control setting, 293

Show Details settings, 294

shared services, creating, 310

SharePoint Designer, filters, creating, 205-206

SharePoint lists, data sources, 105-106, 119

best practices, 119

SharePoint Server 2010

client operating systems, installing on, 262-265

filters, creating, 200, 204-206

installing, 39, 44-53

minimum requirements, 39-43

server farm installation, 47-53

standalone installation, 44

troubleshooting, 312-313

WFE (web front-end) servers, configuring for, 58

show details reports, 194-196

Show Details settings (PPS), 294

Six Sigma, 9

software prerequisites, PPS (PerformancePoint Service), 39-40

Source Value Web Part connection, 208

source values, Web Parts, 209

sources, indicators, 122-123

SPNs (Service Principal Names), data sources, creating for, 256-257

SPPerformancePointServiceApplication cmdlet, 307

SQL 2008 Native Client, 41

SQL Server Analysis Services filters, 204

SQL Server Reporting Services reports, Report Viewer 2008, 87

SQL Server Table data source, creating, 107-108

standalone installation, SharePoint, 44-47

standard indicators (PPS), 122

starting, PPS (PerformancePoint Service), 57-58

STPS syntax, time intelligence, 111-118

    functions, 113-115

    language form, 112

    operators, 113

    time members, 112

strategy map reports, Visio Professional, 87

strategy maps, 188-192

styles, indicators, 122

Sum function, 139

Sync Framework Runtime v1.0, 41

System Center Operations Manager (SCOM), 286

T

tabular data sources, 91

    column types, 100

    custom tabular data source

        class libraries, 270-274

        creating, 269

    time intelligence, configuration, 110-111

text filters, 204

thresholds, scoring, editing, 146

time intelligence, data sources, 108-118

    Analysis Services data source, 109-110

    STPS syntax, 111-118

    tabular data sources, 110-111

Time Intelligence Connection Formula filter (PPS), 201

Time Intelligence filter (PPS), 201

time members, STPS syntax, 112-113

TLS (Transport Layer Security)

    PPS, deploying, 252-253

    PPS web services, configuring on, 254

    web applications, configuring on, 253

trace log files, SharePoint Server 2010, troubleshooting, 313

troubleshooting, SharePoint Server 2010, 312-313

trusted data sources (PPS), 296-297, 311

trusted locations, data sources, 92

U

Unattended Service Account, security, 242-245

Unattended Service Account (PPS)

    connection string, username added to, 242-245

    setting, 61-62

uninstalling Dashboard Designer, 75

    best practices, 87

updating

    custom properties, KPIs, 268

    scorecards, 161

usernames, Unattended Service Account, connection strings, 245

V

Validate Item option (Changes section), 80

validation, PPS (PerformancePoint Service) installation, 67

Visio Professional, strategy map reports, 87

How can we make this index more useful? Email us at indexes@samspublishing.com

W

walkthrough, scoring, 150-153

web applications, TLS, configuring on, 252-253

web page reports, 192

Web Part connections, dashboards, 208-210

Web Parts

Connect To values, 209-210

source values, 209

Web Server Role, 41

WFE (web front-end) servers, configuring, 58

Windows PowerShell 2.0, 41

Windows Token service, claims, configuring, 259

wizards

Configuration Wizard, server farm installation, 47-53

Indicator Template Wizard, 123-126

Scorecard Wizard, 154-158

Workspace Browser (Dashboard Designer), Details pane, 77

Workspace section (Dashboard Design Home tab), 79

Z

zones, dashboards, 216-218

UNLEASHED

Unleashed takes you beyond the basics, providing an exhaustive, technically sophisticated reference for professionals who need to exploit a technology to its fullest potential. It's the best resource for practical advice from the experts, and the most in-depth coverage of the latest technologies.

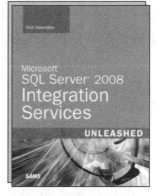

Microsoft SQL Server 2008 Integration Services Unleashed
ISBN-13: 9780672330322

OTHER UNLEASHED TITLES

Windows PowerShell Unleashed
ISBN-13: 9780672329883

Windows Small Business Server 2008 Unleashed
ISBN-13: 9780672329579

ASP.NET 3.5 AJAX Unleashed
ISBN-13: 9780672329739

WPF Control Development Unleashed
ISBN-13: 9780672330339

Microsoft XNA Game Studio 3.0 Unleashed
ISBN-13: 9780672330223

Windows Server 2008 Hyper-V Unleashed
ISBN-13: 9780672330285

System Center Operations Manager 2007 Unleashed
ISBN-13: 9780672329555

System Center Configuration Manager (SCCM) 2007 Unleashed
ISBN-13: 9780672330230

Microsoft Dynamics CRM 4.0 Unleashed
ISBN-13: 9780672329708

Microsoft Dynamics CRM 4 Integration Unleashed
ISBN-13: 9780672330544

LINQ Unleashed
ISBN-13: 9780672329838

Silverlight 2 Unleashed
ISBN-13: 9780672330148

Windows Communication Foundation 3.5 Unleashed
ISBN-13: 9780672330247

C# 3.0 Unleashed
ISBN-13: 9780672329814

Microsoft Expression Blend Unleashed
ISBN-13: 9780672329319

Microsoft SQL Server 2008 Reporting Services Unleashed
ISBN-13: 9780672330261

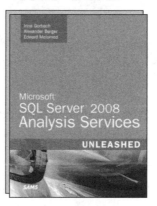

Microsoft SQL Server 2008 Analysis Services Unleashed
ISBN-13: 9780672330018

ASP.NET MVC Framework Unleashed
ISBN-13: 9780672329982

SAMS

informit.com/sams

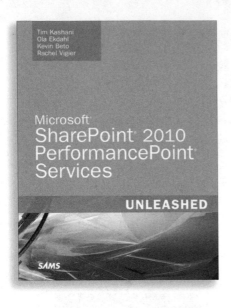

FREE Online Edition

Your purchase of **Microsoft® SharePoint 2010 PerformancePoint® Services Unleashed**
includes access to a free online edition for 45 days through the Safari Books Online
subscription service. Nearly every Sams book is available online through Safari Books
Online, along with more than 5,000 other technical books and videos from publishers
such as Addison-Wesley Professional, Cisco Press, Exam Cram, IBM Press, O'Reilly,
Prentice Hall, and Que.

SAFARI BOOKS ONLINE allows you to search for a specific answer, cut and paste
code, download chapters, and stay current with emerging technologies.

Activate your FREE Online Edition at
www.informit.com/safarifree

> **STEP 1:** Enter the coupon code: YUVYWWA.

> **STEP 2:** New Safari users, complete the brief registration form.
> Safari subscribers, just log in.

If you have difficulty registering on Safari or accessing the online edition,
please e-mail customer-service@safaribooksonline.com